METHODS OF CRIMINOLOGY AND CRIMINAL JUSTICE RESEARCH

SOCIOLOGY OF CRIME, LAW AND DEVIANCE

Series Editors: Mathieu Deflem and Derek M.D. Silva

Previous Volumes:

Volumes 1-5:	Jeffrey T. Ulmer
Volume 6:	Ethnographies of Law and Social Control, edited by Stacey Lee Burns, 2005
Volume 7:	Sociological Theory and Criminological Research, Views from Europe and United States, edited by Mathieu Deflem, 2006
Volume 8:	Police Occupational Culture: New Debates and Directions, edited by Megan O'Neill, Monique Marks and Anne-Marie Singh, 2007
Volume 9:	Crime and Human Rights, edited by Stephan Paramentier and Elmar Weitekamp, 2007
Volume 10:	Surveillance and Governance: Crime Control and Beyond, edited by Mathieu Deflem, 2008
Volume 11:	Restorative Justice: From Theory to Practice, edited by Holly Ventura Miller, 2008
Volume 12:	Access to Justice, edited by Rebecca Sandefur, 2009
Volume 13:	Immigration, Crime and Justice, edited by William F. McDonald, 2009
Volume 14:	Popular Culture, Crime and Social Control, edited by Mathieu Deflem, 2010
Volume 15:	Social Control: Informal, Legal and Medical, edited by James J. Chriss, 2010
Volume 16:	Economic Crisis and Crime, edited by Mathieu Deflem, 2011
Volume 17:	Disasters, Hazards and Law, edited by Mathieu Deflem, 2012
Volume 18:	Music and Law, edited by Mathieu Deflem, 2013
Volume 19:	Punishment and Incarceration: A Global Perspective, edited by Mathieu Deflem, 2013
Volume 20:	Terrorism and Counterterrorism Today, edited by Mathieu Deflem, 2015
Volume 21:	The Politics of Policing: Between Force and Legitimacy, edited by Mathieu Deflem, 2016
Volume 22:	Race, Ethnicity and Law, edited by Mathieu Deflem, 2017
Volume 23:	Homicide and Violent Crime, edited by Mathieu Deflem, 2018

SOCIOLOGY OF CRIME, LAW AND DEVIANCE VOLUME 24

METHODS OF CRIMINOLOGY AND CRIMINAL JUSTICE RESEARCH

EDITED BY

MATHIEU DEFLEM
University of South Carolina, USA

and

DEREK M.D. SILVA
King's University College, Canada

emerald PUBLISHING

United Kingdom – North America – Japan
India – Malaysia – China

Emerald Publishing Limited
Howard House, Wagon Lane, Bingley BD16 1WA, UK

First edition 2019

British Library Cataloguing in Publication Data
A catalogue record for this book is available from the British Library

ISBN: 978-1-78769-866-6 (Print)
ISBN: 978-1-78769-865-9 (Online)
ISBN: 978-1-78769-867-3 (Epub)

ISSN: 1521-6136 (Series)

Printed and bound by CPI Group (UK) Ltd, Croydon, CR0 4YY

CONTENTS

LIST OF FIGURES AND TABLES

CHAPTER 1

CHAPTER 7

CHAPTER 11

ABOUT THE CONTRIBUTORS

Valerie R. Anderson, School of Criminal Justice, University of Cincinnati, USA, conducts research in the areas of human trafficking and juvenile justice. She recently served as the principal investigator on a statewide human trafficking prevalence study funded by the Ohio Office of Criminal Justice Services.

Barak Ariel, Institute of Criminology, University of Cambridge, UK and Institute of Criminology, Hebrew University of Jerusalem, specializes in experimental criminology and evidence-based policy, particularly in respect of technology in policing, place-based interventions, deterrence, legitimacy, and counter terrorism.

Nawal Ammar, Professor and Dean, Rowan University, USA, is an expert on violence against immigrant women. She is the author of over 100 research manuscripts. Her recent work concerns promoting access to justice for immigrant crime victims and children in the US justice system in National Center for State Courts and American Civil Liberties (2018).

Matthew Bland, Institute of Criminology, University of Cambridge, UK, specializes in quantitative and experimental analyses of police-related issues, particularly domestic abuse and the use of algorithms in policing.

Thomas G. Blomberg, Dean and Sheldon L. Messinger Professor of Criminology, College of Criminology and Criminal Justice, Florida State University, USA. His research interests include elderly victimization, the impact of education on delinquency, life course theory, and methods for advancing research in criminal justice.

Julie Brancale, Teaching Faculty Member, College of Criminology and Criminal Justice, Florida State University, USA. Dr Brancale's research interests include the study of elderly victimization, life course theory, and adult and juvenile correctional policies.

Garth Davies, School of Criminology, Simon Fraser University, Canada, specializes in evaluating programs for countering violent extremism, the social psychology of radicalization, and the statistical modeling and projection of violent right-wing extremism. He is a member of the Executive Committee of the Canadian Network for Research on Terrorism, Security, and Society.

Mathieu Deflem, Department of Sociology, University of South Carolina, USA, specializes in the sociology of social control, terrorism, policing, sociology of law, and sociological theory. He is the author of four books, including *The Policing of Terrorism* (Routledge, 2010) and *Sociology of Law* (Cambridge University Press, 2008).

Walter S. DeKeseredy, Anna Deane Carlson Endowed Chair of Social Sciences, West Virginia University, USA, specializes in the areas of violence against women and rural criminology. He received awards for his research from divisions of the American Society of Criminology and sections of the Academy of Criminal Justice Sciences.

Finn-Aage Esbensen is E. Desmond Lee Professor, Youth Crime and Violence, Department of Criminology and Criminal Justice, University of Missouri – St. Louis, USA. He has served as the Principal Investigator of numerous evaluations of school-based prevention programs and is currently PI on the NIJ funded UMSL CSSI project.

Richard Frank, School of Criminology, Simon Fraser University, Canada, specializes in cybercrime, with an interest in hackers and security issues, such as online terrorism and warfare. He is the Director of the International CyberCrime Research Centre and the Associate Editor-in-Chief of Security Informatics.

Tiana Gaudette, School of Criminology, Simon Fraser University, Canada, specializes in extremists' use of fringe online platforms, the alt-right, and right-wing extremism. She is a Research Assistant on a Public Safety Canada-funded project on right-wing extremism in Canada. She is also a Research Assistant at the International CyberCrime Research Centre.

Sadaf Hashimi, School of Criminal Justice, Rutgers University – Newark, USA, is a Doctoral student. Her primary research interests include networks and crime, collective behavior, illicit markets, and criminal justice policy.

Teresa C. Kulig, School of Criminology and Criminal Justice, University of Nebraska at Omaha, USA, specializes in the study of the nature and prevalence of human trafficking, theories of victimization, rape myth acceptance in India, public perceptions on justice-related topics, and laws named after crime victims.

Navin Kumar, Department of Sociology, Yale University, USA, works in the area of sexually transmitted infections (STIs) and Drug Use. Current projects include the effects of social networks on treatment retention among people receiving medication for opioid use disorder, and the use of sexual history in routine health screening to identify targets for behavioral interventions.

Alex Luscombe, candidate, Centre for Criminology & Sociolegal Studies, University of Toronto, Canada. His research interests include policing, corruption, secrecy, and freedom of information law. He has published in a number of academic journals, including *Social Forces*, *British Journal of Criminology*, and *International Political Sociology*.

Timothy McCuddy, Assistant Research Professor, Criminology and Criminal Justice, University of Missouri – St. Louis, USA. His research focuses on how technology affects social processes related to crime. He is currently the Project Director of the UMSL Comprehensive School Safety Initiative.

Jennifer O'Neill is a Doctoral student at the Department of Criminology and Criminal Justice, University of Missouri – St. Louis, USA. She conducts school-based research and her work focuses on schools and deviance, as well as identity and delinquency.

Marie Ouellet, Department of Criminal Justice and Criminology, Georgia State University, USA, is interested in how delinquent groups emerge and evolve, and the role of networks in shaping these dynamics. Her research has been published in *Criminology*, *Criminology and Public Policy*, and *Social Networks*.

Ryan Scrivens, School of Criminal Justice, Michigan State University, USA, specializes in terrorists' and extremists' use of the Internet, right-wing extremism, and computational social science. He is a Research Associate at the International CyberCrime Research Centre, a Visiting Researcher at VOX-Pol, and an Associate Editor of Perspectives on Terrorism.

Derek M. D. Silva, Department of Sociology, King's University College at Western University, Canada, specializes in radicalization and violent extremism, policing, sport, and social control. His most recent work can be found in peer-reviewed journals *Sociological Forum, Race & Class,* and the *Sociology of Sport Journal.*

Christopher J. Sullivan, School of Criminal Justice, University of Cincinnati, USA, works in the areas of developmental and life-course criminology, juvenile justice, and research methodology and analytic methods.

Sarah Turnbull, Department of Criminology, Birkbeck College, University of London, UK, works in the areas of immigration detention and deportation, gender, race, and punishment, reentry, and border criminology. She is the author of *Parole in Canada: Gender and Diversity in the Federal System* (UBC Press, 2016).

Kevin Walby, Associate Professor, Criminal Justice and Chancellor's Research Chair, University of Winnipeg, Canada. He is co-editor of the *Journal of Prisoners on Prisons* as well as book review editor for *Surveillance & Society* and *Security Journal.*

Arshia U. Zaidi, Associate Professor Faculty of Social Science and Humanities, Criminology, University of Ontario Institute of Technology, Canada, she works in the areas of intimate partner violence, issues of immigration, ethnic identity, race, gender, sexuality and family generational issues, survivors of elderly abuse, immigrant youth, information technology/social media, and also specializes in qualitative and quantitative methodology.

INTRODUCTION: MEASURING CRIME AND CRIMINAL JUSTICE

Mathieu Deflem and Derek M. D. Silva

It is not true that the scientific nature of scholarship is primarily determined by its methods. It is a common misconception of science, hopefully made more by non-scientists than by those who practice it, to refer to the merits of scholarship by virtue of the so-called "scientific methods" that are used in a particular field of study. Nothing could be less scientific. In truth, a scientific discipline is defined primarily by the systematic nature in which it builds knowledge about a particular part of reality to account for variation therein. The questions of science are its most foundational component, not the methods with which those questions are answered. Theories clarify what appropriate questions can be formulated and how they should be approached. As such, methods always follow theories. However, this does not mean that methods are any less valuable and indispensable in the scientific process. On the contrary, methods of discovery, data collection, and analysis must be relied upon to test and/or apply propositions on a universe of observable phenomena and their interrelations. In other words, methodology is a necessary but insufficient condition for the accumulation of systematic knowledge the sciences pursue.

From this conception of the relation between theory, methods, and data, the present volume seeks to offer a useful contribution to present an overview of the value and use of a variety of methods and research techniques in criminology and criminal justice research today. There is no doubt that contemporary scholarship in criminology and criminal justice studies is sophisticated in all relevant respects that social science demands. Yet, the value of methodology in research on crime and criminal justice has sometimes been more and sometimes less recognized over the course of the development of these fields of study, with all due consequences.

While today's methodological contributions in crime and criminal justice scholarship are at times not always fully acknowledged, it is to be noted that historically the so-called criminal sciences such as criminal anthropology and criminal justice administration were in fact virtually synonymous with methodology and empirical research. Traditional fields of criminological investigation, such as criminal

Methods of Criminology and Criminal Justice Research
Sociology of Crime, Law and Deviance, Volume 24, 1–4

ISSN: 1521-6136/doi:10.1108/S1521-613620190000024001

statistics in the nineteenth century (Deflem, 1997), were at the center of the evolution of social science. Although the criminological enterprise was distinctly developed to be serviceable to the administration of criminal justice as an instrumental form of knowledge, insights from these social research efforts actually informed the development of the social sciences, especially sociology. Classical scholars such as Auguste Comte, Ferdinand Tönnies, and Emile Durkheim all learned from the rigorous methods used in research on crime and other social-science phenomena, though they also sought to extend those inquiries in a manner that was consistent with the idea of sociology as an independent science.

As a result of developments related to the modernization of social science during the twentieth century, the turn in criminologically relevant work was distinctly theoretical rather than methodological. In fact, whereas methods were at the heart of research on crime and criminal justice in the nineteenth century, central theoretical developments in sociology during the modern era were intimately connected with criminological questions. For example, the masterful insights from crime causation perspectives such as differential association theory, the structural approach to deviant behavior in the context of anomie theory, and the constructionist approach of deviance studies and labeling theory were not only significant to criminology and criminal justice, but also to sociology and social science in general.

The variable positioning of scholarship on crime, deviance, and social control in between theory and methodology, then, is synonymous with the field's development and maturation over time. The scope of the present volume of Sociology of Crime, Law, and Deviance to focus on methodological questions, as such, complements the volume that was published in this series a little over a decade ago to bring out the unique contributions of theory (Deflem, 2006). What this volume hopes to show is that the special connection of criminological work with methodology, which was perhaps lost for a while when the focus was on conceptual questions, is now fully restored and can additionally benefit from not having given up on all useful theoretical considerations. As such, our volume should nicely complement other relevant methodological works, such as the anthologies (Copes, 2012; Piquero & Weisburd, 2010) and textbooks (Bachman, Schutt & Plass, 2017; Maxfield & Babbie, 2015) that our field now can rely on.

The chapters of this volume are not ordered per method applied in the authors' respective research enterprises, nor divided in terms of the dreaded distinction between quantitative and qualitative methods. Instead, precisely in order to show the value of a variety of methods in contemporary criminology and criminal justice research, the chapters are thematically grouped. Part I brings together three chapters that discuss general patterns and relatively broad trends of crime and criminal behavior in different ways. Barak Ariel and Matthew Bland first address the most fundamental question if crime has been rising or falling by comparing police-recorded crime numbers and victim survey results. Based on research on violent crime in England and Wales, they find that both methods have their limitations and that crime classifications need to be rethought and refined. Next, Kevin Walby and Alex Luscombe assess the value of freedom of information requests. They argue that such data can be very useful for the study of a variety of issues in socio-legal studies, criminology, and criminal justice. Marie Ouellet and Sadaf Hashimi examine the use of network methods for modeling the nature of criminal groups and other social systems, rather than focusing on individual-level data. The authors argue that such methodological advances can also have theoretical benefits to examine crime and delinquency in terms of social relations and structure.

Part II focuses on certain special groups and issues of criminological relevance. Concentrating on violence against women, Walter S. DeKeseredy presents novel ways in which relevant survey data can be collected. He finds that such an approach can minimize underreporting and can have several theoretical and policy-related advantages. Focused on male sex workers, Navin Kumar reviews extant research from a methodological viewpoint. He finds that methodology should be carefully considered because research on male sex work is far from well-developed at present, but will need to advance in all relevant respects in view of the fact that the issue will not go away. Devoting attention to the puzzling case of elder financial exploitation, Julie Brancale and Thomas G. Blomberg suggest the advantage of a mixed-methods approach. Based on research in Florida, the authors argue that a variety of methods were used to begin to research the issue because the problem is still very much under-researched, though it will be of growing relevance in the future. Centering on the impact of school violence, in particular the shooting at Stoneman Douglas High School in Parkland, Florida, Jennifer O'Neill, Timothy McCuddy, and Finn-Aage Esbensen have examined a survey of middle and high school students in St. Louis County. The authors show that the Parkland incident greatly influenced students' perception of school safety, affecting the validity of such research.

In Part III, finally, methodological issues are explored on a variety of criminological problems that involve a crossing of boundaries, physical and otherwise. Nawal Ammar and Arshia U. Zaidi study effects of immigration by examining immigrant women in Canada who have been victims of intimate partner violence. They specifically explore the challenges posed in quantitative and qualitative community-based participatory research, which they argue can be relevant to both academics as well as advocacy groups. Sarah Turnbull focuses on another migration-related concern by studying her own attempt to incorporate visual data in research on immigration detention and deportation in Great Britain. Specifically centered on the method of photovoice, she discussed the uses and, especially, the limitations of participant-generated photographic images. Next, studying human trafficking, Valerie R. Anderson, Teresa C. Kulig, and Christopher J. Sullivan study the value and use of agency record data related to victimization, perpetration, and patterns. The authors show that such data have been used in a variety of settings of research on human trafficking and can be further developed and strengthened. Finally, co-authors Ryan Scrivens, Tiana Gaudette, Garth Davies, and Richard Frank study implications of the boundary-crossing aspects of the internet to examine methods for collecting data on extremism and terrorism-related behavior. The authors particularly study how web-crawling technology and sentiment analysis can be relied upon to analyze extremist content that is posted online.

In sum, the authors of this volume represent a usefully broad range of methodologies that are applied to a likewise varied collection of topics related to crime, deviance, and criminal justice. Collectively and through their respective individual chapters, the contributors to this book make for a meaningful addition to the literature that should be of interest to scholars working on a multitude of issues of crime, deviance, and social control.

REFERENCES

Bachman, R. D., Schutt, R. K., & Plass, P. S. (2017). *Fundamentals of research in criminology and criminal justice*. Los Angeles, CA: Sage.

Copes, H. (Ed). (2012). *Advancing qualitative methods in criminology and criminal justice*. Oxford: Routledge.

Deflem, M. (1997). Surveillance and criminal statistics: Historical foundations of governmentality. In A. Sarat & S. Silbey (Eds.), *Studies in law, politics and society* (Vol. 17, pp. 149–184). Greenwich, CT: JAI Press.

Deflem, M. (Ed.). (2006). *Sociological theory and criminological research: Views from Europe and the United States*. Sociology of Crime, Law and Deviance (Vol. 7). Amsterdam, The Netherlands: Elsevier/JAI Press.

Maxfield, M. G., & Babbie, E. R. (Eds.) (2015). *Research methods for criminal justice and criminology* (7th ed.). Stamford, CT: Cengage Learning.

Piquero, A. R., & Weisburd, D. (Eds.). (2010). *Handbook of quantitative criminology*. New York, NY: Springer.

PART I

GENERAL PATTERNS AND TRENDS

CHAPTER 1

IS CRIME RISING OR FALLING? A COMPARISON OF POLICE-RECORDED CRIME AND VICTIMIZATION SURVEYS

Barak Ariel and Matthew Bland

ABSTRACT

Purpose – *Statistics about the level of crime continue to attract public and political attention but are often presented in conflicting ways. In England and Wales, police-recorded crimes are no longer considered "national statistics" and, instead, the crime survey of England and Wales (CSEW) is used. However, it is not clear why partial population data (e.g., police-recorded crime) are considered less reliable or valid for measuring temporal crime trends in society than inferential statistical estimation models that are based on samples such as CSEW. This is particularly the case for approximating rare events like high-harm violence and specific harmful modus operandi (e.g., knife crime and firearms). In this chapter, the authors cross-reference victim survey and police-recorded data to determine similarities and contradictions in trends.*

Methods – *Using police data and CSEW estimates, the authors contrast variance and logarithmic trend lines since 1981 across a range of data categories and then triangulate the results with assault records from hospital consultations.*

Findings – *Change in crime rates in recent years is neither as unique nor extreme as promulgated in media coverage of crime. Moreover, analyses show conflicting narratives with a host of plausible but inconclusive depictions of the*

Methods of Criminology and Criminal Justice Research
Sociology of Crime, Law and Deviance, Volume 24, 7–31

ISSN: 1521-6136/doi:10.1108/S1521-613620190000024004

"actual" amount of crime committed in the society. The authors also conclude that neither source of data can serve as the benchmark of the other. Thus, both data systems suffer from major methodological perils, and the estimated crime means in CSEW, inferred from samples, are not necessarily more valid or accurate than police-recorded data (particularly for low-frequency and high-harm crimes). On the other hand police-recorded data are susceptible to variations in recording practices. As such, the authors propose a number of areas for further research, and a revised taxonomy of crime classifications to assist with future public interpretations of crime statistics.

Originality – *There is much public and academic discourse about different sources of crime measurement yet infrequent analysis of the precise similarities and differences between the methods. This chapter offers a new perspective on long-term trends and highlights an issue of much contemporaneous concern: rising violent crime.*

Keywords: Rising crime; victim surveys; recorded crime; violent crime; crime statistics; police records

INTRODUCTION

Is crime going up or down in society? This question is frequently the subject of public debate, being of particular interest to politicians and police professionals alike (Mercer, 2019). Being able to answer this question accurately is also essential for policing scholars who seek to identify appropriate targets (Sherman, 2013), as well as for scholars interested in research methods and crime trajectory analyses (Farrington, 1979; Jennings, Gray, Hay, & Farrall, 2015). However, temporal patterns – that is, what are often referred to as "trends" in crime volume and type – are difficult to measure and interpret (Nguyen & Loughran, 2018). For example, is an arithmetic increase in crime volume during a particular time period a genuine upward crime trend? The answer is not simple, as the increase can be explained through other theories: crime-recording practices, crime reporting patterns, or changes in the definitions of crime, which are all plausible explanations vis-á-vis the case for explaining an arithmetic increase as an "actual" change in crime volume or type.

One major reason for the difficulty in interpreting crime figures is that the ways in which they are measured, or estimated, determine the outcome. From a methodological perspective, when crime levels are dependent on the data collection methodology, it raises suspicions about the integrity of claims about increases or reductions in crime levels over time. Put differently, if the measurement tool "causes" the fluctuations in the figures, we experience statistical noise, to a point that we may not trust the measurement at all.

Given these concerns, in England and Wales, police-recorded crimes were recently declared to be invalid national statistics of crime. Statisticians made the case that police-recording practices affect crime records to such an extent that we can no long trust them. This is a logical deduction, because police crime figures largely depend on the extent to which the police deal with crime and record it accurately. Instead, national crime statistics have been "replaced" by the Crime Survey of England and Wales (CSEW). At least for the Home Office, the CSEW is a superior instrument, because it directly surveys victims. Statisticians who use CSEW suggest that they are the best available tools to estimate from a large sample onto the populations of England and Wales. Therefore, the question about the rise or fall of overall crime in England and Wales is broadly answered based on the evidence presented in the CSEW.

However, the CSEW is not infallible either. The survey systematically excludes crime categories and subgroups of participants who are likely to be the most vulnerable to become victims or commit crimes: the young, the homeless, the transient, and the non-respondents. It also excludes crimes against businesses and those where there is no apparent personal victim. The CSEW is, after all, a survey of a sampled subset of households in society. By definition, a survey requires sampling techniques, estimation models, and statistical correction to account for various sampling errors and "design effects". Therefore, the CSEW population estimates miss much of the low-frequency but high-harm crimes. Violence estimates are a case in point. These and other methodological issues underscore the problems that the CSEW faces, and for at least some crime categories, it ought not to be blindly accepted that a national survey of 35,000 households is the "best practice" for understanding crime patterns. Further, it is not *necessarily* the appropriate yardstick against which the validity and reliability of police-reported crime statistics ought to be evaluated.

One solution is to triangulate data with a third source of information. For example, National Health Services (NHS) hospital records can be contrasted with the two data sources (police records and CSEW). It is often argued that the NHS data are not affected by police crime-recording practices, nor are they susceptible to victim survey methodology flaws (Sivarajasingam et al., 2010). Therefore, hospital admission records give indications about the validity of the data sources, as well as the direction of crime trends. Naturally, hospital population data may only be useful for against-person crime figures that resulted in injury, but the data also provide additional evidence on crime patterns in society.

With these contemplations in mind, this chapter has a modest aim: to compare publicly available, population-level data from both the police as well as the CSEW, and to then contrast these "data narratives" with NHS records. Particular emphasis will be given to the argument that *all* crime statistics fail to reflect the actual amount of crime committed in society.

The chapter has the following structure: first, the study of temporal crime patterns is introduced, with a presentation of the two major data sources for the study of crime trends: police records and victim surveys. Unofficial versions of data collection instruments – localized surveys of offenders, victims, places, etc. – are purposely excluded, as these do not establish national crime policies or lead the political discourse on the necessary response to crime like official statistics do. For each source, the methodologies used to collate data are explored, with particular attention paid to the concerns of which source is exposed (reliability and validity).

Next, the procedures used in this chapter are laid out, with our focus being on temporal trend analyses and comparisons between the datasets. The analysis is then followed by a discussion of the results in the context of policy, as well as research recommendations for future research.

POLICE-RECORDED CRIME VERSUS ESTIMATES FROM VICTIM SURVEYS

There are two major sources for crime count statistics: victim surveys and police-recorded crimes (Maguire, 2002, chapter 3; Skogan, 1984; Wittebrood & Junger, 2002). For a broader review of these two instruments, see Newburn (2018). At least in England and Wales, statisticians have argued for the superiority of the CSEW over police-recorded data (Home Office, 2018b); as discussed in more detail below, the UK Statistics Authority made the case that police records do not provide accurate estimates of crime reported to the police. On the other hand, it is not immediately clear why we accept this argument unconditionally (Baumer & Lauritsen, 2010). Relying on surveys creates at least as many challenges to the validity and reliability of the data as are in police records (Home Office, 2018a). Thus, we review the prominent difficulties of these data sources below.

Methodological Issues with Police-recorded Crimes

There are a number of hazards to police-recorded data protocols, and we will focus on two primary issues – recording practices and insufficient differentiation between police-generated and victim-generated crimes.

Police records are notoriously susceptible to changes in recording practices (MacDonald, 2002). The Greater Manchester Police (GMP) is a case in point; for a certain period of time, the GMP –the second largest force in the country – was excluded from national police records due to challenges with their crime-recording practices (ONS, 2017). Therefore, recorded crime statistics are affected by recording practices – which makes them more vulnerable to threats of validity and reliability.

To increase the reliability – that is, the consistency of recording – the Home Office Counting Rules (HOCR) were introduced to govern crime classification practices. The HOCR was established in 1998 and later supplemented by the National Crime Recording Standard (NCRS) in 2002. These guidelines are aimed to increase the consistency of crime recording between English and Welsh forces. They also sought to establish a victim-oriented approach in crime statistics, in which every victim of a crime event was allocated an individual crime record – a policy colloquially known as "one victim, one crime". The result was greater numbers of crimes recorded for multiple victim events and a rise in overall crime, accordingly.

Still, Her Majesty's Inspectorate of Constabulary and Fire & Rescue Services (HMICFRS) conducted reviews into the way police forces recorded crimes in 2009 and 2014, and while there were improvements over the years, recording issues were nearly always detected. Consequently, the UK Statistics Authority (House of Commons Public Affairs Select Committee, 2014) assessed police records, and concluded that the "underlying data on crimes recorded by the police may not be reliable." Thus, the "National Statistics" quality badge was removed from police-recorded crime data, with the most concerning issue being the under-recording of certain crime categories by the police (HMICFRS, 2014): more than 20% of crimes that received police attention did not get recorded as such (for instance, violence with or without injury – 33%). Immediately after the 2014 report, the HMICFRS announced that it would conduct an "unannounced programme of rolling inspections of crime recording on an ongoing basis." The results of these inspections are periodically published on the HMICFRS's website.

Furthermore, a clear distinction between police-generated and witness/victim-generated records is required, but the police database (as well as the CSEW estimates) overlook this crucial discrepancy. We need to isolate outcomes from outputs (Ariel, Weinborn, & Sherman, 2016). Outputs are produced through proactive productivity, and outcomes are the result of the outputs. Traffic offences, drugs, and tax evasion are all examples of behaviors that are unlikely to be reported by the public (exceptions to these can be found in Ellis & Arieli, 1999 and Near & Miceli, 1985). Therefore, increases in confiscations, arrests, and detentions of these crime categories are directly linked to the "dosage" of law enforcement, not crime per se (Wain & Ariel, 2014). Therefore, the more attention a crime problem receives from the police, the higher the police crime figures will be.

On the other hand, crimes that come to the attention of the police through victims and witnesses have a different journey: they are reported to the police independent of a *necessary* specific police intervention. When victims "generate" crimes, it is often considered that the trend is not affected by immediate police practices but rather the willingness of the victim/witness to cooperate with the police (Macbeth & Ariel, 2017).

Policing experiments have taken this approach in the context of place-based interventions, when the unit of analysis is the crime hotspot and the test measures police effectiveness (Ariel et al., 2016; Sherman & Weisburd, 1995; Ariel, 2018). Nonetheless, the same approach is often not taken in epidemiological and longitudinal studies of crime (however, *cf.* Sherman, Neyroud, & Neyroud, 2016). When this distinction is applied, it then becomes unclear whether the police's data represent a genuine variation in crime rates. One alternative explanation is that police tactics and recording strategies dictate fluctuations in some crime figures (Ariel, Bland, & Sutherland, 2017; Ariel & Partridge, 2017). Further, when the police target drug or gun offences, these output figures would go up (Sherman & Rogan, 1995). At least in crime categories that are conditional of police outputs – stop and search, arrests, seizes, crackdowns, etc. – we would expect an increase in these categories when the police increase attention on them, because the police have placed these behaviors as performance targets (Martin, Downe, Grace, & Nutley, 2010; Talbot, 2008).

Methodological Issues with the CSEW

The CSEW surveys households about their victimization experiences across various crime categories. Approximately 35,000 face-to-face interviews are conducted across the country every survey wave, with response rates ranging between 70% and 75%. Respondents are asked about crime, antisocial behavior, and perceptions about certain dangerous lifestyles. According to its creators, the CSEW is "powerful in providing the most reliable victimisation estimates possible" (ONS, 2017).

Despite its size and aims, inferring from sample means ($n = 35{,}000$ households) to population means ($n = 27{,}000{,}000$ households) involves complex statistical modeling and estimating the error and variance of the data is even more difficult. Technically, the CSEW's error terms are used to construct the confidence intervals (CI) around the sample estimates, which are the range of possible scores that the "true" population means are. The CI are meant to "reflect the stratified and semi-clustered design of the survey," and complex models are then applied to "correct" the statistical design. This implies that since the survey design is not a simple random sample (in order to adjust for remote and infrequent populations), statistical modifications are required. Yet, like any inferential statistical model, by definition, the equations introduce statistical noise.

Another issue the CSEW faces is that the estimates are at the household level rather than the individual level (the unit of analysis is the household, rather than the victim, per se). Approximation methods are then used to correct the fact that the two populations – households and adults – are not the same (although correlated). These methods use population-weighted variances associated with two approximated estimates for overall crime:

> The first approximation is derived by apportioning household crime equally among adults within the household (in other words, converting households into adults), and second, by apportioning personal crimes to all household members (converting adults into households). The variances are calculated in the same way as for the standard household or personal crime rates (that is, taking into account the complex sample design). An average of the two estimates of the population-weighted variances is then taken. The resulting approximated variance is then used in the calculation of CI for the estimate of all CSEW crime and in the calculation of the sampling error. (Office for National Statistics, ONS, 2019)

Next, by calculating the mean of the two approximations, the method deals with the possible effect on the estimates of differing response rates (and therefore, calibration rates) by household size.

Why are these statistical issues important? Despite some of the elegance in these modeling techniques, surveys remain surveys, and questions about sample representativeness can always be raised. Further, the survey depends on the willingness of the respondent to engage, the interaction between the interviewer and the interviewee, or how rare particular events are in the representative population for the survey to "pick up" the prevalence and frequency of a phenomenon (Gideon, 2012). Sharing with a stranger about being a victim of car theft is one thing; telling them you have been a victim of domestic violence, a knife crime, or knowing a serious violent offender, is another (Holbrook, Green, & Krosnick, 2003).

The problem is exacerbated by the fact that the true population means are unknown, so the representation error rate can only be induced from the very sample that is assumed to represent the population. While 35,000 respondents may "feel" like a large number, the analytical tools are estimations, approximations, and assessments induced from samples. Therefore, stating the sample *is* the population, across rare victimization incidents, is incorrect (see discussion in Nulty, 2008).

Recent Trends in Police-recorded Crimes and CSEW

The official stance in England and Wales is that the CSEW is more reliable and valid for longitudinal trends (ONS, 2018). However, the ONS itself argues that rare events such as violence might best be measured through police-recorded crimes. In addition, there are crime events that are not included in the CSEW at all (including the aforementioned police-generated crimes). As such, recorded crimes are still relevant and continue to be the source of much public and scholarly scrutiny.

With this in mind, what do the two measurement sources tell us about the ways in which crime has fluctuated during the latest generation?

DATA AND ANALYSIS PLAN

To answer these questions, then, analysis was conducted on open source data (as of January 2019), published by the ONS and the NHS (www.ons.gov.uk, Digital.nhs.uk, respectively). The ONS provides police-recorded crime data as well as CSEW records. Data from 1981 to 2018 were contrasted between the three datasets. These rich datasets include annual figures on police actions (stop-and-searches, arrests, etc.) as well as crimes reported to the police, including homicides and injuries to victims. Rates per 1,000 population, per year, were computed for all crimes, and then for violent crimes. Analyses of the absolute figures were used for certain subgroups of data, particularly violence. These rare but high-harm incidents can be interpreted in different ways; thus, unweighted figures are presented so that readers may form their own views of the interpretation of these patterns. The usual measures of central tendencies were computed (means and rates), and variance was measured in terms of the 95% CI and standard deviations.

To assist in this task, logarithmic trend lines were calculated based on these annual records and then added in the graphic presentation of the data. Crime fluctuates, sometimes greatly, over the course of many years (Linning, Andresen, & Brantingham, 2017), so drawing a linear model (i.e., a straight-line explanation) will not represent the accurate movement of the trend. Linear models assume consistent change between the data points, but as seen in the figures, the data exhibit quick increases and reductions, particularly the spike in certain crime categories (2014–2018, as a case in point). Instead, logarithmic models use logarithmic transformations to bring variances closer together by adjusting the data for the lack of constant rate of change. Put differently, these trend lines are best fit when the rate of the change in the data increases or decreases quickly, which has been arguable in terms of the crime level in England and Wales. Therefore, the logarithmic model is "useful if the assumptions of homogeneity in variance, normality, and additivity used in linear regression are not met" (Picard, 1998, p. 49).

Health warning: this chapter does not attempt to predict, nor does it apply inferential estimations on the data (for examples thereof, see Nagin, 1999). For these, subject-level data are required and more sophisticated statistical modeling should be consulted, all of which go beyond the scope of this paper. Instead, the technical literature should be referred to (see e.g., Andresen & Felson, 2009;

Goldsmith, McGuire, Mollenkopf, & Ross, 1999; Gove, Hughes, & Geerken, 1985). The analyses do, however, correspond with the wider narrative that each data source presents, and how these "stories" are problematized in terms of their validity and reliability (Litwin & Fink, 1995).

A second limitation of the data is the lack of strong temporal congruency between all the data available from ONS and NHS. "Annual figures" are defined differently, such as fiscal or calendar years. Similarly, the CSEW survey asks questions about crime experiences over the course of the "previous 12 months," so it is difficult to estimate the precise moment of the reported event. We know some crime types are temporal (Haberman, Sorg, & Ratcliffe, 2018), so crimes over the course of a year can be misassigned to the wrong corresponding year in the comparison dataset. Police crime recording trends may also exacerbate this issue. Moreover, police-recorded crime statistics are compiled based on the date a crime was recorded by the police, not the date that it occurred. Such "non-recent" crimes have increased in the last few years, particularly in violent and sexual crime classifications (ONS, 2018). Therefore, the comparability of the two timelines is suspect, to some degree, to temporal sequencing error. These drawbacks limit the validity of the conclusions. Still, the analyses provide grounds for new explorations of the ways in which we interpret crime measurement.

FINDINGS

Overall Crime Trends

Fig. 1 reports the year-to-year differences in the two leading crime-recording systems – police records and CSEW estimates. Both measures suggest a 6–9% year-to-year change – approximately 415,000 additional incidents. Does this dramatic increase represent a true change in crime rates in England & Wales? Two data points do not provide sufficient information and trend analyses are too speculative with only two "waves" of records. Without more evidence, this increase in incidence is difficult to interpret.

However, when looking at a greater number of such point to point comparisons, substantial context is gained. Take police records as a case in point. As Fig. 2 shows, the use of year on year percentage change only masks important facts about cyclical changes. Longer follow-up periods in the datasets allow us to compute the variance of the fluctuation of incidents on a year-to-year basis, rather than the fluctuation itself. This means we can contextualize how extraordinary a particular observation (i.e., annual data) is from the overall pattern of change. As shown, the latest year is not unique.

Fig. 3 shows the fluctuation for both police-recorded crimes as well as for CSEW. Crime fluctuated, on average, by 300,000 police-recorded incidents every year and about one million victimization estimations per year (Mean(Crime) = 4,665,647; 95% CI [4,397,168.82, 4,934,125.18]; and Mean(CSEW) = 11,084,760.0; 95% CI [9,927,270.54, 12,242,249.46]). As shown, the *mean* year-to-year variation for police records is ±6% (31 years of data) and ±5% for CSEW records (16 years). A total of 17 out of 37 years of police records experienced more than a ±6%

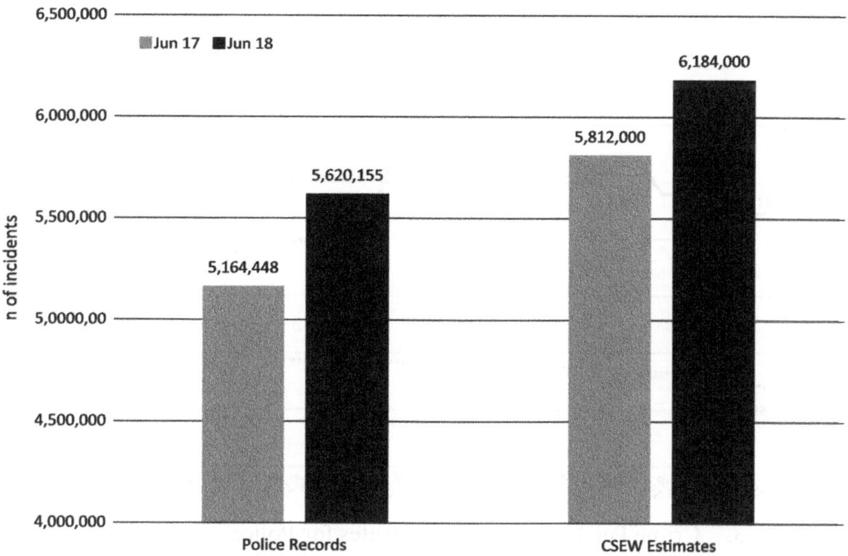

Fig. 1. Police Records Versus CSEW Estimates (2017 and 2018).

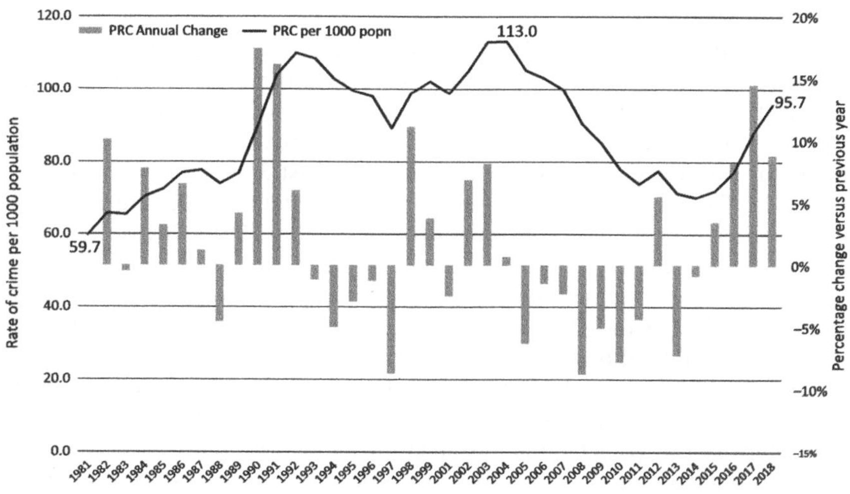

Fig. 2. Crime Per 1,000 Population Rates for Police-recorded Crime and Year-to-Year Annual Change for England and Wales (1981–2018).

difference from the overall crime mean, and 8 years of CSEW data experienced more than ±5% difference from the overall mean. In a historical context, the most recent spike in crime is not unusual, statistically speaking.

Fig. 3 presents the rate of crime/victimization per 1,000 population according to both police records and CSEW estimates over more than 35 years.

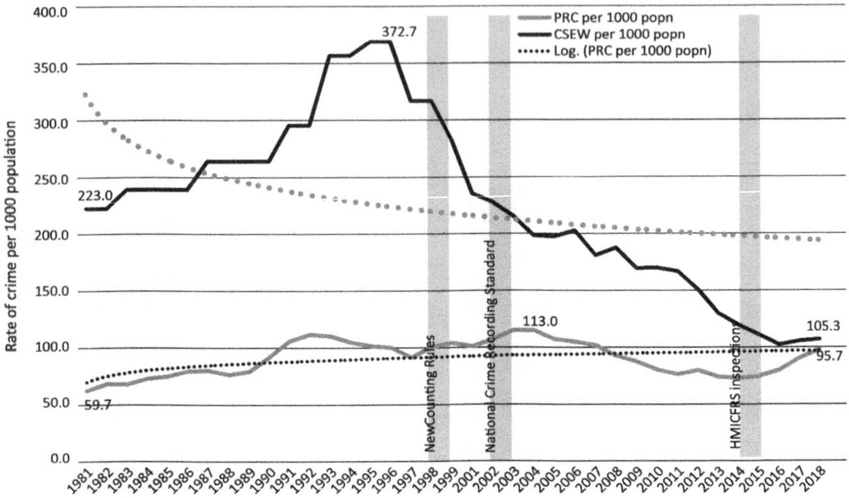

Fig. 3. Crime Per 1,000 Population Rates for Police-recorded Crime Versus Crime Survey for England and Wales (CSEW; 1981–2018) with Logarithmic Trendlines.

Further, it provides more contexts to the increase in crime illustrated in Figs. 1 and 2. The logarithmic trend lines for both datasets are presented as well, for ease of comparability between the two. As shown, there was a steep decline in victimization estimations starting in the mid-1990s, of approximately 80 incidents per 1,000 population ($y = -37.93\ln(x) + 301.89$). On the other hand, the rate of police records has increased over the last 31 years ($y = 7.3406\ln(x) + 60.712$). The rate per 1,000 population in both data sources are the closest to each other over the last two years of observations (2017–2018) than in the previous three decades.

New rules have increased the number of crimes the police forces record – and the possible effect of these rules and practices can be seen in Fig. 3. As shown on the in-chart annotations, the introduction of new counting rules corresponded with new trends in recorded crime. Modification of the rules changes administrative and operational decisions, and with this, the measurement of crime may fluctuate even without "real" fluctuations in crime figures (Maguire, 2012, chapter 5). Therefore, a reduction in the number of crimes recorded by the police may not necessarily mean that the level of crime has decreased (Bowles, Reyes, & Garoupa, 2009; Loveday, 2006; Neyroud, 2008). Not all crimes are reported, and not all crimes that are reported are then logged. Since the year of the UK Statistics Authority's report and the HMICFRS' enhanced involvement in improving the integrity of crime statistics (2014), the overall level of recorded crime rose sharply, and Fig. 3 shows this trend most clearly: increases in crime. Of course, this is a correlational observation; however, the noticeable variations following new accounting regimes raises alternative explanations for the "rise-in-crime" interpretation of the algebraic increase in the figures.

Trends in Violence Data

The distinction between the police records and CSEW datasets can be expressed by comparing data on violence. Figs. 4 and 5 show the overall downward trend in the incidence of violence computed by the CSEW (2003–2018) – with the graph plateauing in more recent years. This trend occurred for violence with and without injuries to the victims [($y = -146{,}439.49\ln(x) + 1{,}090{,}910.73$), and $y = -258{,}407.87\ln(x) + 1{,}411{,}615.64$), respectively].

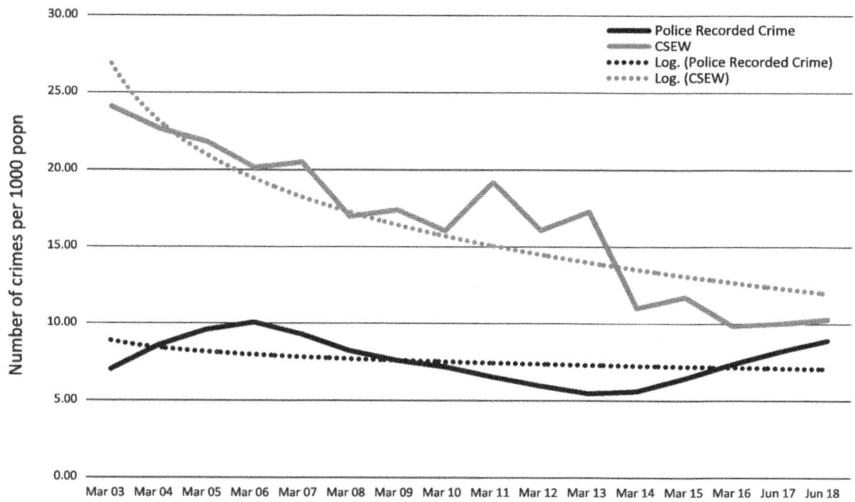

Fig. 4. Violence with Injury: Police-recorded Crime Versus CSEW (2003–2018).

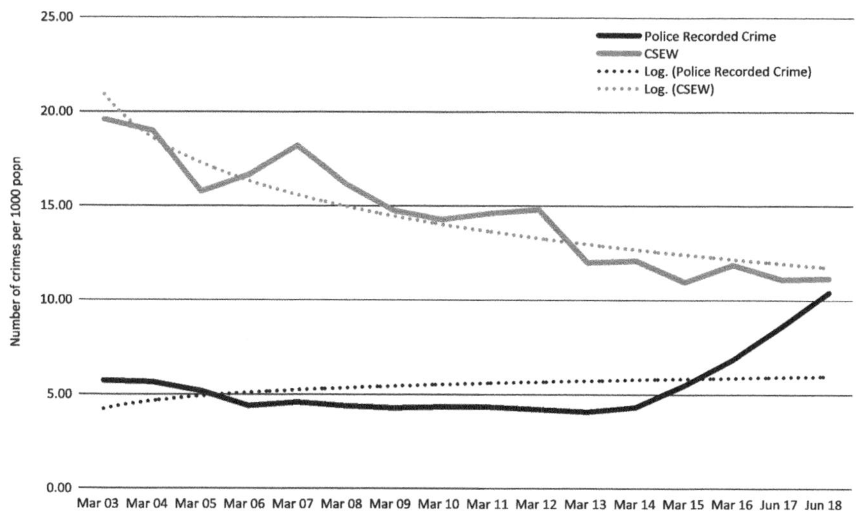

Fig. 5. Violence without Injury: Police-recorded Crime Versus CSEW (2003–2018).

On the other hand, these CSEW patterns of violence in society are not shown in the police-recorded violence data. Instead, violence seems to increase, particularly in 2014. Police crime figures point to an overall long-term increase in recorded violence *without* injuries to the victims ($y = 45{,}219.95\ln(x) + 214{,}876.26$, but a decrease in violence *with* injuries to the victims $y = -20{,}456.67\ln(x) + 463{,}465.25$).

Therefore, the figures for injurious assaults have declined over time according to both data sources. However, CSEW estimates suggest that non-injurious assaults are declining over time as well, while police records show a conflicting trend. These patterns are most noticeable after 2014 – and as will be shown hereafter, there are logical (and rival) explanations for these trends.

Homicide Data

Homicide can only be analyzed through police records, as the CSEW does not cover this crime category. More conceptually, homicide data are often used to strengthen the argument that violent crime is either increasing or decreasing over time (see Mercer, 2019 as a recent example of public media portrayal), since this crime type is considered less susceptible to crime-recording biases. Homicide rates and violence rates seem to be linked and correlate with social inequality (Fajnzylber, Lederman, & Loayza, 2002). Therefore, homicide data can provide a proxy for the population violence estimates by illustrating how violence fluctuates over time, common modus operandi, and about the relationship between the offenders and the victims.

First, as shown in Fig. 6, the number of homicides appeared to drop until the year 2012, plateau until 2015, and then escalate back to the level seen in 2006–2008. In the 16 years of data available for analysis from the ONS, the mean homicides per year are 683.1 (95% CI [620.3, 745.8]), and the overall trend is downwards ($R^2 = 70.1\%$; $y = -132.3\ln(x) + 936.66$). However, in the most recent years of observations, there had been an increase in homicide figures, which coexists with a similar increase in police-recorded violence.

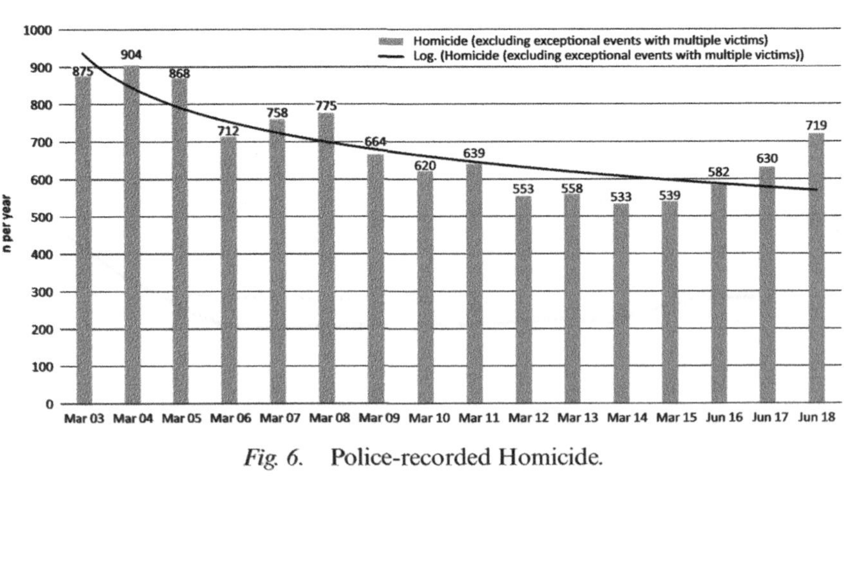

Fig. 6. Police-recorded Homicide.

Second, the recent media attention on violence in England and Wales has largely been in the context of knife and gunshot homicides (Google.co.uk; https://bit.ly/2RtHS5l). However, police records indicate that the proportion of violent incidents involving a sharp instrument had been relatively stable over the years, ranging between 186 and 272 incidents per year (Fig. 7). Similarly, on average, 36.0% of homicides are caused by a sharp instrument, with relatively little fluctuation in the standard deviation from year to year ($M = 0.36$, 95% CI [0.35, 0.37]). Thus, the increase in violence and homicide is not necessarily attributed to knife crime, as these police-recorded trends have been relatively stable over the years.

Finally, the relationship between the deceased and the suspect provides further information about these violence trends. According to the police records, while there had been a steady and continuous decline in homicide committed against family members or an acquaintance of the victim (e.g., domestic violence; $y = -38.36\ln(x) + 294.4$), as well as homicide committed by a stranger ($y = -39.34\ln(x) + 187.41$), the spike in recent homicide rates is attributable to the "homicides without a suspect" category, particularly since 2013–2014 ($y = 20.275\ln(x) + 30.467$). To place these figures in perspective, the number of homicides without a suspect moved between 2013 and 2014 and 2016 and 2017 from 32 to 46 and 84 to 210, respectively (Fig. 8). Without additional evidence on nearly one third of all victims in a given year, it is difficult to estimate population predictors that explain homicide trends in England and Wales.

However, these figures do not correspond with the CSEW data. When we look closely at the reported use of weapons since 2006–2007, we see that the percentage of incidents *victims* reported that involved weapons (out of all reported victimization due to violence) has been relatively stable over time, ranging between 18% and 24% (Fig. 9). Thus, there is no apparent major shift in recent years (2014/2015–2016/2017). On the other hand, wider fluctuations were reported by

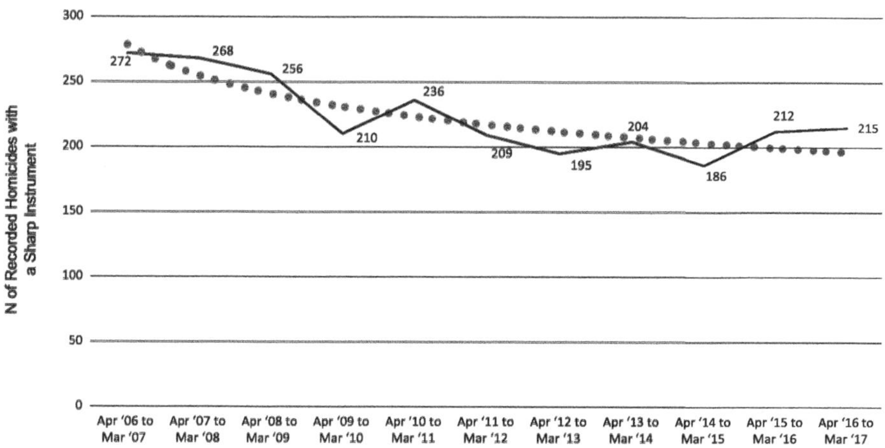

Fig. 7. Homicide Police Records: Offences Recorded by the Police as Homicide by a Sharp Instrument (2007–2017).

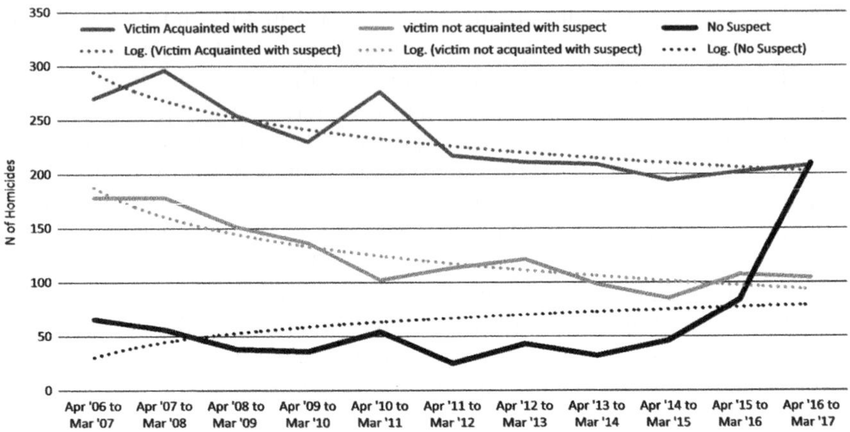

Fig. 8. Homicide Police Records: Relationship between Victim and Suspect.

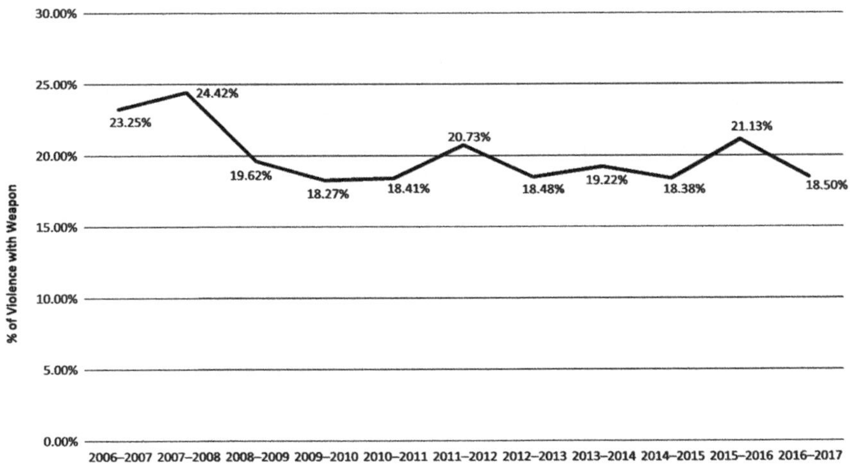

Fig. 9. Use of Weapons in Violent Incidents (2007–2017).

individuals from 29 years old and below in terms of carrying a weapon, particularly very young persons (ages 10–15). As shown in Fig. 10, less than 1% of respondents said they had carried a weapon, but the bandwidth of young people carrying a weapon moved between 0.3% and 0.7% during this period.

Police "Outputs": Stop and Search Data

Stop and search data – a major output activity for the police to tackle crime proactively and directly – provide an additional layer of information about crime trends, with Fig. 11 illustrating national stop and search data. The analysis takes 2006/2007 as an anchor and shows how the trends diverged since then (a score

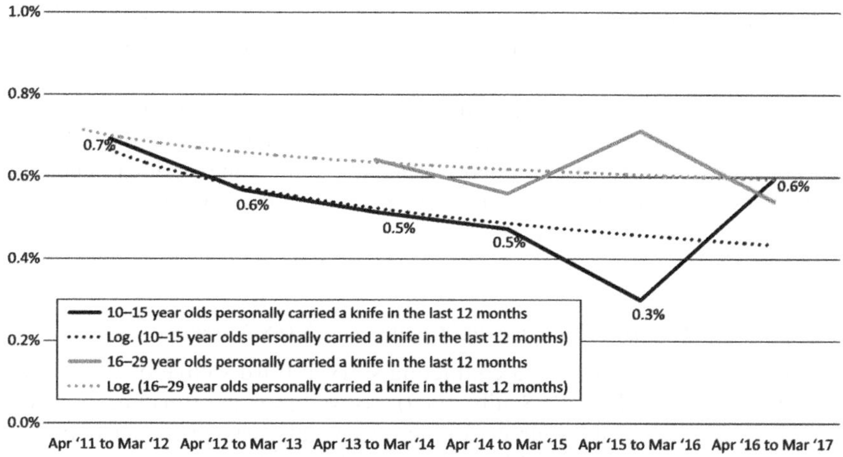

Fig. 10. Prevalence of Knife Carrying among 10–15 Year Olds and 16–29 Year Olds (2007–2017).

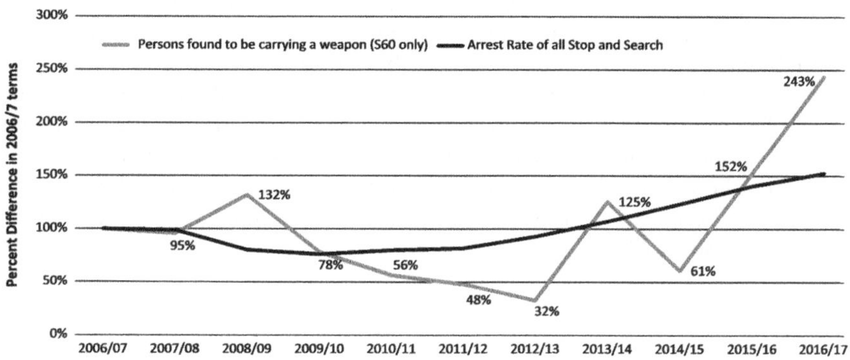

Fig. 11. Police Stop-and-Search Data (2006/07–2016/07).

lower than 100% suggests a reduction from 2006/2007 figures, and a score above 100% suggests an increase from this anchor year). On the one hand, the data show that the police have increased their arrest ratios following stops-and-searches (11% in 2006/2007 vs 17.1% in 2016/2017), which may indicate improved practices (e.g., "only" stopping the "right" people). Simultaneously, the number of stops and searches in which the suspect was found to be carrying a weapon went up by 2.5 times compared to 2006/2007 and 50% more than the year before. Therefore, while the police may have specifically targeted violent crimes in recent years on gun-related and knife-related crime, which manifested the increase in these "S60" searches and thus resulting in the confiscation of weapons. The more the police target these crime categories, the higher their incidence. Notice that the trend mimics that for police-recorded violence for the most recent years.

However, there is a completely different narrative when looking at the "bigger picture." Police have dramatically reduced the overall number of stops-and-searches since the recording of these outputs exist. Overall, the number of people stopped and searched plunged from 2006/2007 to 2016/2007, from 1,007,604 recorded stops and searches to 303,845 in 2016/2017 (and total arrests reduced from 1,474,843 to 779,660 during the same time period). Therefore, while the police may have cracked down specifically on violent crime in recent years, *overall* police activities have dramatically been reduced during the same time period.

Trends in Violence and Crime: The NHS Narrative

When two sources of data tell a conflicting story, a third source of data may be used (Shepherd, Shapland, & Scully, 1989). As we have seen thus far, the CSEW and police-recorded crime sources conflict in several areas, particularly in terms of injurious violence figures. When observing hospital records data, it appears that medical records follow the same pattern as the CSEW, rather than the police records (Fig. 12). The slope of the trend line resembles that of the CSEW dataset [$y = -7681\ln(x) + 46749$], with year-to-year reductions, except the last year on record, which has seen an increase of 2,000 incidents over the previous year (a 7% change) – and this latter pattern resembles police recorded crimes. Therefore, the NHS data provides partial support for both narratives.

However, for data on patients of assaults of certain violent modus operandi (i.e., knife crime), there is a noticeable trend that is similar to the trend purported by police records. As shown in Figs. 13 and 14, finished hospital admissions with the cause of assault of sharp objects have increased sharply since 2014, while the increase of treatment of firearm assault victims is even more pronounced (86 vs 170).

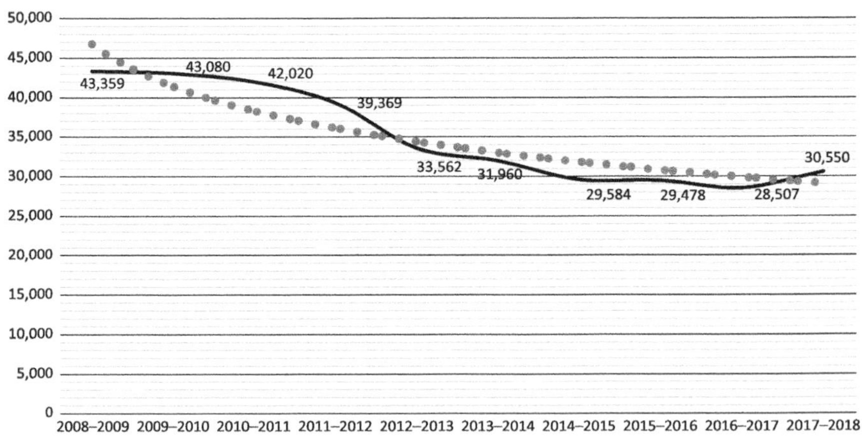

Fig. 12. Finished Hospital Consultant: All Assaults Episodes, 2008–2018 (with Logarithmic Trend Line).

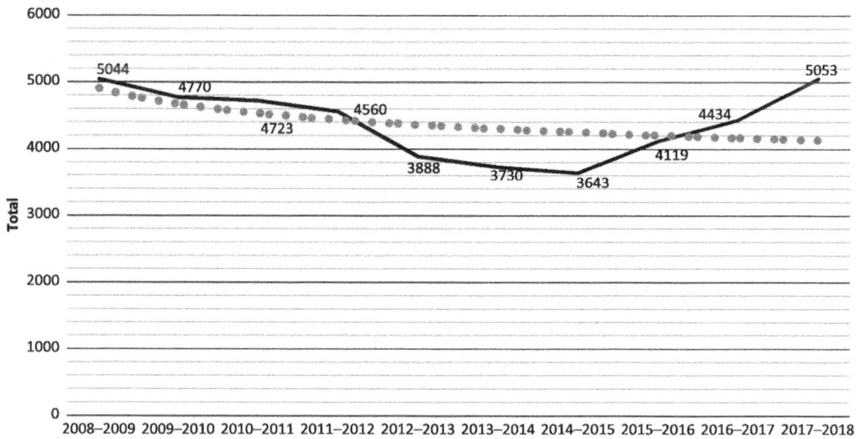

Fig. 13. Finished Hospital Consultant for Assault by Sharp Object Episodes, 2008–2018 (with Logarithmic Trend Line).

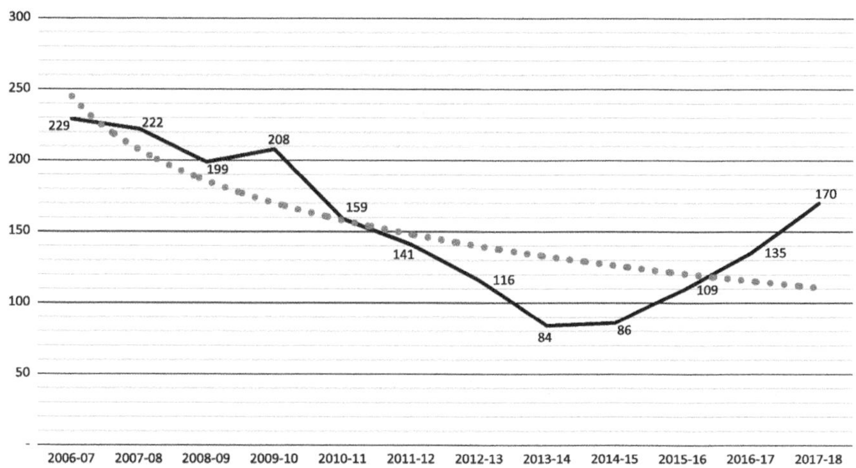

Fig. 14. Finished Hospital Admission Episodes with Cause Code of Firearm Assault, 2008–2018 (with Logarithmic Trend Line).

DISCUSSION

A Rise in Crime or Faulty Wires?

An estimated one million more victimization incidents occurred in one year. A total of 400,000 more crimes recorded by the police. A 10-year spike in homicides ("more murders in London than in New York"). Two- and threefold increases in weapons and particularly knife crime. Without context, these figures feel as if they describe Brazil's favelas, not the Borough of Westminster. Has crime in England and Wales gone up dramatically in recent years?

Algebraically, some crime categories increased, so the percent differences from year to year seem striking. However, *any* crime is *still* a rare event in England and Wales (Eisner, 2001, 2003; Pinker, 2011), and violence is even rarer. For this reason alone, the data trends exhibit high volatility: year-to-year percentage differences become larger as the number of observations decreases. This means that violence rates can fluctuate a great deal in medium to short-term analysis. Moreover, the infrequency of incidents can lead to erroneous conclusions about apparent changes in crime trends during these time periods (Maguire, 2012, chapter 5). Say, for example, that a particular city experiences, on average, 50 homicides every year, but one particular year, there had been 70 and then the following year, 65 homicides were recorded. These 30–40% increases can be interpreted as being quite a dramatic development for this city. Yet statistically, the increase is not likely to be significant, but rather just a natural variation in the data. On the other hand, if the same city experiences 500,000 thefts every year, then it would have to see an increase of nearly 700,000 incidents of theft per year to meet the abovementioned 40% increase – an extremely unusual pattern in crime trends. Thus, the percent differences from year to year are susceptible to strong fluctuations when the overall base rates of crime are low (Hinkle, Weisburd, Famega, & Ready, 2013). The rule of mathematical patterns is that the rate of low-frequency events "violently" expands and contracts over time. Therefore, any variation from year to year can translate into large percentage differences, even though in absolute terms, the change may be less notable (Von Storch, 1999).

The rare-event problem in analyzing temporal patterns is then amplified by the fact that different crime-recording instruments produce different or even conflicting stories during comparable same time periods (Blumstein, Cohen, & Rosenfeld, 1991). It is not uncommon in some periods to have crime rates rise using certain crime measurement tools while others show a reduction (see e.g., https://www.bbc.co.uk/news/uk-41677046). The methodology, sampling techniques, and definitional structure can alter the narrative to a large degree (Maguire, 2012, chapter 5). How can we conclude that short-term variations in data represent the "true" fluctuations of the crime phenomenon and not an artificial change if the data collection instruments are not correlated?

Therefore, setting aside the question of whether the recent spike is "dramatic" compared to other years, a more fundamental question is whether the data upon which these conclusions are drawn are valid and reliable. As we do not have access to the true population means, we have to use filtered data – police records and the CSEW estimates. However, both are susceptible to measurement errors. If they pointed in the same direction and with the same magnitude, then the representativeness question would not be raised. Yet, they tell conflicting narratives. On the one hand, police records show increases in (a) overall crime rates since 1981; (b) reported violent crimes, particularly non-injurious assaults; (c) homicide figures; and (d) police activities surrounding firearms and knife crime more recently (despite a long-time trend downwards). As such, CSEW estimates do not follow these trends, or do not have comparable data.

NHS data support the police narrative in the short term, but not in the long-term trend. During the last year of the data, there has been an increase of approximately 2,000 assaults treated in hospitals – but the overall assaults trend since 2008 is nevertheless negative (which supports the CSEW narrative about a long-term reduction trend). Within this overall hospital data trend, the slope of change for assaults by sharp objects has also been declining; however, since 2014, there has been an increase in the figures, as suggested by police records as well. The same pattern emerges for firearms assaults, with an even more pronounced speed of change. The number of incidents is still very low (a handful of firearm assaults every month), and some may be linked to domestic violence, which should be measured and analyzed separately; however, we lack this granularity in the available data.

At the same time, it is not entirely clear if population means are represented in any of these figures. Temporal variations in the data can be attributed to other factors, not necessarily to the actual variations in crime levels in society. For example, changes in crime figures can be attributed to the increased (or reduced) willingness of the public to report crimes to the police – or share any personal information, for that matter (see Weitzman, Kelemen, Kaci, & Mandl, 2012; Whiddett, Hunter, Engelbrecht, & Handy, 2006). This may explain the increase in non-injurious assaults recorded by the police found in the present analysis. It is possible that people in England and Wales report more violence to the police, particularly less harmful incidents, than they have in the past, and it is equally possible that police are more likely to classify such reports as official crimes than ever before. Longitudinal analyses of willingness to report crime are needed to validate this conclusion. This hypothesis is plausible and should be controlled for before we can safely conclude that violence in society is rising rather than "just" its reporting.

This reporting behavior may explain at least some of the patterns and the link between police and NHS records. Thus, there seems to be a causal link between perceptions of trust and confidence in the police: the greater the legitimacy accorded to the police, the more we should observe higher rates of cooperation and reporting incidents to the police (Mazerolle, Bennett, Davis, Sargeant, & Manning, 2013; Tyler & Bies, 1990). The more incidents are reported to the police, the higher the overall number of events *both* the police and the hospital records register. The two systems collaborate on the same "jobs," and therefore, a rise in one would be met with a rise in the other – especially with suspects with mental health issues (see Herrington, 2012; Sutherland, Sivarajasingam, & Sheperd, 2002; Zealberg, Christie, Puckett, McAlhany, & Durban, 1992). But is this relationship correlational or does one cause the other? One plausible mechanism is, again, that the more crime reported to the police, the more the police handle; the more victims the police handle, the more the NHS handles as well. Some evidence supports this interpretation, at least in terms of hotspots of crime (Ariel, Weinborn, & Boyle, 2015; Boyle, Snelling, White, Ariel, & Ashelford, 2013).

In a similar way, increases in police "crimes" can be related to reforms in recording practices, which have been introduced several times over the years. A "push" from the HMICFRS was particularly noteworthy; since 2014, when the Inspectorate began to audit the recording practices of English and Welsh forces, upward trends in police-recorded crimes were observed – particularly non-injurious violence, stalking, and domestic violence – the very crime categories that are susceptible to changes in crime-recording patterns. The increased levels of registration of crimes may have led to an increase in police response to crime, followed by an increased number of medical treatments.

Is Crime Going Up in Society?

Despite our critique, it remains plausible that the mechanism at play in the figures is a genuine rise in crime (not just the reporting or recording of it), followed by a simultaneous increased response by the police (and health professionals). This suggests that the increase in both police and hospital records of assaults may simply be a result of a genuine trend. Aggression may be more prevalent in society in 2019 than what it was just five years ago. This is suggested by the homicide rates, which have increased during this time period. In this case, we must therefore understand the antecedents of this phenomenon.

The causal mechanism is a larger question than we can address here. However, one possible explanation that resonates from the data is de-policing (Ariel, Sutherland, Henstock, Young, & Sosinski, 2017; Oliver, 2017). Over the years, the number of violent crimes has increased in society, while the number of police "activities" has reduced – dramatically. There has been some debate recently about the possible reductions of police activity and what may have led to them, such as the Ferguson Effect in the United States, budgetary pressures in England and Wales, or technological auditing systems (Oliver, 2017; Shjarback, Pyrooz, Wolfe, & Decker, 2017; Wallace, White, Gaub, & Todak, 2018). If measures of arrests and stops and searches represent police "proactive actions" (though clearly not all of them), then the police in England and Wales continuously do much "less." These outputs have continued to go down over the years, and the trend is negatively correlated with increases in police-recorded violence.

Therefore, reduced police actions may be an antecedent to the increase in recorded crime in recent years (see O'Brien, 1996). This is a logical argument; when the police do not proactively engage with offenders – fewer arrests, a reduction in stop and search activity, etc. – crime then increases. If this argument is true, then given the recent public expenditure measures, there are scarcer resources for prevention and systematic intervention policies. As such, this may explain the sharp reductions in total arrest and stops-and-searches across England and Wales on the one hand, and an increase in violence on the other hand. Whether de-policing exists, and whether the link between it and crime is causal remains unclear, but the argument is logical: less police activity means more non-police-generated crimes but fewer police-generated crimes. As such, there is a case for the separate presentation of statistics relating to "police-generated" and "police received" crimes. The former, which may include drug supply offences or possession of weapon offences, is a proxy measure of the proactivity of the police. The latter consists of reports made by victims of the types of crime that one may expect to increase when the police are less active in communities and are therefore unable to prevent crime from happening – hence, the increase in violence. Response to violence has increased (more recorded crimes), but interventions through proactive police actions (searches, arrests, street engagements, arrests, etc.) were reduced.

When Should We Use CSEW as a Measurement of Violent Crime?

If violence *is* rising in society and if police-recorded assaults, homicides, and hospital admissions represent a genuine increase in violence, then why are the CSEW estimates not picking up on this trend? The answer is methodological. CSEW surveys populations that are necessarily "permanently resident in households," so many population types are not included in this estimator. Crime committed by or against the homeless, undocumented or illegal immigrants, businesses, murders, the hundreds of languages spoken not covered in the survey, night-shift workers, minors, communal establishments, or "visitors from abroad" can reach millions of people/incidents. These are precisely the populations in society that are most susceptible to victimization (see Gaetz, 2004; Garland, Richards, & Cooney, 2010; Snow, Baker, &Anderson, 1989; Walklate, 2006), and they are systematically discounted from the data, year after year.

Similarly, the cost and size of the CSEW should not necessarily lead us to conclude that it is large "enough" to provide a valid representation of crime in England and Wales. Surveying 35,000 households might seem high but given the rate of violence in England and Wales (2 in every 100 adults were a victim of violence in 2017), the survey is likely to capture fewer than 1,000 respondents that can answer relevant questions about this high-harm crime type. Any cross-sectional analysis quickly becomes underpowered when estimating the rate of victimization for 16–29 year-old low-income males, ethnic minorities who experience knife crime, sexual offences, harassment, gang crime, or have had their identity stolen. Finally, no-one has to take part in the CSEW if they do not want to. A response rate of 70% may be deemed "sufficient," but we can speculate that many of the violence and sex crime victims and offenders are located in the non-respondent group. Collectively, all these reasons suggest that CSEW should not necessarily serve as a benchmark for measuring violence in society.

Future Research Implications

The most immediate implication for scholars and practitioners interested in crime patterns is that year-to-year comparisons (e.g., contrasting 2018 with 2019) are misleading and misguided. Illustrating a 40% increase in rare events such as violent crimes between two or three adjacent years loses context – just like a 40% reduction in crime can be an outlier performance rather than the result of a sustainable change in crime patterns. Similarly, comparing the most recent high or low points (e.g., comparing the current year with a value from 10 years ago) is as misleading because there is usually no theoretical or fundamental reason to make such a comparison.

Year-to-year comparisons are particularly problematic if the aim of the statement is to suggest a causal link between an implemented crime strategy and the outcome measure because singling out the treatment effect is difficult if not impossible without proper control conditions; thus, a before–after–only analysis is graded low on the Scientific Maryland Scale (Farrington, Gottfredson, Sherman, & Welsh, 2002). This (second) conclusion is that we should be careful to infer causality from correlational data. Longitudinal analyses are observational only, and any effort to ascribe a causal link between time periods or between crime reporting and crime trends, or even crime-recording patterns and crime trends, is doomed to failure without controlled settings. As such, conclusions based on correlations are speculative by nature.

As obvious as these two conclusions may seem to some, they are unlikely to prevent individuals and agencies with a vested interest (commercial, personal, or political) in drawing on such comparisons if they are favorable. While alternative methods of comparisons have been suggested (Guilfoyle, 2013), none have yet taken root. The immediate challenge for policing scholars is to develop a better case and instrument for the presentation of such information.

Finally, the analysis underscores the need to differentiate between police-generated and public-generated crimes. Hotspots studies allocate officers to take action in specific crime areas, so drawing a difference between the two types is operationally necessary (as arrests of police-generated crimes at the hotspots would lead to an increase rather than a decrease in crime rates, in the treatment areas). To remove the bias, drug offences, outcomes following stops and searches, or crimes that came to police attention first-hand, should be taken out and analyzed separately. Neither the CSEW nor summary statistics on police-recorded crime overtly observe this difference, so we are mixing between outcomes (crimes) and outputs (police activity). Future research ought to apply this distinction more robustly.

CONCLUSION

The level of crime in society is a matter of great interest to scholars as well as practitioners. It is not unusual for elections to be fought on premises of tackling such issues, so it follows that the instrument for measuring the occurrence of crime should be reliable and valid. In practice, things are not this simple. In England and Wales, victim-led surveys arguably take primacy as a measure of crime. Yet while police statistics have been "downgraded" and roundly criticized for quality, we argue that they continue to play an important role in the discussion about the level of crime in society. Both methodologies have flaws, and they examine different aspects of the "crime" phenomenon. The methodological approach, the findings and, consequently, the policy recommendations from each instrument are different. Neither can serve as the benchmark of the other.

REFERENCES

Andresen, M. A., & Felson, M. (2009). The impact of co-offending. The *British Journal of Criminology*, *50*(1), 66–81.

Ariel, B. (2018). "Not all evidence is created equal": on the importance of matching research questions with research methods in evidence based policing. Evidence based policing: An introduction, 63.

Ariel, B., Bland, M., & Sutherland, A. (2017). 'Lowering the threshold of effective deterrence'—Testing the effect of private security agents in public spaces on crime: A randomized controlled trial in a mass transit system. *PLoS One*, *12*(12), e0187392.

Ariel, B., & Partridge, H. (2017). Predictable policing: Measuring the crime control benefits of hotspots policing at bus stops. *Journal of Quantitative Criminology*, *33*(4), 809–833.

Ariel, B., Sutherland, A., Henstock, D., Young, J., & Sosinski, G. (2017). The deterrence spectrum: Explaining why police body-worn cameras 'work' or 'backfire' in aggressive police–public encounters. *Policing: A Journal of Policy and Practice*, *12*(1), 6–26.

Ariel, B., Weinborn, C., & Boyle, A. (2015). Can routinely collected ambulance data about assaults contribute to reduction in community violence? *Emergency Medicine Journal, 32*(4), 308–313.

Ariel, B., Weinborn, C., & Sherman, L. W. (2016). "Soft" policing at hot spots—Do police community support officers work? A randomized controlled trial. *Journal of Experimental Criminology, 12*(3), 277–317.

Baumer, E. P., & Lauritsen, J. L. (2010). Reporting crime to the police, 1973–2005: A multivariate analysis of long-term trends in the National Crime Survey (NCS) and National Crime Victimization Survey (NCVS). *Criminology, 48*(1), 131–185.

Blumstein, A., Cohen, J., & Rosenfeld, R. (1991). Trend and deviation in crime rates: A comparison of UCR and NCS data for burglary and robbery. *Criminology, 29*(2), 237–263.

Bowles, R., Reyes, M. G., & Garoupa, N. (2009). Crime reporting decisions and the costs of crime. *European Journal on Criminal Policy and Research, 15*(4), 365.

Boyle, A. A., Snelling, K., White, L., Ariel, B., & Ashelford, L. (2013). External validation of the Cardiff model of information sharing to reduce community violence: Natural experiment. *Emergency Medicine Journal, 30*(12), 1020–1023.

Eisner, M. (2001). Modernization, self-control and lethal violence. The long-term dynamics of European homicide rates in theoretical perspective. *British Journal of Criminology, 41*(4), 618–638.

Eisner, M. (2003). Long-term historical trends in violent crime. *Crime and Justice, 30*, 83–142.

Ellis, S., & Arieli, S. (1999). Predicting intentions to report administrative and disciplinary infractions: Applying the reasoned action model. *Human Relations, 52*(7), 947–967.

Fajnzylber, P., Lederman, D., & Loayza, N. (2002). Inequality and violent crime. *The Journal of Law and Economics, 45*(1), 1–39.

Farrington, D. P. (1979). Longitudinal research on crime and delinquency. *Crime and Justice, 1*, 289–348.

Farrington, D. P., Gottfredson, D. C., Sherman, L. W., & Welsh, B. C. (2002). The Maryland scientific methods scale. In *Evidence-based crime prevention* (pp. 13–21). London: Routledge.

Gaetz, S. (2004). Safe streets for whom? Homeless youth, social exclusion, and criminal victimization. *Canadian Journal of Criminology and Criminal Justice, 46*(4), 423–456.

Garland, T. S., Richards, T., & Cooney, M. (2010). Victims hidden in plain sight: The reality of victimization among the homeless. *Criminal Justice Studies, 23*(4), 285–301.

Gideon, L. (2012). *Handbook of survey methodology for the social sciences*. New York, NY: Springer.

Goldsmith, V., McGuire, P. G., Mollenkopf, J. B., & Ross, T. A. (1999). *Analyzing crime patterns: Frontiers of practice*. Thousand Oaks, CA: Sage.

Gove, W. R., Hughes, M., & Geerken, M. (1985). Are uniform crime reports a valid indicator of the index crimes? An affirmative answer with minor qualifications. *Criminology, 23*(3), 451–502.

Guilfoyle, S., (2013). *Intelligent policing: How systems thinking methods eclipse conventional management practice*. Axminister: Triarchy Press.

Haberman, C. P., Sorg, E. T., & Ratcliffe, J. H. (2018). The seasons they are a changin' testing for seasonal effects of potentially criminogenic places on street robbery. *Journal of Research in Crime and Delinquency, 55*(3), 425–459.

Herrington, V. (2012). Inter-agency cooperation and joined-up working in police responses to persons with a mental illness: Lessons from New South Wales. Policing: *A Journal of Policy and Practice, 6*(4), 388–397.

Hinkle, J. C., Weisburd, D., Famega, C., & Ready, J. (2013). The problem is not just sample size: The consequences of low base rates in policing experiments in smaller cities. *Evaluation Review, 37*(3–4), 213–238.

HMICFRS. (2014). *Crime-recording: Making the victim count – The final report of an inspection of crime data integrity in police forces in England and Wales*. Retrieved from https://www.justiceinspectorates.gov.uk/hmicfrs/wp-content/uploads/crime-recording-making-the-victim-count.pdf

Holbrook, A. L., Green, M. C., & Krosnick, J. A. (2003). Telephone versus face-to-face interviewing of national probability samples with long questionnaires: Comparisons of respondent satisficing and social desirability response bias. *Public Opinion Quarterly, 67*(1), 79–125.

Home Office. (2018a). *Crime in England and Wales: Year ending June 2018*. Retrieved from https://www.ons.gov.uk/peoplepopulationandcommunity/crimeandjustice/bulletins/crimeinenglandandwales/yearendingjune2018

Home Office. (2018b). *Methodology: Crime in England and Wales quality and methodology information report* Retrieved from https://www.ons.gov.uk/peoplepopulationandcommunity/crimeandjustice/methodologies/crimeinenglandandwalesqmi

House of Commons Public Affairs Select Committee. (2014). *Caught red-handed: Why we can't count on Police recorded crime statistics* Retrieved from https://publications.parliament.uk/pa/cm201314/cmselect/cmpubadm/760/760.pdf

Jennings, W., Gray, E., Hay, C., & Farrall, S. (2015). Collating longitudinal data on crime, victimization and social attitudes in England and Wales: A new resource for exploring long-term trends in crime. *British Journal of Criminology*, *55*(5), 1005–1015.

Linning, S. J., Andresen, M. A., & Brantingham, P. J. (2017). Crime seasonality: Examining the temporal fluctuations of property crime in cities with varying climates. *International Journal of Offender Therapy and Comparative Criminology*, *61*(16), 1866–1891.

Litwin, M. S., & Fink, A. (1995). *How to measure survey reliability and validity* (Vol. 7). New York: Sage.

Loveday, B. (2006). Policing performance: The impact of performance measures and targets on police forces in England and Wales. *International Journal of Police Science & Management*, *8*(4), 282–293.

Macbeth, E., & Ariel, B. (2017). Place-based statistical versus clinical predictions of crime hot spots and harm locations in Northern Ireland. *Justice Quarterly*, *36*, 1–34.

MacDonald, Z. (2002). Official crime statistics: Their use and interpretation. *The Economic Journal*, *112*(477), F85–F106.

Maguire, M. (2002). Crime statistics: The 'data explosion' and its implications. In *The Oxford handbook of criminology* (pp. 322–370). Oxford: Oxford University Press.

Maguire, M. (2012). Criminal statistics and the construction of crime. In *The Oxford Handbook of Criminology* (pp. 206–244). Oxford: Oxford University Press.

Martin, S., Downe, J., Grace, C., & Nutley, S. (2010). Validity, utilization and evidence-based policy: The development and impact of performance improvement regimes in local public services. *Evaluation*, *16*(1), 31–42.

Mazerolle, L., Bennett, S., Davis, J., Sargeant, E., & Manning, M. (2013). Procedural justice and police legitimacy: A systematic review of the research evidence. *Journal of Experimental Criminology*, *9*(3), 245–274.

Mercer, D. (2019). *Crime figures: Sharp rise in homicides fuels call for more police funding*. Retrieved from https://news.sky.com/story/crime-figures-sharp-rise-in-homicides-fuels-call-for-more-police-funding-11616115

Nagin, D. S. (1999). Analyzing developmental trajectories: A semiparametric, group-based approach. *Psychological Methods*, *4*(2), 139.

Near, J. P., & Miceli, M. P. (1985). Organizational dissidence: The case of whistle-blowing. *Journal of Business Ethics*, *4*(1), 1–16.

Newburn, T. (2018). *Criminology: A very short introduction*. Oxford: Oxford University Press.

Neyroud, P. (2008). Past, present and future performance: Lessons and prospects for the measurement of police performance. *Policing: A Journal of Policy and Practice*, *2*(3), 340–348.

Nguyen, H., & Loughran, T. A. (2018). On the measurement and identification of turning points in criminology. *Annual Review of Criminology*, *1*, 335–358.

Nulty, D. D. (2008). The adequacy of response rates to online and paper surveys: What can be done? *Assessment & Evaluation in Higher Education*, *33*(3), 301–314.

O'Brien, R. M. (1996). Police productivity and crime rates: 1973–1992. *Criminology*, *34*(2), 183–207.

Office for National Statistics. (2017). Crime in England and Wales: Year ending March 2017. Retrieved from https://www.ons.gov.uk/peoplepopulationandcommunity/crimeandjustice/bulletins/crimeinenglandandwales/yearendingmarch2017/previous/v1. Accessed on January 22, 2019.

Office for National Statistics. (2018). *Crime in England and Wales: Year ending March 2018*. Retrieved from https://www.ons.gov.uk/peoplepopulationandcommunity/crimeandjustice/bulletins/crimeinenglandandwales/yearendingmarch2018/previous/v1. Accessed on January 22, 2019.

Office for National Statistics. (2019). *Crime in England and Wales QMI*. Retrieved from https://www.ons.gov.uk/peoplepopulationandcommunity/crimeandjustice/methodologies/crimeinenglandandwalesqmi. Accessed on February 4, 2019.

Oliver, W. M. (2017). Depolicing: Rhetoric or reality? *Criminal Justice Policy Review*, *28*(5), 437–461.

Picard, R. G. (1998). A note on the relations between circulation size and newspaper advertising rates. *Journal of Media Economics*, *11*(2), 47–55.

Pinker, S. (2011). *The better angels of our nature: Why violence has declined* (Vol. 75). New York, NY: Viking.

Shepherd, J., Shapland, M., & Scully, C. (1989). Recording by the police of violent offences; an accident and emergency department perspective. *Medicine, Science and the Law*, *29*(3), 251–257.

Sherman, L., Neyroud, P. W., & Neyroud, E. (2016). The Cambridge crime harm index: Measuring total harm from crime based on sentencing guidelines. *Policing: A Journal of Policy and Practice*, *10*(3), 171–183.

Sherman, L. W. (2013). The rise of evidence-based policing: Targeting, testing, and tracking. *Crime and Justice*, *42*(1), 377–451.

Sherman, L. W., & Rogan, D. P. (1995). Effects of gun seizures on gun violence: "Hot spots" patrol in Kansas City. *Justice Quarterly*, *12*(4), 673–693.

Sherman, L. W., & Weisburd, D. (1995). General deterrent effects of police patrol in crime "hot spots": A randomized, controlled trial. *Justice Quarterly*, *12*(4), 625–648.

Shjarback, J. A., Pyrooz, D. C., Wolfe, S. E., & Decker, S. H. (2017). De-policing and crime in the wake of Ferguson: Racialized changes in the quantity and quality of policing among Missouri police departments. *Journal of Criminal Justice*, *50*, 42–52.

Sivarajasingam, V., Wells, J. P., Moore, S., Page, N., Morgan, P., Matthews, K., & Shepherd, J. P. (2010). Violence in England and Wales in 2010: An accident and emergency perspective. Cardiff: Violence and Society Research Group.

Skogan, W. G. (1984). Reporting crimes to the police: The status of world research. *Journal of Research in Crime and Delinquency*, *21*(2), 113–137.

Snow, D. A., Baker, S. G., & Anderson, L. (1989). Criminality and homeless men: An empirical assessment. *Social Problems*, *36*(5), 532–549.

Sutherland, I., Sivarajasingam, V., & Shepherd, J. P. (2002). Recording of community violence by medical and police services. *Injury Prevention*, *8*(3), 246–247.

Talbot, C. (2008). Performance regimes—The institutional context of performance policies. *International Journal of Public Administration*, *31*(14), 1569–1591.

Tyler, T. R., & Bies, R. J. (1990). Beyond formal procedures: The interpersonal context of procedural justice. *Applied Social Psychology and Organizational Settings*, *77*, 98.

Von Storch, H. (1999). Misuses of statistical analysis in climate research In *Analysis of climate variability* (pp. 11–26). Berlin: Springer.

Wain, N., & Ariel, B. (2014). Tracking of police patrol. *Policing: A Journal of Policy and Practice*, *8*(3), 274–283.

Walklate, S. (2006). *Imagining the victim of crime*. McGraw-Hill Education (UK). Maidenhead.

Wallace, D., White, M. D., Gaub, J. E., & Todak, N. (2018). Body-worn cameras as a potential source of depolicing: Testing for camera-induced passivity. *Criminology*, *56*(3), 481–509.

Weitzman, E. R., Kelemen, S., Kaci, L., & Mandl, K. D. (2012). Willingness to share personal health record data for care improvement and public health: A survey of experienced personal health record users. *BMC Medical Informatics and Decision Making*, *12*(1), 39.

Whiddett, R., Hunter, I., Engelbrecht, J., & Handy, J. (2006). Patients' attitudes towards sharing their health information. *International Journal of Medical Informatics*, *75*(7), 530–541.

Wittebrood, K., & Junger, M. (2002). Trends in violent crime: A comparison between police statistics and victimization surveys. *Social Indicators Research*, *59*(2), 153–173.

Zealberg, J. J., Christie, S. D., Puckett, J. A., McAlhany, D., & Durban, M. (1992). A mobile crisis program: Collaboration between emergency psychiatric services and police. *Psychiatric Services*, *43*(6), 612–615.

CHAPTER 2

USING FREEDOM OF INFORMATION REQUESTS IN SOCIO-LEGAL STUDIES, CRIMINAL JUSTICE STUDIES, AND CRIMINOLOGY

Kevin Walby and Alex Luscombe

ABSTRACT

Purpose – *The chapter explores the use of freedom of information (ATI/FOI) requests in social science research, with specific focus on using ATI/FOI requests in socio-legal studies, criminal justice studies, and criminology.*

Methodology/approach – *ATI/FOI requests constitute a novel method of data collection that has methodological and also epistemological implications for researchers.*

Findings – *The chapter explains how to use ATI/FOI requests in social science as well as how to navigate challenges and barriers ATI/FOI users regularly face.*

Originality/value – *There is a paucity of writings on use of ATI/FOI requests in socio-legal studies, criminal justice studies, and criminology. The chapter reveals the value of using ATI/FOI in social science and the originality of the data that ATI/FOI requests can result in.*

Keywords: Freedom of information; qualitative methods; access; methods; methodology; law

Methods of Criminology and Criminal Justice Research
Sociology of Crime, Law and Deviance, Volume 24, 33–46

ISSN: 1521-6136/doi:10.1108/S1521-613620190000024005

INTRODUCTION

Access to information (ATI) and freedom of information (FOI) requests can be used to collect data from government agencies. In most countries, this includes agencies working in the areas of law and criminal justice. Hundreds of countries have now enacted ATI/FOI laws, which bestow citizens with the right to request information from government offices (Ackerman & Sandoval-Ballesteros, 2006; Birkinshaw, 2010a, 2010b; Byrne, 2003; Hazell, 1989). ATI/FOI laws exist alongside or in lieu of other open government initiatives that provide citizens more direct access to government records, such as public archives and proactive disclosure (Afful-Dadzie & Afful-Dadzie, 2017; García-Tabuyo, Sáez-Martín, & Caba-Pérez, 2016). ATI/FOI is a partial, limited mechanism of information access, but it can still be an effective tool for data collection when used systematically. In terms of its use and place in the popular imagination, ATI/FOI law is most often associated with opposition political parties or investigative journalists. In recent years, however, more and more scholars from a range of disciplines have begun using ATI/FOI laws to supplement their other data collection strategies. Often, it is the nature of the topic which dictates these scholars' inclusion of ATI/FOI into their research designs. When exploring government practices that the public knows little about but which can have major implications for justice and the state of democracy, ATI/FOI law becomes a crucial means of gaining access (Brown, 2009; Greenberg, 2016; Keen, 1992; Lee, 2005; Savage & Hyde, 2014).

Using ATI/FOI requests in the social sciences is thus an investigative, critical endeavor. Investigative research guards against deceptive appearances, warns of the perils of ignorance, and operates as a guardian of social conscience and public interest (Douglas, 1976; Ho, Ho, & Ng, 2006). ATI/FOI laws afford researchers access to a diverse range of records. Such records may be qualitative or quantitative, mundane, or controversial. Although ATI/FOI records can indeed be "staged" or altered before disclosure, in general they are qualitatively different than the kinds of "official discourse" that government agencies publish on their websites or communicate in speeches. Most ATI/FOI records could be said to constitute "insider documents" in the sense that they were never intended for public release. ATI/FOI records are also qualitatively different from files that are "pro-actively disclosed" by government agencies, since these tend to be carefully selected and potentially even manicured prior to release. Put simply, records disclosed through ATI/FOI can comprise "dirty data" (Marx, 1984) and these can be revealing of government practices and processes in ways that other data types might not be. At the same time, we stress that ATI/FOI law is only one strategy of data collection and as such is best combined with others, such as surveys, interviews, or media analysis. ATI/FOI requests are not a yellow brick road to knowing about how government "really works." Indeed, literature on ATI/FOI has demonstrated that there are many barriers to government transparency and accountability even when ATI/FOI is used (Rappert, 2012; Walby & Larsen, 2011; Worthy, John, & Vannoni, 2016).

This chapter is organized in four parts. First, this chapter addresses some of the key issues that we have encountered using ATI/FOI for social science research. Second, we reflect on some of the major strategies that scholars can use to overcome barriers and challenges. Third, we make specific arguments about the benefits of using ATI/FOI requests in socio-legal studies, criminal justice studies, and criminology. While the boundaries between socio-legal studies, criminal justice studies, and criminology might sometimes be slippery and full of holes, we use these categories illustratively to reveal the different objects of analysis and texts that ATI/FOI requests can be used to investigate. Finally, we conclude with thoughts on future use of ATI/FOI requests in social science research.

ATI/FOI IN THE SOCIAL SCIENCES: THE BASICS

There are two myths that thwart use of ATI/FOI in the social sciences. The first is that ATI/FOI is strictly a tool for journalistic muck-raking and should not be incorporated into academic research designs (Luscombe, Walby, & Lippert, 2017). When conducted carefully and systematically, we argue that ATI/FOI requests can be as valid and rigorous a method for producing data in the social sciences as any other (Walby & Luscombe, 2017). Indeed, any scholar with a research project that focuses on a government agency (assuming it is subject to ATI/FOI laws in the country of interest) can use ATI/FOI requests to gain access. There are often two levels to a country's ATI/FOI legal regime, consisting of a federal law and a series of state, provincial, or municipal ones. There can be fees associated with processing a request, but these can be anticipated in research grant applications and/or waived by the government agency if it can be shown that the information is in the public interest. A second myth about ATI/FOI requests is that these requests are easy to use. This is not the case. ATI/FOI is a craft like any other mode of inquiry and is thus no simpler to use than a survey or interview guide. Any experienced user of ATI/FOI will tell you it takes time to master the art of "brokering access," a term we use to capture the interactive dynamics of communicating, negotiating, and arguing with government agents to obtain access to kinds of records ATI/FOI users are looking for.

Although it is conceivable to gain access to dirty data through interviews or participant observation, opportunities are rare. In Canada, Ericson (1981) gained access to a wealth of dirty data using interviews and by shadowing detectives in their day to day work, but such studies are the exception rather than the norm. And although there are indeed strategies for generating meaningful data in interviews with elites (Aberbach & Rockman, 2002), the real difficulty is always access. The methodological pathways to interviewing elites about practices they do not wish to publicly discuss are slim (Alvesalo-Kuusi & Whyte, 2018; Cousin, Khan, & Mears, 2018). The potential to directly observe elites while they engage in sensitive or illegal acts is even slimmer. There may be a number of gatekeepers (Broadhead & Rist, 1976) who limit entry or access to such personnel. In addition, even if one did gain access, elite government personnel are often trained to follow scripted lines or espouse crafted government rhetoric. It is these difficulties with researching government elites that has driven many researchers to use ATI/FOI requests in lieu of (or in addition to) more traditional means.

ATI/FOI requests are not a simple form of unobtrusive research. Unobtrusive research involves archival studies or analyses of existing statistics (Auriacombe, 2007). Unobtrusive research is thought to be devoid of human actors. The same cannot be said about ATI/FOI use. It does involve people, namely the people who work in government agencies and who enact government practices. These are some of the most powerful people in society. The decisions they make affect the lives of hundreds of thousands of people. Use of ATI/FOI is therefore a form of "studying up" (Nader, 1974) and entails examining the work of professionals and elites in the public sector. Use of ATI/FOI constitutes an obtrusive form of research bound by its own set of ethical considerations (Walby & Luscombe, 2018; Yeager, 2006). In this sense, use of ATI/FOI in the social sciences could even be viewed as a conflict methodology (Lehmann & Young, 1974) that accepts it is necessary to be somewhat obtrusive to gain access to certain types of information and to make critical arguments relevant for social change.

ATI/FOI researchers believe that written texts constitute a powerful source of social science data. Insider texts disclosed through ATI/FOI contain insight into the logics, organization, and everyday practices of governing. For this reason, ATI/FOI disclosures might be particularly well-suited to abductive analysis, which Timmermans and Tavory (2012, p. 170) define as "an inferential creative process of producing hypotheses and theories based on surprising research evidence. A researcher is led away from old to new theoretical insights." The files obtained through ATI/FOI have typically never been consumed by outsiders and thus can be quite revealing. Looking at these files can often change the way an audience conceives of the government practice in question. To acquire this kind of insight, however, usually requires access to a large corpus of text. It is rare when using ATI/FOI to obtain a single document that tells much of a story on its own. ATI/FOI requests are best used to build up an archive of records that reveal something about government practices over time (Walby & Larsen, 2011). It can take months or years to acquire enough data through ATI/FOI requests for a research project on government. And even when a researcher does acquire valuable information through ATI/FOI, it still necessary to triangulate these records with other kinds of data (interviews, observations, and open source material). Records obtained through ATI/FOI provide only a single perspective on the issue under study.

There are many ways to triangulate ATI/FOI records with other data forms (also see Moran-Ellis et al., 2006). For example, ATI/FOI records can be combined with qualitative interviews. ATI/FOI requests can be used first, with interviews following subsequently to confirm or check the information in ATI/FOI disclosures, or to generate more insightful questions for interviews. We have also found that ATI/FOI can be a useful means of determining who to potentially interview. Interviews can also be conducted before ATI/FOI requests as a means of figuring out how to frame and where to target future ATI/FOI requests. Asking interviewees about types of documents and the textual organization of a particular department can provide extremely useful background information to help file a subsequent ATI/FOI request. ATI/FOI disclosures can be compared to news articles and government reports, where inconsistencies in the claims of journalists and political leaders may emerge in light of what is stated "backstage." This comparison can be made with website or internet-based material that government entities post ATI/FOI as well. The possibilities of incorporating ATI/FOI requests into nested, sequential, and concurrent research designs are limitless.

The important message is that the researcher, where possible, should avoid relying solely on ATI/FOI records without consulting other data sources. ATI/FOI records may contain only part of the story and there are always risks to drawing inferences from insider texts alone (Rappert, 2012).

We should note that ATI/FOI requests are not limited to contemporary or recent records. ATI/FOI requests are often used in historical research as a means of declassifying records (Clément, 2015; Hewitt, 2012). In many jurisdictions, ATI/FOI is needed to engage in the work of declassification. The other temporal dimension to use of ATI/FOI requests in research is that these may be sequenced in a longitudinal manner. ATI/FOI users seeking data representing sequenced intervals (Thomson & Holland, 2003) can help to reveal changes in government activities over time.

DIGGING DEEPER

Challenges, Barriers, and Tricks of the Trade

Although the idea of "filing a request" may sound simple, ATI/FOI is fraught with layers of barriers, delays, and unexpected setbacks, which can be conceptualized as broader organizational barriers to transparency (Pasquier & Villeneuve, 2007). Navigating these barriers is a normal part of the process. Even the most seasoned ATI/FOI user encounters barriers to access with near every request they make (Lippert, Walby, & Wilkinson, 2016; Savage & Hyde, 2014). Every access regime is different (Roberts, 2006), but exceptions to the rule exist within all of them. Despite advocacy aimed at strengthening access laws, the ATI/FOI laws in most countries continue to be weakened (Halstuk & Chamberlin, 2006; Pozen, 2005; Roberts, 2000). Public offices and their ATI/FOI coordinators have a number of tools at their disposal to withhold entire records or redact parts of them before disclosure. Most ATI/FOI laws, for example, afford governments the right to withhold information about private third parties, whether it be an individual or a corporation. In an era of increasing government privatization, however, such a clause makes research on government matters involving private actors exceptionally difficult (Bunker & Davis, 1998). Some record types are exempt from ATI/FOI by definition. To borrow Galison's (2004) phrase, they are "born secret." In Canada, where we conduct most of our research, any records from the Cabinet are excluded from ATI/FOI. In some ATI/FOI regimes, entire public agencies can be exempted from ATI/FOI. In the United Kingdom, for example, ATI/FOI law does not apply to national security agencies. In the United States, national security provisions are often abused by over-redacting and exempting materials that in principle should be disclosed (Cramer, 2018). In many ATI/FOI regimes, ATI/FOI coordinators can deem a request vexatious (Cherry & McMenemy, 2013) if the reasoning in the request appears odd or if the requester has made a similar request before. We have experienced instances where the power of ATI/FOI coordinators to label requests vexatious has been abused (see Luscombe et al., 2017).

There are also extra-legal barriers to access. ATI/FOI coordinators have a number of informal techniques at their disposal that they can use to mitigate disclosure. In our use of ATI/FOI in Canada and the United States, we have occasionally encountered some ATI/FOI coordinators who are overtly obstructionist and keen on promoting obfuscation rather than access (Luscombe et al., 2017; Luscombe & Walby, 2015; also see Katz, 1969). Such coordinators thrive on the general impunity and lack of accountability characteristic of most ATI/FOI regimes. To entice the user to alter the scope of their request or block access outright, ATI/FOI coordinators can fall back on a number of informal techniques including exaggerating cost estimates and threatening longer than normal processing times. Claiming to have "missed calls," "lost emails," or to simply not understand the nature of a request are also regular means of trying to get a user to abandon their pursuit of records. These techniques that promote opacity can be conceived of as internal or infra laws (Roberts, 2002) that limit the access of researchers and other ATI/FOI users. By engaging in these forms of information control, ATI/FOI coordinators are akin to gatekeepers in social control research (Broadhead & Rist, 1976). Yet in many jurisdictions they also have a duty to assist that ATI/FOI users can use as a wedge to gain access to records and to ask questions about how the agency is conceptualizing the request and managing or mitigating access to the records requested. Not all coordinators are out to scuttle these requests, and coordinators often feel like the meat in the sandwich (Mann, 1986) being chewed on from both sides. Limited research on ATI/FOI coordinators show that they have a variety of opinions on transparency and a number of ideas on how ATI/FOI regimes can be improved (Kimball, 2012; Swallow & Bourke, 2012; Shepherd, Stevenson, & Flinn, 2010).

Experienced users of ATI/FOI requests try to be hyperaware when such techniques are being deployed by ATI/FOI coordinators to scuttle access. By recognizing these techniques of information control, ATI/FOI researchers can employ counterstrategies in attempting to get around them. ATI/FOI users, for instance, can call ATI/FOI coordinators out on their bluffs when they claim that a record "probably doesn't exist" or that a request will "probably costs thousands of dollars to process." It is also strategic for ATI/FOI users to collect extensive fieldnotes during these brokering phases of the request (which can later become the object of reflexive study). The researcher should make fieldnotes about their exchanges with ATI/FOI coordinators and put everything in writing, so as to keep track of the process and account for it later on when writing up the study or filing an appeal. Before filing a request, ATI/FOI users should always carefully plan the best way to produce fieldnotes (also see Tessier, 2012).

If an ATI/FOI user is not satisfied with the process or with the disclosure, they can appeal to ATI/FOI commissioners in any given jurisdiction. Appeals to ATI/FOI accountability agencies such as the offices of ATI/FOI commissioners can be successful, but they are often delayed for months or years due to underfunding of these offices (Larsen & Walby, 2012; Rowat, 1993). Nevertheless, dealing with such delays and difficulties is part and parcel of the process of brokering access to data and wrestling with government agencies that are not always acting in good faith (Larsen & Walby, 2012; Luscombe et al., 2017).

We would also note that ATI/FOI disclosures do not speak for themselves. What is recorded in organizational texts is not a complete and objective account of what happens (Trace, 2002). To make sense of ATI/FOI disclosures, researchers therefore need to use social theories and techniques of data analysis just as they would when analyzing other kinds of information. Analysis of ATI/FOI disclosures also needs to be carefully validated by the researcher, using established procedures like triangulation and reflexivity. ATI/FOI requests can give a researcher access to different types of information. Some of this information can be analyzed quantitatively, using either conventional statistical procedures or social network analysis, or analyzed using qualitative analysis techniques like discourse analysis or grounded theory (or some mix of both). In addition, government record-keeping and communication is increasingly digitized, and this has implications for future research and analysis. Governments are collecting and digitally storing increasing amounts of information about their operations and this is opening up new possibilities for new research questions and computer-assisted analysis.

Based on our experiences using ATI/FOI requests to research issues of policing and security, we have devised a number of strategies to share with researchers and improve their use of the craft. First, ATI/FOI requests require extensive background research. Scholars should do preliminary research on the agencies they plan to task before they submit requests. The more an ATI/FOI user knows about the government process or practice they are interested in studying, the easier it will be to craft a targeted request and negotiate with ATI/FOI coordinators over access to salient records (Larsen & Walby, 2012; Luscombe et al., 2017).

Second, multiple simpler requests are better than complex, omnibus ones. We recommend that the researcher always break up their request into multiple requests to avoid more complex or sensitive requests from delaying the total time to disclosure. The time it takes to process a request varies from weeks to years. Even if several items in a multiple item request can be processed quickly, the disclosure package will be withheld until every item has been processed, some of which may take significantly longer than others. Breaking up requests makes the whole process more manageable, efficient (for the user), and affordable.

Third, researchers should determine if it is a single agency or agenc*ies* that hold the records relevant to their research question. Government agencies and offices operate in a network and it is rare for only one node to have access to a particular kind of public record. Plus, multi-agency requests are often more interesting than single agency ones and increase the chances of receiving information. We advise scholars to send the same ATI/FOI requests to multiple agencies to see what different files and record formats are available and/or learn about different practices that disparate agencies might use in relation to the same theme or phenomenon. This tactic can be revealing of differences between agencies and how they address the same governance issues. Engaging in this process also helps to illuminate variations in how different agencies handle requests.

Fourth, it is worth sending multiple requests to an agency, with slightly different framing, even if they seem somewhat redundant. This will ensure that all actionable files are retrieved and considered by the ATI/FOI coordinator. It can be difficult to know exactly how a particular coordinator interpreted the wording of one request, so submitting multiple requests with different wording can ensure greater breadth of record search. This can further reveal how government agencies classify and manage information.

Finally, we would suggest that depending on the countries one is interested in ATI/FOI can be used to produce comparative datasets. For example, most jurisdictions across the United States allow people from outside the United States to submit requests for records. Using ATI/FOI in comparative fashion can provide additional insights into cross-national variation in government practices and decision-making.

Using ATI/FOI Requests in Socio-legal Studies

Socio-legal studies examines law in action, or the difference between law on the books and how law works in practice. Valverde, Levi, and Moore (2005, p. 96) note that scholars who study law in action tend to focus strictly on people, abandoning focus on legal texts and other material things that are part of legal processes. ATI/FOI can act as a major methodological corrective in this regard for socio-legal scholars. ATI/FOI requests can be used to locate records that reveal patterns in how different types of law are used (or not) by particular kinds of petty sovereigns (Rose & Valverde, 1998) to govern people's lives. The scope of analysis is certainly not limited to criminal law or criminalization. Socio-legal scholars could access qualitative materials on any types of communications by petty sovereigns. But they could also seek quantitative records on their performance, rates of use of laws, and so on.

An example of this is the work of Luscombe et al. (2017) in their analysis of fieldnotes generated throughout the processing of ATI/FOI requests in 90 police jurisdictions in Canada and 16 in the United States. They comparatively examined how requests for the same information were processed by different police departments. The information sought (police deployment logs and financial records) were treated variably by different police departments whose coordinators used the law in diverse ways to process the disclosure. It was also a study of ATI/FOI law in action. Luscombe et al. showed how ATI/FOI law works in action and how users have to act in a different capacity than legal discourse on ATI/FOI frames the "user." Skilled users of ATI/FOI law must creatively broker and navigate the barriers they face when trying to get information from state agencies like police that may try to block them.

Beyond examining ATI/FOI law itself, ATI/FOI could be used in socio-legal studies to examine municipal law more broadly as well as health law. Sheaff's (2017) examination of National Health Service's decision-making in England and the lack of transparency fit this use of ATI/FOI (also see Wilson, 2011). Socio-legal studies does not as far as we can see have a methodological core. It is caught between the doctrinal approach of traditional law and the more textual approach of cultural studies of law and legality. More development of the methodological approach of socio-legal studies is needed (also see Mopas & Turnbull, 2011). Elsewhere, we have suggested that use of ATI/FOI requests is one way to do this (Luscombe & Walby, forthcoming).

Using ATI/FOI Requests in Criminal Justice Studies

Criminal justice studies examines the institutional practices of criminal justice personnel (Kraska & Brent, 2011). Criminal justice studies, also examines the process of making criminal justice policy. ATI/FOI requests can be used to locate records on the types of work criminal justice personnel undertake. ATI/FOI requests can also be used to locate records on how policy was formed. Criminal justice scholars can use ATI/FOI to access qualitative materials on project or operation planning or rationales for some types of activities. They can also seek access to quantitative records on deployments of some types of personnel.

In their analysis of racial disparities in marijuana misdemeanor arrests in New York City, Geller and Fagan (2010) used ATI/FOI to gain access to New York City Police Department stop activity logs, which recorded every time a citizen was stopped by an officer along with other relevant sociodemographic (including race) and contextual information. Geller and Fagan combined this information with other sources and analyzed their dataset using content analysis alongside more sophisticated statistical techniques to measure disparities resulting from flawed "broken windows" and racist war on drugs policies in New York City. They found that Blacks in New York City were much more likely to be arrested for cannabis possession than Hispanics and Whites, despite Black people having similar if not lower rates of use. They also found that there was a high concentration of "stop, frisk, and search" actions leading to cannabis arrests in neighborhoods with high concentrations of Black residents.

Another example of using ATI/FOI in criminal justice studies is the work of Roziere and Walby (2018). Roziere and Walby conducted an analysis of police files on militarization of public police and special weapons and tactics (SWAT) teams in Canada. In official discourse, police in Canada typically claim their SWAT teams are for emergency (mass public casualty) purposes only. However, an examination of records disclosed through ATI/FOI revealed a different picture. Analyzing the frequency and type of SWAT team deployment in Canadian cities, Roziere and Walby found that municipal SWAT teams across Canada are now used for routine policing activities, including traffic stops, community policing, response to mental health and domestic violence calls, and execution of warrants. Mummolo (2018) used a similar research design involving ATI/FOI requests in the United States to study police militarization.

A final example comes from Piché (2014) who used ATI/FOI requests to gain access to unpublished records documenting prison expansion across Canadian provinces and territories. He found that despite claims about prison expansion being driven by increasing crime rates and a need to punish criminals, the vast majority of expansion efforts were being effected to create more space for prisoners on remand.

Using ATI/FOI Requests in Criminology

Criminology examines lawbreaking activity, how "crime" is categorized and made intelligible by criminal justice agencies, and how criminal classifications are designed and applied. ATI/FOI requests can be used to locate documents about how "crime" is classified, recorded, processed, and analyzed. ATI/FOI requests can also be used to locate records on rates of some types of criminalized activities. Nelson, Wooditch, and Gabbidon (2014) argue that criminology is at risk of appearing out of date due to its overreliance on archaic data sources and because it often takes for granted state categories of crime. Perhaps ATI/FOI can be of some methodological service in this regard. Criminologists could access qualitative materials on how some types of categories are devised. But they could also seek quantitative records on how often those categories are used or locate internal statistics to compare to state-released descriptions of crime.

Crosby and Monaghan's (2016) work on the policing of Indigenous protest is an example for the use of ATI/FOI for criminological research. Using ATI/FOI requests, they were able to generate insider records detailing the Royal Canadian Mounted Police's (RCMP) use and understanding of the term "aboriginal extremism," which they deployed as analogous to a category of crime to frame Indigenous protest groups as dangerous. Crosby and Monaghan (2016) were also able to locate documents about how the RCMP and other security agencies used hotspot analysis to map and target Indigenous resistance and protest.

Another example comes from Owusu-Bempah and Wortley (2014). In their research on the representation of ethnoracial groups in Canada's prisons, Owusu-Bempah and Wortley (2014, p. 292) conducted ATI/FOI requests with provincial and territorial prisons across the country. Unlike at the federal level, Canadian provincial and territorial prisons do not proactively disclose information on the ethnoracial makeup of their prisoner populations, making ATI/FOI a necessary means of access. The data (Owusu-Bempah & Wortley, 2014) gained access to under ATI/FOI showed clear evidence of Indigenous and African Canadian overrepresentation in provincial and territorial prisons.

Bows (2017) used ATI/FOI to access police records to show underreporting and under-policing of specific categories of crime, notably sexual violence against older people. In this way, Bows shows that some categories of crime do not receive the same attention as others because of stereotypes about what crime is. The ATI/FOI data were crucial to reveal frequencies of sexual violence against older people compared to other types of victimization, and she argues that this insight should be taken further and applied to other types of criminal classification and criminalization as well.

A final example is Reeves-Latour and Morselli (2017). Reeves-Latour and Morselli used ATI/FOI data to acquire decades of public construction tenders in Laval, Quebec, a city historically fraught with high levels of procurement corruption. Using social network analysis, the authors were able to show how evidence for bid-rigging and price-fixing by construction companies went back as far as the mid-1960s.

CONCLUSION

Like any method of data production in the social sciences, ATI/FOI can be used well, when conducted in accordance with the principles of quality social science, but it can also be used poorly. Using ATI/FOI does not make a project inherently better. Nor is it necessary to use ATI/FOI for every research project on issues related to government. We believe that the decision to use ATI/FOI, like the decision to use any method, should always be determined by what question the researcher is asking. Whether or not a project that uses ATI/FOI is a quality one depends on much more than just how carefully and systematically they conducted the ATI/FOI requests. All research needs a clear, determinate research question, proper case selection strategies, multiple data sources, and clearly justified and explained procedures for analysis. As social scientists, research quality must always be at the forefront of our minds (Tracy, 2010). And we would suggest that researchers should use agreed-upon criteria for quality (see Guba & Lincoln, 1994; Tracy, 2010) when designing research that incorporates use of ATI/FOI and compares the disclosures obtained to other data types.

ATI/FOI is not just an investigative enterprise, but also a collaborative one. ATI/FOI users benefit from working together, both with academics as well as those outside of academia (Walby & Larsen, 2012). Often the questions being investigated are broader than any one researcher can manage on their own. Other researchers (journalists and lawyers) are usually investigating similar questions. These multiple users can share disclosures or can work together on joint projects. This will ensure they dig as deep as possible into what can be troubling and controversial government practices. The promise of ATI/FOI is its investigative character, but impact comes from collaboration. When records are found that reveal government practices going against the public interest, especially in areas of criminal justice and security, it is necessary to share these findings as widely as possible in an effort to inform the various publics who are impacted.

REFERENCES

Aberbach, J. D., & Rockman, B. A. (2002). Conducting and coding elite interviews. *PS: Political Science & Politics*, *35*(4), 673–676.

Ackerman, J. M., & Sandoval-Ballesteros, I. E. (2006). The global explosion of freedom of information laws. *Administrative Law Review*, *58*(1), 85–130.

Afful-Dadzie, E., & Afful-Dadzie, A. (2017). Liberation of public data: Exploring central themes in open government data and freedom of information research. *International Journal of Information Management*, *37*(6), 664–672.

Alvesalo-Kuusi, A., & Whyte, D. (2018). Researching the powerful: A call for the reconstruction of research ethics. *Sociological Research Online*, *23*(1), 136–152.

Auriacombe, C. J. (2007). Unobtrusive research methods: Critical issues. *Journal of Public Administration*, *42*(6), 458–471.

Birkinshaw, P. (2010a). *Freedom of information: The law, the practice and the ideal*. Cambridge: Cambridge University Press.

Birkinshaw, P. (2010b). Freedom of information and its impact in the United Kingdom. *Government Information Quarterly*, *27*(4), 312–321.

Bows, H. (2017). Researching sexual violence against older people: Reflecting on the use of freedom of information requests in a feminist study. *Feminist Review*, *115*(1), 30–45.

Broadhead, R. S., & Rist, R. C. (1976). Gatekeepers and the social control of social research. *Social Problems*, *23*(3), 325–336.

Brown, K. J. (2009). COUNTERBLAST: Freedom of information as a research tool: Realising its potential. *The Howard Journal of Criminal Justice*, *48*(1), 88–91.

Byrne, M. (2003). Freedom of information in the post-communist world. *Problems of Post-Communism, 50*(2), 56.

Bunker, M. D., & Davis, C. N. (1998). Privatized government functions and freedom of information: Public accountability in an age of private governance. *Journalism & Mass Communication Quarterly, 75*(3), 464–477.

Cherry, M., & McMenemy, D. (2013). Freedom of information and 'vexatious' requests—The case of Scottish local government. *Government Information Quarterly, 30*(3), 257–266.

Clément, D. (2015). 'Freedom' of information in Canada: Implications for historical research. *Labour/Le Travail, 75*(1), 101–131.

Cousin, B., Khan, S., & Mears, A. (2018). Theoretical and methodological pathways for research on elites. *Socio-Economic Review, 16*(2), 225–249.

Cramer, B. W. (2018). Old love for new snoops: How exemption 3 of the freedom of information act enables an irrebuttable presumption of surveillance secrecy. *Communication Law and Policy, 23*(2), 91–124.

Crosby, A., & Monaghan, J. (2016). Settler colonialism and the policing of idle no more. *Social Justice, 43*(2), 37–57.

Douglas, J. D. (1976). *Investigative social research: Individual and team field research*. Beverley Hills, CA: Sage.

Ericson, R. V. (1981). *Making crime: A study of detective work*. Toronto, Canada: Butterworths.

Galison, P. (2004). Removing knowledge. *Critical Inquiry, 31*(1), 229–243.

García-Tabuyo, M., Sáez-Martín, A., & Caba-Pérez, M. D. C. (2016). Mandatory versus voluntary disclosures: Drivers of proactive information provision by local governments in Central America. *Information Development, 32*(4), 1199–1215.

Geller, A., & Fagan, J. (2010). Pot as pretext: Marijuana, race, and the new disorder in New York City street policing. *Journal of Empirical Legal Studies, 7*(4), 591–633.

Greenberg, P. (2016). Strengthening sociological research through public records requests. *Social Currents, 3*(2), 110–117.

Guba, E., & Lincoln, Y. (1994). Competing paradigms in qualitative research. In N. Denzin & Y. Lincoln (Eds.), *Handbook of qualitative research* (pp. 105–117). Thousand Oaks, CA: Sage.

Halstuk, M. E., & Chamberlin, B. F. (2006). The freedom of information act 1966–2006: A retrospective on the rise of privacy protection over the public interest in knowing what the government's up to. *Communication Law and Policy, 11*(4), 511–564.

Hazell, R. (1989). Freedom of information in Australia, Canada and New Zealand. *Public Administration, 67*(2), 189–210.

Hewitt, S. (2012). He who controls the present, controls the past: The Canadian security state's imperfect censorship under the access to information act. In M. Larsen & K. Walby (Eds.), *Brokering access: Power, politics, and freedom of information process in Canada* (pp. 194–208). Vancouver, Canada: UBC Press.

Ho, D., Ho, R., & Ng, S. (2006). Investigative research as a knowledge-generation method: Discovering and uncovering. *Journal for the Theory of Social Behaviour, 36*(1), 17–38.

Katz, J. M. (1969). Games bureaucrats play: Hide and seek under the freedom of information act. *Texas Law Review, 48*, 1261–1284.

Kimball, M. B. (2012). Shining the light from the inside: Access professionals' perceptions of government transparency. *Communication Law and Policy, 17*(3), 299–328.

Kraska, P., & Brent, J. (2011). *Theorizing criminal justice*. Long Grove, IL: Waveland.

Larsen, M., & Walby, K. (2012). Power, politics and freedom of information process in Canada. In M. Larsen & K. Walby (Eds.), *Brokering access: Power, politics and freedom of information process in Canada* (pp. 1–34). Vancouver, Canada: University of British Columbia Press.

Lee, R. M. (2005). The UK freedom of information act and social research. *International Journal of Social Research Methodology, 8*(1), 1–18.

Lehmann, T., & Young, T. R. (1974). From conflict theory to conflict methodology: An emerging paradigm for sociology. *Sociological Inquiry, 44*(1), 15–28.

Lippert, R., Walby, K., & Wilkinson, B. (2016). Spins, stalls, and shutdowns: Pitfalls of qualitative policing and security research. *Qualitative Social Research, 17*(1), 1–20.

Luscombe, A., & Walby, K. (2015). High policing and access to information. *Police Practice and Research, 16*(6), 485–498.

Luscombe, A., & Walby, K. (forthcoming). Practicing freedom of information as 'Feral Law' and theorizing FOI in socio-legal studies. In M. Alam, P. Dwyer, K. Roots, & J. Williams (Eds.), *Socio-legal imaginations: A field in development*. Vancouver, BC: University of British Columbia Press.

Luscombe, A., Walby, K., & Lippert, R. (2017). Brokering access beyond the border and in the wild: Comparing freedom of information law and policy in Canada and the United States. *Law & Policy*, *39*(3), 259–279.

Marx, G. T. (1984). Notes on the discovery, collection, and assessment of hidden and dirty data. In J. Schneider & J. Kitsuse (Eds.), *Studies in the sociology of social problems* (pp. 78–113). Norwood, NJ: Ablex.

Mann, B. (1986). The federal information coordinator as meat in the sandwich. *Canadian Public Administration*, *29*(4), 579–582.

Mopas, M. S., & Turnbull, S. (2011). Negotiating a way in: A special collection of essays on accessing information and socio-legal research. *Canadian Journal of Law & Society*, *26*(3), 585–590.

Moran-Ellis, J., Alexander, V., Cronin, A. Dickinson, M., Fielding, J., Sleney, J., & Thomas, H. (2006). Triangulation and integration: Processes, claims and implications. *Qualitative Research*, *6*(1), 45–59.

Mummolo, J. (2018). Militarization fails to enhance police safety or reduce crime but may harm police reputation. *Proceedings of the National Academy of Sciences*, *115*(37), 9181–9186.

Nader, L. (1974). Up the anthropologist – Perspectives gained from studying up. In D. Hymes (Ed.), *Reinventing anthropology* (pp. 284–311). New York, NY: Vintage Books.

Nelson, M. S., Wooditch, A., & Gabbidon, S. L. (2014). Is criminology out-of-date? A research note on the use of common types of data. *Journal of Criminal Justice Education*, *25*(1), 16–33.

Owusu-Bempah, A., & Wortley, S. (2014). Race, crime, and criminal justice in Canada. In S. Bucerius & M. Tonry (Eds.), *The Oxford handbook of ethnicity, crime, and immigration* (pp. 281–320). New York, NY: Oxford University Press.

Pasquier, M., & Villeneuve, J. P. (2007). Organizational barriers to transparency: A typology and analysis of organizational behaviour tending to prevent or restrict access to information. *International Review of Administrative Sciences*, *73*(1), 147–162.

Piché, J. (2014). A contradictory and finishing state. Explaining recent prison capacity expansion in Canada's provinces and territories. *Champ pénal/Penal field*, *11*. doi:10.4000/champpenal.8797

Pozen, D. E. (2005). The mosaic theory, national security, and the freedom of information act. *Yale Law Journal*, *115*, 628–679.

Rappert, B. (2012). States of ignorance: The unmaking and remaking of death tolls. *Economy and Society*, *41*(1), 42–63.

Reeves-Latour, M., & Morselli, C. (2017). Bid-rigging networks and state-corporate crime in the construction industry. *Social Networks*, *51*, 158–170.

Roberts, A. S. (2000). Less government, more secrecy: Reinvention and the weakening of freedom of information law. *Public Administration Review*, *60*(4), 308–320.

Roberts, A. (2002). Administrative discretion and the access to information act: An "internal law" on open government? *Canadian Public Administration*, *45*(2), 175–194.

Roberts, A. (2006). *Blacked out: Government secrecy in the information age*. Cambridge: Cambridge University Press.

Rose, N., & Valverde, M. (1998). Governed by law? *Social & Legal Studies*, *7*(4), 541–551.

Rowat, D. (1993). Freedom of information: The appeal bodies under the access laws in Canada, Australia and New Zealand. *Australian Journal of Public Administration*, *52*(2), 215–222.

Roziere, B., & Walby, K. (2018). The expansion and normalization of police militarization in Canada. *Critical Criminology*, *26*(1), 29–48.

Savage, A., & Hyde, R. (2014). Using freedom of information requests to facilitate research. *International Journal of Social Research Methodology*, *17*(3), 303–317.

Sheaff, M. (2017). Constructing accounts of organisational failure: Policy, power and concealment. *Critical Social Policy*, *37*(4), 520–539.

Shepherd, E., Stevenson, A., & Flinn, A. (2010). Information governance, records management, and freedom of information: A study of local government authorities in England. *Government Information Quarterly*, *27*(4), 337–345.

Swallow, D., & Bourke, G. (2012, June). *The freedom of information act and higher education: The experience of FOI officers in the UK*. Report, The Constitution Unit, University College London.

Tessier, S. (2012). From field notes, to transcripts, to tape recordings: Evolution or combination? *International Journal of Qualitative Methods*, *11*(4), 446–460.

Thomson, R., & Holland, J. (2003). Hindsight, foresight and insight: The challenges of longitudinal qualitative research. *International Journal of Social Research Methodology*, *6*(3), 233–244.

Timmermans, S., & Tavory, I. (2012). Theory construction in qualitative research: From grounded theory to abductive analysis. *Sociological Theory*, *30*(3), 167–186.

Trace, C. B. (2002). What is recorded is never simply 'what happened': Record keeping in modern organizational culture. *Archival Science*, *2*(1–2), 137–159.

Tracy, S. (2010). Qualitative quality: Eight "big-tent" criteria for excellent qualitative research. *Qualitative Inquiry*, *16*(10), 837–851.

Valverde, M., Levi, R., & Moore, D. (2005). Legal knowledges of risk. In Law Commission of Canada (Ed.), *Law and risk* (pp. 86–121). Vancouver, Canada: UBC Press.

Walby, K., & Larsen, M. (2011). Getting at the live archive: On access to information research in Canada. *Canadian Journal of Law and Society*, *26*(3), 623–634.

Walby, K., & Larsen, M. (2012). Access to information and freedom of information requests: Neglected means of data production in the social sciences. *Qualitative Inquiry*, *18*(1), 31–42.

Walby, K., & Luscombe, A. (2017). Criteria for quality in qualitative research and use of freedom of information requests in social research. *Qualitative Research*, *17*(5), 537–553.

Walby, K., & Luscombe, A. (2018). Ethics review and freedom of information requests in qualitative research. *Research Ethics*, *14*(4), 1–15.

Wilson, J. (2011). Freedom of information and research data. *Research Ethics*, *7*(3), 107–111.

Worthy, B., John, P., & Vannoni, M. (2016). Transparency at the parish pump: A field experiment to measure the effectiveness of freedom of information requests in England. *Journal of Public Administration Research and Theory*, *27*(3), 485–500.

Yeager, M. (2006). The freedom of information act as a methodological tool: Suing the government for data. *Canadian Journal of Criminology and Criminal Justice*, *48*(4), 499–521.

CHAPTER 3

CRIMINAL GROUP DYNAMICS AND NETWORK METHODS

Marie Ouellet and Sadaf Hashimi

ABSTRACT

Purpose – *Criminal groups have long been central to explanations of crime and deviance. Yet, challenges in measuring their dynamic and transient nature meant that group-level explanations were often displaced in favor of individual-level ones. This chapter outlines how network methods provide a powerful tool for modeling the dynamic nature of criminal groups.*

Approach – *The chapter starts by providing a brief introduction to social network analysis, including key concepts and terminology. The chapter then focuses on the types of relational data available to study criminal groups, and how network methods can be used to delineate group boundaries. The chapter concludes by presenting a framework for understanding group dynamics from a network perspective, describing the contributions of network analysis to theories of group processes.*

Findings – *Network methods have provided meaningful advances to the study of group dynamics, leading scholars to revisit assumptions about the impact of group' structure on delinquent behavior. Network studies of group dynamics have primarily focused on the cohesion–delinquency link (within-group structure) and the social contagion of conflict (between-group structure), highlighting important opportunities for the intersection of these two inquiries.*

Value – *Network methods provide a means to revisit and extend theories of crime and delinquency with a focus on social structure. The unique affinity between group dynamics and network methods highlights immense opportunities for expanding the knowledge of collective trajectories.*

Methods of Criminology and Criminal Justice Research
Sociology of Crime, Law and Deviance, Volume 24, 47–65

ISSN: 1521-6136/doi:10.1108/S1521-613620190000024006

Keywords: Network methods; group dynamics; relational data; group boundaries; delinquency peer influence

INTRODUCTION

The wide array of criminal groups has been well documented by decades of research (e.g., Klein, 1971; Miller, 2001; Thrasher, 1927). There are groups that seize to exist beyond a single crime incident, and others that survive for decades. There are groups that maintain stable membership, and those that undergo high turnover. There are groups that engage in episodic delinquent activity, and those for which delinquency is a staple of their existence.

These variations create difficulties for defining, delimiting, and measuring criminal groups. Earlier explanations of criminal group processes often relied on extensive field research, spanning years of observations of group members and their interactions. This research has yielded important insights about group processes and delinquency, including the role of a group's structural features in shaping group processes. Indeed, this was the basic premise of Short and Strodtbeck's (1965) seminal piece on Chicago gangs. They observed that delinquent behavior was directly related to social processes that emerged in the day-to-day of gang members lives, including their interactions with one another and with other groups. Similarly, Block's (1979) work on organized crime in mid-century New York City showed that criminal syndicates operated in "alliance networks" that structured around the groups ability to maximize profits and evade sanctions. Yet, despite many decades of research, group-level studies have been primarily descriptive in nature, creating important gaps in explanatory accounts of group dynamics.

The gaps in our knowledge are, in part, due to a lack of group-level data. Although group dynamics were once central to explanations of crime, advances in survey research during the 1970s shifted individual-based research to the forefront of criminology (e.g., Bursik, 1998; Kreager, Rulison, & Moody, 2011). The shift allowed for important methodological and theoretical developments, including the ability to generate representative samples, a major critique of early field research on criminal groups. However, it virtually displaced group-level explanations of crime – a phenomenon that was observed across the study of gangs (Pyrooz & Mitchell, 2015), criminal enterprises (Paoli, 2002), delinquent peer groups (Kreager et al., 2011), and terrorist organizations (Miller, 2012).

This chapter aims to outline how a network framework can be leveraged to address these gaps and foster explanatory research. Network methods are uniquely suited to measure the dynamic and transient nature of groups, mapping out social relations, delineating group structure, and allowing for cross-comparisons across groups. Network methods have led to meaningful advances in the structure of criminal operations[1]; however, a large proportion of these studies have conventionally focused on the role that networks play in shaping individual behavior (Carrington, 2011). This chapter aims to foster group-level research, by demonstrating how network methods can be used to move up the analytical ladder to examine variation in collective trajectories.

In this chapter, we start by providing a brief introduction to a network perspective, including key terminology and concepts. We then outline the various relational data sources that scholars have relied on to study group dynamics, and how network methods provide a set of methodological techniques for delineating group boundaries. Next, we present a framework for examining group dynamics, distinguishing between studies that focus on within-group and between-group social structures. We conclude by highlighting how these two areas intersect, and opportunities for moving the field forward.

A NETWORK PERSPECTIVE OF DELINQUENT GROUPS

Networks refer to the mathematical representations of the relationships that link different units within a system. These units – referred to as *vertices* – may represent entities across different levels of analysis, including individuals (e.g., gang members and youth), groups (e.g., gangs and peer groups), or larger collectives (e.g., gang task forces). The links – referred to as *edges* – represent relationships between the vertices. Edges may be operationalized as binary links – the presence or absence of a relationship (however defined) or can be built up to further characterize the relationship. For instance, edges may be directed, representing the flow of information or resources (e.g., A phones B, but B never phones A); valued, indicating the intensity or frequency of interaction (e.g., the number of times A phones B), and/or multiplex, representing the presence of multiple relationship types (e.g., A and B are both part of the same gang and siblings). Network methods provide a set of tools to identify and describe the structural properties of these networks, as well as a set of models and techniques to examine the sources and patterns of interactions in social relationships (Carrington, Scott, & Wasserman, 2005).

To start, the application of network methods to the study of delinquent groups requires distinguishing between complete-network data and ego-network data. Studies of criminal groups require complete-network data when the unit of analysis are individuals (e.g., gang members), providing a complete representation of all the actors and their links within the social system. Network analysis can then be used to assess the structural properties of a group, including the degree to which it is structured as a cohesive entity or centralized around a subset of highly connected members. In contrast, when the unit of analysis is groups (e.g., gangs), studies of criminal groups may rely on either complete-network data, the full set of relationships between all groups, or ego-network data, capturing the "local" connections around any one group. These relationships can be used to examine larger network structure, including the degree to which a group is embedded in a network of alliances and/or rivalries, and how interdependence between these groups influences social processes.

NETWORK DATA

Studies relying on network methods to examine criminal group dynamics have acquired network data from various sources, including: (1) field observations, (2) police records, (3) archived materials, (4) self-reports, and (5) online data. Ideally, network data should reflect the full population of interest; however, who to include or exclude is often restricted by practical constraints – "who is in the data" rather than theoretical questions "who should be considered part of the network." While some data sources may be more reliable, they may be less relevant, and conversely, while some data sources are relevant, they may be less reliable.

Some of the earliest applications of network analysis to criminal groups drew from field observations of gang members. For instance, the Boston Special Youth Project a study of juvenile delinquency founded in the 1950s by Water J. Miller, relied heavily on detached workers and their interactions with gangs and gang members to obtain relational data. Specifically, contact cards maintained by the workers detailing the nature of their interactions with gang members (e.g., name, date, location, and group), the author's interactions with outreach workers, as well as the author's personal interactions with gang members, and group meetings were used to address gang delinquency and restructure the activities of adolescence street gangs (see Miller, 1957, 1958, 1962). More recently, scholars have revisited the detailed field notes of early gang scholars to reconstruct the social structure of gangs and their members (See Papachristos, 2009). Relational data collected from field observations provide a valuable source of network data, affording in-depth coverage of the set and types of relationships between actors. However, data collection is labor-intensive and often restricted to a subset of groups, that are more readily accessible, creating concerns about the representativity of results.

More recent research has relied on relational data present in police records, including arrest and field incident reports. Arrest records afford information on two types of ties: (1) Offender-offender relationships, cases where more than one individual has been arrested for the same criminal incident and (2) offender–victim relationships, cases where the crime incident records both an alleged perpetrator(s), and the alleged victim(s). In contrast, field incident records provide information on non-criminal ties, cases where officers document the individuals they encounter in their daily routines (e.g., Hashimi & Bouchard, 2017). These non-criminal ties may overlap with criminal-ties found in arrest records, or present distinct relationships not previously recorded. Police records thus provide a two-mode data structure (ties to incidents), where individuals are linked based on their joint involvement in the same incident or behavior. Researchers can then rely on a one-mode projection (ties between individuals) of these incidents, connecting individuals through their co-involvement in the same event. Police records have been increasingly used to understand group dynamics to delineate the scope of organized crime groups (e.g., Hashimi, Bouchard, Morselli, & Ouellet, 2017), examine trends in group crime (e.g., Carrington, 2002; Lantz & Hutchison, 2015; Sarnecki, 2001), and conflict between groups (e.g., Papachristos, 2009; Hashimi & Bouchard, 2017).

Police records are impressive in their scope, creating networks of co-offenders, co-arrestees, and co-associates, on a scale that may not otherwise be available. But the breadth of the data comes at a cost to its depth and representativity. Official records are limited to the individuals for which there was available evidence, were present at the crime incident, and who were detected by police, thus imposing boundaries on groups that may be much more fluid and dynamic than they seem. Discrepancies in how agencies record and define crime incidents, departmental mandates, and variation in resources mean that some individuals (and their interactions) are more likely to be detected than others. Further, police records only tell us about behavioral ties, instances where individuals were observed (or alleged) to be engaging in the same type of behavior together. These networks only provide a subset of an individual's larger network, and limits our considerations of individuals beyond those involved in the behavior and the larger group from which the behavior emerged.

Archived records, including court files, meeting minutes, and public inquiries, have also formed the foundation of many network studies. The sources of archived records are extensive. For instance, Crossley, Edwards, Harries, & Stevenson (2012) relied on the UK Home Office files, which detailed all individuals who were in court for suffragette-related incidents from 1906 to 1914. This allowed them to extract "co-offending" links between suffragettes who appeared in court together for the same incident. Others have relied on archived electronic surveillance records of illicit organizations, such as wiretaps, to map out the networks of their operations (e.g., Campana, 2011; Malm, Bichler, & Nash, 2011; Morselli, 2009). Electronic wiretaps provide valuable information on both the network of phone calls, but also the content of these phone calls, which allows researchers to understand the context of the relationships between callers (Campana, 2015; Campana & Varese, 2012; Baker and Faulkner, 1993). Similar to police sources, archived records provide valuable information, but are restricted to the individuals and interactions detected and then recorded into files.

Self-report data collected from surveys and interviews provide a valuable resource for researchers wanting to surmount limitations in official and archived sources. Surveys and interviews may be marshaled to collect network data by asking respondents to nominate or select their peers according to a pre-defined criterion. As part of the National Longitudinal Study of Adolescent to Adult Health (Add Health) in-school questionnaire, students were asked to nominate up to five male and five female friends from all students enrolled in the respondent's school or their sister school (Harris et al., 2009). Importantly in 16 of the 145 schools (i.e., the "saturation" sample), all students were solicited to participate in the network component of the survey. From this sub-sample, the complete network of friendships within a high school may be analyzed through student nominations (see Gallupe & Gravel, 2018).

Surveys provide researchers with the flexibility to specify the number, type, and characterization of relationships. The control that researchers have over the data collection procedure is a major strength of this approach, especially when compared to police or archived records. Survey data of complete networks – where all members within a bounded population have been sampled – has been used to study the social structure of peer friendship groups (Kreager et al., 2011), gang networks (Hughes, 2013), and inmate groups (Schaefer, Bouchard, Young, & Kreager, 2017). However, the use of survey data to study criminal groups is limited to the degree that all members of a bounded population can be sampled. Bounded populations may be more clearly defined in some samples, such as high school students, but more ambiguous in others, such as gangs where fluid boundaries preclude the existence of a roster or even be known to all members.

Further, network studies may rely on data collection tools already in the criminologist repertoire, such as snowball sampling of hidden populations (e.g., Decker, 1996). An extension of this technique, respondent-driven sampling, relies on patterns in repeated waves of recruitment to make statistical inferences about the full population under study, and help infer group boundaries (e.g., Heckathorn, 1997; Heckathorn & Cameron, 2017). In addition, the rise in social media provides additional sources for extending the pool of available data, by reaching populations that would be too difficult to study with traditional methods. Social media has already proven to be a valuable source to understand group dynamics with social networking platforms like Twitter (e.g., Patton, Lane, Leonard, MacBeth, & Smith Lee, 2017) and Facebook (e.g., Lane, 2019), along with email records (e.g., Palla, Barabási & Vicsek, 2007), mobile phone data (e.g., Eagle, Pentland, & Lazer, 2009; Morselli, 2009; Sugie, 2018) and other electronic tools such as the Global Positioning System (Schmidt, 2012), tracking and recording information on the ways in which groups interact and organize themselves in the "online" versus "offline" world. With this comes an unprecedented opportunity to adopt an interdisciplinary approach and employ computational techniques to mine network data. The impact of media communication and its capability to reach others by decreasing both social and spatial distance allows individuals to establish new forms of social ties and creates new forms of group structure (Castells, 2000).

The selection of a data source is the fundamental building block to design reliable and valid network studies, as it guides who will and will not be included in the network, along with the types of relationships to be considered. The various data collection strategies are not mutually exclusive, and there is ample evidence of scholars merging multiple sources (e.g., Malm et al., 2011; Stevenson & Crossley, 2014). Some works have been done to examine the validity of structural inferences across official records and self-reports (e.g., Ouellet & Bouchard, 2018; Sarnecki, 2001); however, these have focused on case studies, and more systematic efforts on the precise measurement biases, including how network data converges (or diverges) across sources is needed.

Additionally, an often-overlooked step is the time-varying nature of relations. To date, much research has focused on static networks, directing their attention to a single time snapshot or an aggregate view over time, yet networks are dynamic. Ties form, grow stronger and weaker, and eventually dissolve, with change being dependent on the characteristics of those that make up the network along with the structure of the network itself. As such, periods on which group-level data are sampled are essential. Data aggregated across extended periods may misconstrue the true group structure at any one-time point. Klein and Crawford (1967) highlighted this point when discussing the scope of gangs, finding that some numbered over a few hundred when data were aggregated across multiple time points, but in reality, only consisted of 30–40 members at any single point in time. This is particularly important for network studies, where many metrics depend on the number of actors. Just like inaccuracies in network data can lead to fundamentally different representations of the same group, so can a singular snapshot at an arbitrary time point.

A NETWORK APPROACH TO DELINEATING GROUP BOUNDARIES

The available relational data provides cues for researchers looking to design network-based studies of criminal groups. While relational data may provide information on the relationships between individuals in the dataset, they are not necessarily telling of established boundaries amongst groups. We may know, for instance, the full set of interactions between students in a school, inmates in a prison, or offenders in a police district, but not much about the social groups that these actors belong to. Network methods provide a unique approach to resolve this issue, offering a set of methodological techniques to partition network data into groups according to patterns of social relations. Techniques such as block modeling, hierarchical clustering, and community detection have largely been applied by scholars grounded in computer science, physics, as well as the biological and social sciences.

In the study of crime, scholars have primarily relied on community detection techniques to delineate groups from relational data. The overall aim of community detection is to extract subgroups from the larger network that correspond with meaningful conceptualizations of social groups. Theoretically, community detection draws on suggestions by early scholars, such as Simmel (1955) who emphasized that while individuals are embedded in various webs of affiliations, strong(er) social ties are more likely to form with those who are in one's immediate vicinity; their local "circle" as opposed to their larger social environment. It is through these immediate, local ties that larger heterogeneous networks of individuals filter into smaller homogenous groups. Methodologically, community detection aims to quantify the "intuitive concept of community structure" by arranging edges (ties between actors) into groups (Newman, 2006, p. 8578) – thus, identifying areas of structural homogeneity within the larger heterogeneous network graph. Community detection methods can be broadly divided into two classes of techniques: modularity- and clique-based approaches.

Modularity-based approaches partition network graphs into densely connected sub-groups with loose connections between groups. This approach takes into account both the proportion of within-group edges (high within-group connectivity) and between-group edges (low between-group connectivity) (e.g., Girvan & Newman, 2002; Newman & Girvan, 2004). The degree to which a network graph can be partitioned into subgraphs is assessed via a modularity score, which represents a weighted function of within- as compared to between-group ties. The modularity score ranges from 0 to 1, with scores closer to 1 representing a better fit. There are multiple modularity-maximization techniques; some of the most popular include the Girvan–Newman (Girvan & Newman, 2002); Newman (Clauset, Newman, & Moore, 2004), and Louvain (Blondel, Guillaume, Lambiotte, & Lefebvre, 2008). The selection of the appropriate method often depends on the solution with the highest modularity score and greatest face validity, as compared to other solutions.

Modularity-based techniques provide a flexible approach to detect group boundaries; they can be used for weighted, directed, and longitudinal graphs (e.g., Mucha, Richardson, Macon, Porter, & Onnela, 2010). Kreager et al. (2011) demonstrated the utility of a modularity-based approach to discern peer friendship groups across students in 27 Iowan and Pennsylvania high schools. Relying on friendship nominations across 9,385 ninth-grade students, the authors delineated 897 distinct peer groups. These groups formed the unit of analysis for the study, which examined the link between a group's delinquency and structural features. Scholars have since applied modularity-based approaches to extract groups of co-offenders (e.g., Lantz & Hutchison, 2015; Ouellet, Charette, & Bouchard, 2019), gangs (e.g., van Gennip, Hu, Hunter, & Porter, 2012), inmates (e.g., Schaefer et al., 2017), criminal organizations (e.g., Calderoni, Brunetto, & Picardi, 2017), and cryptomarket vendors (e.g., Duxbury & Haynie, 2018). Though widely used, modularity-based approaches have been critiqued for being limited in nature and scope. Methodologically, modularity-based techniques suffer from degeneracy, where a high number of alternative high scoring partitions may be extracted from the full network graph (Good, de Montjoye, & Clauset, 2010), and resolution limits, where subgroups are unable to be detected if they are too small relative to the overall size of the network (Fortunato & Barthélemy, 2007). Theoretically, modularity-based techniques have been critiqued for limiting membership to a single group, imposing "an artificial constraint on the groupings they are seeking to uncover" (Everett & Borgatti, 1998, p. 49).

Clique-based approaches distinguish themselves from modularity-based techniques primarily by their ability to produce overlapping groups, where group membership is not mutually exclusive (also see mixed membership stochastic blockmodels, Airoldi et al. (2008)). Cliques represent the most fundamental notion of a subgroup where each actor is connected to every other actor, with triads – a set of three actors who are all connected – the simplest notion of a clique. The clique percolation method (CPM) represents a clique-based technique to detect subgroups from relational data (Palla, Derényi, Farkas, & Vicsek, 2005). The CPM works by first identifying all cliques of size k in a network graph. It then generates a new graph where each vertex represents one of the k-cliques. Vertices (i.e., k-cliques) are then clustered into larger groups if they are adjacent to other vertices, where adjacency is defined by any k-cliques that share $k-1$ members. Because an actor can belong to more than one k-clique, these groups can overlap.

In contrast to modularity-based approaches, the number of optimal groups is selected by the researcher who determines the size of the initial k-clique. Consequently, individuals may be excluded from any grouping as not all individuals in a network graph may belong to a clique of size k though, solutions of k-size should aim to maximize coverage of the actors within the graph (Palla et al., 2005). Although CPM offers clear advantages for delineating group boundaries, it is not without its limits, performing poorly in network graphs with few cliques (see Newman, 2018).

Schaefer et al. (2017) applied the CPM to delineate subgroups of residents housed in a medium-security prison. Relying on "get-along" nominations, the authors uncovered 12 social groups among the residents. Representing one of the few studies to compare modularity and clique-based social groupings, the authors showed that modularity-based approaches identified eight groups. Rather than pit the two approaches, the authors demonstrated how they offered complementary information and reinforced the finding that residents were organized into racial and religious heterogeneous social groups. The study also highlighted how the two approaches created important differences in the distribution of groups, with the modularity-based groups ranging from 8 to 26 residents, and the clique-based groups uncovering one larger social grouping of 61 residents, followed by several smaller ones.

Important methodological advances have been made to delineate group boundaries from relational data, including the ability to account for the frequency and duration of interactions, as well as more advanced methods such as the mixed-membership stochastic block model (Airoldi et al., 2008). However, there have been limited efforts to validate these groups. One of the rare examples to validate groups extracted using these techniques in criminology includes van Gennip et al.'s (2012) validation of algorithmically detected communities extracted from the networks of individuals as recorded in field incident cards by the Los Angeles Police Department. Indeed, studies may also rely on methodological approaches to validate the extracted partitions, such as similarity and dissimilarity measures that can be used to assess the effect of different distance measures on the quality of community detection algorithm results (Shirkhorshidi, Aghabozorgi, & Wah, 2015).

RESEARCH ON CRIMINAL GROUP DYNAMICS

Studies equipped with criminal network data are uniquely positioned to revisit and extend theories of crime and delinquency. Early applications of network analysis provided descriptive accounts of the social structure of criminal groups, challenging dominant perspectives that gangs and other criminal entities flowed vertically in a hierarchical structure (e.g., McGloin, 2005; Morselli, 2009), while also examining the sources of this structure (e.g., Bright, Koskinen, & Malm, 2018; Crossley et al., 2012; Morselli, Giguère, & Petit, 2007), and its impact on offending pathways (e.g., Haynie, 2001; McGloin & Piquero, 2010; Morselli & Tremblay, 2004; Morselli, Tremblay, & McCarthy, 2006). The underlying premise of these studies was that the etiology of crime was inherently a social phenomenon that shaped the emergence and evolution of delinquent activity. More recent studies have aimed to test these premises on collective trajectories, by providing explanatory accounts of how group dynamics influence behavior. These studies can be broadly categorized into two classes: studies that examine *intra*-group dynamics (within-group structure), and studies that examine *inter*-group dynamics (between-group structure).

Intra-group Network Dynamics

Intra-group explanations make use of within-group interactions to account for group behavior. Much of this work has focused on the internal connectivity – or *cohesiveness* – of a group. Cohesion has long been central to theorizing about criminal group processes, often viewed as a key governing force of group behavior, influencing patterns in group delinquency and violence (e.g., Decker, 1996; Jansyn, 1966; Short & Strodtbeck, 1965; Vigil, 1988). Conceptually, cohesion refers to the degree of solidarity and unity between members within a group (e.g., Collins, 1988; Decker & Curry, 2002). However, challenges in directly measuring cohesion have meant that many theories of cohesion have remained largely untested (see Papachristos, 2013). Network methods have aimed to fill this gap by providing a set of measures to quantify group cohesion, based on patterns in members' social interactions, and the degree to which groups are structured into tightly knit entities.

A classic study of gangs by Klein & Crawford (1967) made direct connections between a group's cohesion and delinquency. Its key concept – cohesion – was defined as the "mutual liking or acceptance, attraction to group, degree of shared norms or values, and resistance to disruptive forces" (Klein & Crawford, 1967 p. 69). However, the authors rejected traditional approaches to operationalizing cohesion in favor of a network approach that directly measured member interactions. Relying on detached worker contact cards, which recorded workers' daily observations of gang members and who they were seen with, the authors mapped out the interactions between 576 gang members across four gang clusters. The cohesiveness of each gang cluster was operationalized as the degree to which members formed tightly connected groups, according to nine different network indices, including a measure of the overall density of the group (i.e., the number of connections between gang members as a proportion of all possible connections). Comparing a group's cohesiveness with their delinquency, the authors found a positive association between cohesiveness and delinquency, with the most cohesive groups being the most delinquent.

Despite the important contribution of network methods to operationalize cohesion, it would be nearly half a century before scholars would re-test the cohesion–delinquency link with statistical models across samples of delinquent and non-delinquent groups. Kreager et al. (2011) examined the sources of a group's cohesion across 897 peer friendship groups with varying levels of delinquency. Cohesion in this study reflected measures of: transitivity (degree to which groups consisted of triads), reciprocity (the percent of friendship nominations within a group that were reciprocated), and structural cohesion (the mean number of node independent paths). However, in contrast to Klein and Crawford (1967), the findings did not support a consistent relationship between a group's cohesiveness and delinquency. Once behavioral and attitudinal measures were controlled for, only transitivity was found to be positively associated with a group's overall delinquency.

The relationship, or better yet, a lack thereof, of relationship between a group's delinquency and cohesion was also supported by Hughes (2013) study of Chicago gangs. Resurrecting relational data embedded in surveys of 248 gang members conducted during Short and Strodtbeck's (1965) field research in Chicago, she examined variation in delinquency and cohesion across 11 gangs. Measuring cohesion as the average number of friends nominated by each gang member within the gang, results showed that a group's cohesion did not predict its general delinquency levels, but it did negatively predict a group's violence.[2]

Network approaches have provided meaningful advances in unpacking the cohesion–delinquency relationship – allowing us to look at cohesion across large samples of delinquent and non-delinquent groups and forcing us to revisit assumptions about the impact of a group's structure on collective behavior. However, the relationship between a group's cohesion and delinquency is far from conclusive. One way forward would be to extend these examinations to focus on the temporal order of the cohesion–delinquency relationship. Scholars working on cohesion and delinquency typically focus on one strategy and point the causal arrow in a single direction. However, the direction of the relationship is unclear. Cohesion ebbs and flows across a group's life cycle, and the relationship with delinquency may not be linear, but rather reflect dynamic, reciprocal, or cumulative processes. In some contexts, non-cohesive groups are more likely to engage in delinquent acts bringing members together for a singular event (e.g., Jansyn, 1966). In other contexts, cohesive groups are more likely to engage in delinquency, such that, members are embedded in tightly knit structures that facilitate the transfer of norms and behaviors (e.g., Klein, 1969; Thornberry, Krohn, Lizotte, & Chard-Wierschem, 1993). As part of this research agenda, it would be meaningful to investigate whether sources of cohesion change across a group's evolution. It may be that cohesion is important when the group is still forming, but its effect dwindles as group activities shift or exhibit greater mobility.

Efforts to look at the flow of cohesion over time may draw from research in the social movement literature, which has conducted detailed accounts of a group's evolution over time. Focusing on a case study of the Provisional Irish Republican Army, Stevenson and Crossley (2014) demonstrated that despite high turnover, the group remained structurally stable. The group maintained a core set of members who became more central over time and connected the group as it evolved. This study suggests that subgroups within the criminal group were just as important as the overall structure of the group itself.

Inter-group Network Dynamics

Groups, criminal or otherwise, are rarely isolated entities but embedded in webs of relations. Decades of research have shown that neighboring groups play important roles in shaping a group's own identity and behavior, influencing group-based identities, serving as reference points, and structuring the spread of behaviors (e.g., Decker, 1996; Decker & Curry, 2002; Klein, 1971; Sanchez-Jankowski, 1991; Thrasher, 1927). Although these studies did not explicitly rely on formal network methods or terminology, their early insights into inter-group social processes shaped the network agenda. Network scholars have since mapped out the networks of collaboration and conflict between groups as a means to explicitly test these early perspectives and their implications for group behavior.

In a study of Chicago gangs, Papachristos (2009) provided an influential demonstration of the relevance of network methods for understanding the spread of gang violence. Defining gang conflict, as "first and foremost an interaction" (p. 75) he mapped out the network of conflict between all gangs who had been involved in a homicide, either as a perpetrator or a victim, for nearly two decades in Chicago. Extracted from law enforcement records, these data provided the full network of lethal rivalries between gangs. From this network, Papachristos (2009) estimated the likelihood that any two gangs would engage in lethal conflict with one another based on previous patterns of conflict. The results highlighted a social contagion process, such that the likelihood of violence was governed by cycles of reciprocal murders – cases where gangs were more likely to target gangs that they had targeted or had been targeted by in the past – creating institutionalized patterns of violence (p. 118).

Extending this research, Papachristos, Hureau, and Braga (2013) tested claims that violence served as a means for gangs to assert their social standing, creating the presence of dominance hierarchies. Specifically, they drew from a body of literature that observed the consequences of dominance hierarchies through interchanges of aggression (see Chase, 1980). Drawing analogies with the gang dominance literature, Papachristos et al. (2013) tested whether gangs that successfully use violence to settle disputes, or retaliate, were less likely to become victims such that they have asserted their dominance. And whether the converse was equally true, where a failure to react to violence was detrimental to the reputation of the gang, given that others within their network perceive their lack of action as a sign of weakness, making the gang and its members susceptible to future aggressors (Gould, 2003, p. 118; Papachristos, 2009). The main construct – dominance hierarchies – was measured as a network variable, whereby more aggressive gangs (more out-group ties) were presumed to have a higher status than victimized gangs (more in-group ties). Specifically, a transitive triad term allowed them to test for whether gangs exhibited different status rankings according to their violence profiles.[3] Findings from exponential random graph models showed that dominance hierarchies were not associated with gang conflict; rather, results bolstered earlier findings: lethal violence between gangs was primarily a function of reciprocal violence, where gangs were more likely to engage in conflict if a member of their gang had previously been targeted.

Since Papachristos's (2009) seminal study, scores of research findings have affirmed that gang violence spreads through a social contagion process in Boston (Papachristos et al., 2013), Chicago (Papachristos, 2009; Papachristos et al., 2013), and Los Angeles (Radil, Flint, & Tita, 2010; Tita & Radil, 2011). These studies provide important insights, and shed light on ways forward. For instance, studies of violence have primarily focused on the role of "conflict" ties rather than "collaborative" ties between gangs. We know from earlier studies that network rivalries are not necessarily independent. Alliances have been shown to form between gangs that share a common enemy, rival, or exhibit a similar gang-related motive. These alliances are responsible for how gangs respond to conflict, shaping retaliatory patterns of conflicts that may not have been there otherwise (see Bouchard & Hashimi, 2017; Morselli, Tanguay, & Labalette, 2008; Papachristos et al., 2013). In extreme cases, it may even create a polarized state whereby participants who otherwise would not have been involved in the conflict, or those located on the periphery of the network, may be inclined to choose a side (Morselli et al., 2008).

Relatedly, other studies emphasize that rivalries and alliances are not mutually exclusive categories. For instance, in Montreal, Canada, focus group interviews with 20 gang members belonging to 15 different gangs found that many gang members count their friends among their enemies; reporting instances of conflict between members of allied gangs (Descormiers & Morselli, 2011). Similarly, in Newark, New Jersey, McGloin (2005) found that gang members did not display a homogenous set of allegiances or "gang networks" per se, rather they operated in a series of loosely knit cliques, maintaining associations with individuals outside of their "explicit named sets" and members of other gangs (p. 619). This perspective underlies the main demonstration of Morselli's (2009) examination of drug distribution networks, namely that the modal form of criminal entities are ephemeral groups, where collaborations develop between groups opportunistically, to facilitate the commission of crimes and increase profitability (also see Bouchard & Morselli, 2014).

CONCLUSION

In many ways, network studies of criminal group dynamics are just getting started. This chapter provides an overview of prior research aimed at integrating group dynamics and also points to future directions for expanding such efforts. Here, we review three promising areas for moving the area forward.

A hybrid approach to group dynamics. The bulk of research on criminal group dynamics considers either a group's internal connectivity (i.e., *intra*-group) or external connectivity (i.e., *inter*-group), but rarely merges the two. Both perspectives can create important shortcoming in our understanding of group dynamics; groups are considered independent entities, in the former, or as unitary actors lacking variation in their structural features, in the latter. Yet, from the earliest studies of criminal groups we know this is not the case. Early theories emphasized that the main source of criminal groups' internal cohesion was due to this "group effect" whereby conflicts sustained with other groups increased within-group ties. Conversely, a group's cohesion has been viewed to be threatened by alliance structures that may pull members to other groups. Indeed, a hybrid approach – looking at both a group's internal and external network structure – may help explain discrepancies in whether a group elects to engage, or not engage in violence, with scholars emphasizing that a group's cohesiveness and solidarity moderates whether inter-group violence escalates or desists (see Gould, 2003; Morselli et al., 2008).

Advances in network modeling suggest there is much to be gained from looking at the intersection of these categories. For instance, Shi, Fedor, Genkin, and

Brashears (2017) demonstrated that a group's ability to persist depended on bridging internal, and external structures, maintaining cohesiveness to retain members, and creating ties to other organizations to facilitate recruitment (also see Vedres & Stark, 2010). Drawing from this literature, Ouellet et al. (2019) examined the network dynamics of criminal group persistence with an explicit focus on a group's internal and external connections. Results showed that groups at different stages in their evolution required distinct network structures to survive. More established groups, with high levels of membership, profited from adopting closed structures to maintain their existing position. Whereas, smaller groups, in their early stages of formation, benefited from more versatile structures, opening up to outside associates to expand their access to illicit opportunities. Importantly it was the balance between how a group structured its internal- and external-connectivity that shaped how the group was able to persist over time.

Beyond delinquency. Another important direction would be extend research on criminal groups to look over and beyond delinquent activities. Even among the most delinquent groups, only a fraction of social activities is spent in the commission of the actual criminal act. Similarly, many of the individuals who may be considered members of a criminal group, may or may not participate in criminal incidents. A focus purely on the delinquent aspects of a group may cloud the more peripheral, but equally important factors that bring together groups, allowing them to forge bonds, and eventually shift into collective actions. For instance, Ouellet and Bouchard's (2018) study of a domestic terrorist organization demonstrated that only a minority of the participants interacting with the group were charged for a crime. Yet, it was the majority who had an impact on the group's evolution into violence. Network methods provide a means to look beyond delinquent acts and shed light on the factors that allow groups to emerge and evolve (see Bright et al., 2018; Fitzhugh & Butts, 2018), and stress the importance of non-delinquent actors that bring together their delinquent counterparts (Morselli, 2009). These insights could assist in explaining a host of group-level outcomes, including the distribution of criminal groups, their resiliency to interdictions, and changes in group activity over time.

Cross-level analysis. Network methods are not just an opportunity for advancing our understanding of collective trajectories. More importantly they provide a path for bridging the divide between how individual- and group-level pathways intersect (see Matsueda, 2017).

Although the focus of this chapter was on the group-level dynamics associated with crime, it also advances an individual-level research agenda that suggests individual-level variation can only be understood within the context of a group's overall trajectory (see Tremblay et al., 1989). From this perspective, we view individual- and group-level research as complementary fields of inquiry. Notably, one of the strengths of social network analysis is in it's ability to seamlessly move between different levels of while work has been done on investigating how group membership structures an individual's offending pathway, group membership is often designated as a static or binary variable, creating binary cleavages between individuals who belong to a group, and those who do not. Here, we propose nesting individuals within these groups, and distinguishing between different types of groups. For instance, individuals who belong to highly cohesive gangs may have distinct offending pathways, as compared to individuals who belong to more decentralized, opportunistic entities. The same could be said for individuals who join a gang as it is just forming, in comparison to those who join a gang after it has been established. This perspective is consistent with a long line of research that considers offending pathways as structured by opportunities (e.g., Conway & McCord, 2002; McGloin & Piquero, 2010) and the underlying premise of Tremblay et al.'s (1989) work on the collective trajectories of organized crime groups.

Relatedly, cross-level analysis disentangles social interaction effects by representing network dependencies in statistical models. Analytical approaches such as stochastic actor-oriented models help transition from the macro- to the micro-level by teasing exogenous (individual level effects), endogenous (structural network effects) from non-effects, longitudinally (Snijders, 2011). Alternatively, analysis of multilevel data with statistical techniques, such as hierarchal linear modeling, incorporates effects at various hierarchical levels, modeling cross-level interactions while controlling for their shared variance (Bryk & Raudenbush, 1992). When supplemented with community detection techniques, statistical models used to deal with complex network dependencies pave the way forward to generate statistical inference, causality, and spillover effects.

NOTES

1. Evidence of this increase can be observed across ample, high quality reviews of applications of network analysis to the study of criminal phenomena, including Bouchard and Malm (2016), Campana (2016), Carrington (2011), Faust and Tita (2019), Gallupe (2016), Gravel and Tita (2017), Haynie and Kreager (2013), McGloin and Kirk (2010a, 2010b), Papachristos (2006, 2011), and Sierra-Arévalo and Papachristos (2015).
2. The authors also estimated models where cohesion was operationalized as the mean number of friendship nominations received, the proportion of intra-gang nominations (i.e., density) with a control for size, and the maximum *k*-core (based on undirected ties). All substantive results remained the same.
3. To identify the presence of gangs: (a) high in status, perpetrated violence against other gangs, but were not the targets of violence; (b) low in status, did not perpetrate violence, but were the targets of violence; and (c) gangs in the middle of the hierarchy who were both perpetrators and targets of gang violence.

REFERENCES

Airoldi, E. M., Blei, D. M., Fienberg, S. E., & Xing, E. P. (2008). Mixed membership stochastic blockmodels. *Journal of Machine Learning Research*, *9*, 1981–2014.

Baker, W. E., & Faulkner, R. R. (1993). The social organization of conspiracy: Illegal networks in the heavy electrical equipment industry. *American Sociological Review*, *58*(6), 837–867.

Block, A. A. (1979). The snowman cometh: Coke in progressive New York. *Criminology*, *17*(1), 75–99.

Block, A. (1983). *East side, west side: Organizing crime in New York, 1930–1950*. New Brunswick, NJ: Transaction Books.

Blondel, V. D., Guillaume, J.-L., Lambiotte, R., & Lefebvre, E. (2008). Fast unfolding of communities in large networks. *Journal of Statistical Mechanisms: Theory and Experiment*, *10*, P10008.

Bouchard, M., & Hashimi, S. (2017). When is a "war" a "wave?": Two approaches for the detection of waves in gang homicides. *Canadian Journal of Criminology and Criminal Justice*, *59*(2), 198–226.

Bouchard, M., & Malm, A. (2016). Social network analysis and its contribution to research on crime and criminal justice. In *Oxford handbooks online*. Retrieved from http://www.oxfordhandbooks.com/view/10.1093/oxfordhb/9780199935383.001.0001/oxfordhb-9780199935383-e-21

Bouchard, M., & Morselli, C. (2014). Opportunistic structures of organized crime. In L. Paoli (Ed.), *The Oxford handbook of organized crime* (pp. 288–302). Oxford: Oxford University Press.

Bright, D., Koskinen, J., & Malm, A. (2018). Illicit network dynamics: The formation and evolution of a drug trafficking network. *Journal of Quantitative Criminology*. Online First. https://doi.org/10.1007/s10940-018-9379-8

Bryk, A. S., & Raudenbush, S. W. (1992). *Hierarchical linear models: Applications and data analysis methods*. Newbury Park, CA: Sage Publications.

Bursik, R. J. (1998). Social disorganization and theories of crime and delinquency: Problems and prospects. *Criminology*, *26*(4), 519–551.

Calderoni, F., Brunetto, D., & Piccardi, C. (2017). Communities in criminal networks: A case study. *Social Networks*, *48*, 116–125.

Campana, P. (2011). Eavesdropping on the mob: The functional diversification of Mafia activities across territories. *European Journal of Criminology*, *8*(3), 213–228.

Campana, P. (2015). The structure of human trafficking: Lifting the bonnet on a Nigerian transnational network. *The British Journal of Criminology*, *56*(1), 68–86.

Campana, P. (2016). Explaining criminal networks: Strategies and potential pitfalls. *Methodological Innovations*, *9*, 1–10.

Campana, P., & Varese, F. (2012). Listening to the wire: Criteria and techniques for the quantitative analysis of phone intercepts. *Trends in Organized Crime*, *15*(1), 13–30.

Carrington, P. J. (2002). Group crime in Canada. *Canadian Journal of Criminology*, *44*(3), 277–315.

Carrington, P. J. (2011). Crime and social network analysis. In J. Scott & P. J. Carrington (Eds.), *The SAGE handbook of social network analysis* (pp. 236–255). Thousand Oaks, CA: Sage Publications.

Carrington, P. J., Scott, J., & Wasserman, S. (2005). *Models and methods in social network analysis*. Cambridge: Cambridge University Press.

Castells, M. (2010). Globalisation, networking, urbanisation: Reflections on the spatial dynamics of the information age. *Urban Studies*, *47*(13), 2737–2745.

Chase, I. V. (1980). Social process and hierarchy formation in small groups: A comparative perspective. *American Sociological Review*, *45*(6), 905–924.

Clauset, A., Newman, M. E. J., & Moore, C. (2004). Finding community structure in very large networks. *Physical Review*, *70*(6), 1–6.

Collins, R. (1988). *Theoretical sociology*. New York, NY: Harcourt Brace Jovanovich.

Conway, K. P., & McCord, J. (2002). A longitudinal examination of the relation between co-offending with violent accomplices and violent crime. *Aggressive Behavior*, *28*(2), 97–108.

Crossley, N., Edwards, G., Harries, E., & Stevenson, R. (2012). Covert social movements and the secrecy-efficiency trade off: The case of the UK suffragettes (1906–1914). *Social Networks*, *34*, 634–644.

Decker, S. H. (1996). Collective and normative features of gang violence. *Justice Quarterly*, *13*(2), 243–264.

Decker, S. H., & Curry, D. G. (2002). Gangs, gang homicides, and gang loyalty: Organized crimes or disorganized criminals. *Journal of Criminal Justice*, *30*, 343–352.

Descormiers, K., & Morselli, C. (2011). Alliances, conflicts, and contradictions in Montreal's street gang landscape. *International Criminal Justice Review*, *21*(3), 297–314.

Duxbury, S. W., & Haynie, D. L. (2018). The network structure of opioid distribution on a darknet cryptomarket. *Journal of Quantitative Criminology*, *34*, 921–941.

Eagle, N., Pentland, A. S., & Lazer, D. (2009). Inferring friendship network structure by using mobile phone data. *Proceedings of the National Academy of Sciences*, *106*(36), 15274–15278.

Everett, M. G., & Borgatti, S. P. (1998) Analyzing clique overlap. *Connections*, *21*(1), 49–61.

Faust, K., & Tita, G. E. (2019). Social networks and crime: Pitfalls and promises for advancing the field. *Annual Review of Criminology*, *2*, 99–122.

Fitzhugh, S. M., & Butts, C. T. (2018). Patterns of co-membership: Techniques for identifying subgraph composition. *Social Networks*, *55*, 1–10.

Fortunato, S., & Barthélemy, M. (2007). Resolution limit in community detection. *Proceedings of the National Academy of Sciences*, *104*(1), 36–41.

Gallupe, O. (2016). Network analysis. In B. M. Huebner & T. S. Bynum (Eds.), *The handbook of measurement issues in criminology and criminal justice* (pp. 555–575). Oxford: John Wiley.

Gallupe, O., Gravel, J. (2018). Social network position of gang members in schools: Implications for recruitment and gang prevention. *Justice Quarterly*, *35*(3), 505–525.

Girvan, M., & Newman, M. E. J. (2002). Community structure in social and biological networks. *Proceedings of the National Academy of Sciences*, *99*(12), 7821–7826.

Good, B. H., de Montjoye, Y.-A., & Clauset, A. (2010). Performance of modularity maximization in practical contexts. *Physical Review E*, *81*, 046106.

Gould, R. V. (2003). *Collison of wills: How ambiguity about social rank breeds conflict.* Chicago, IL: University of Chicago Press.

Gravel, J., & Tita, G. E. (2017). Network perspectives on crime. In S. Messner & H. Pontel (Eds.), *Oxford Research Encyclopedia of Criminology*, (pp. 1–42). Oxford: Oxford University Press.

Harris, K. M., Halpern, C. T., Whitsel, E., Hussey, J., Tabor, J., Entzel, P., & Udry, J. R. (2009). *The national longitudinal study of adolescent to adult health: Research design.* Retrieved from http://www.cpc.unc.edu/projects/addhealth/design. Accessed on January 30, 2019.

Hashimi, S., & Bouchard, M. (2017). On to the next one? Using social network data to inform police target prioritization. *Policing: An International Journal of Police Strategies & Management*, *40*(4), 768–782.

Hashimi, S., Bouchard, M., Morselli, C., & Ouellet, M. (2017). A method to detect criminal organizations from police data. *Methodological Innovations*, *9*, 1–14.

Haynie, D. L. (2001). Delinquent peers revisited: Does network structure matter? *American Journal of Sociology*, *106*(4), 1013–1057.

Haynie, D. L., & Kreager, D. A. (2013). Peer networks and crime. In F. T. Cullen & P. Wilcox (Eds.), *The Oxford handbook of criminological theory* (pp. 257–273). New York, NY: Oxford University Press.

Heckathorn, D. D. (1997). Respondent-driven sampling: A new approach to the study of hidden populations. *Social Problems*, *44*(2), 174–199.

Heckathorn, D. D., & Cameron, C. J. (2017). Network sampling: From snowball and multiplicity to respondent-driven sampling. *Annual Review of Sociology*, *43*, 101–119.

Hughes, L. A. (2013). Group cohesiveness, gang membership prestige, and delinquency and violence in Chicago, 1959–1962. *Criminology*, *51*, 795–832.

Jansyn, L. R. (1966). Solidarity and delinquency in a street corner group. *American Sociological Review*, *31*(5), 600–614.

Klein, M. W. (1969). Gang cohesiveness, delinquency, and a street-work program. *Journal of Research in Crime and Delinquency*, *6*(2), 135–166.

Klein, M. W. (1971). *Street gangs and street workers.* Englewood Cliffs, NJ: Prentice-Hall.

Klein, M. W., & Crawford, L. Y. (1967). Groups, gangs, and cohesiveness. *Journal of Research in Crime and Delinquency*, *4*(1), 63–75.

Kreager, D. A., Rulison, K., & Moody, J. (2011). Delinquency and the structure of adolescent peer groups. *Criminology*, *49*(1), 95–127.

Lane, J. (2019). *The digital street: Adolescence, technology, and community in the inner city.* New York, NY: Oxford University Press.

Lantz, B., & Hutchison, R. (2015). Co-offender ties and the criminal career: The relationship between co-offender group structure and the individual offender. *Journal of Research in Crime and Delinquency*, *52*(5), 658–690.

Malm, A., & Bichler, G. (2011). Networks of collaborating criminals: Assessing the structural vulnerability of drug markets. *Journal of Research in Crime and Delinquency*, *48*(2), 271–297.

Malm, A., Bichler, G., & Nash, R. (2011). Co-offending between criminal enterprise groups. *Global Crime*, *12*, 112–128.

Matsueda, R. L. (2017). Toward an analytical criminology: The micro–macro problem, causal mechanisms, and public policy. *Criminology*, *55*(3), 493–519.

McGloin, J. M. (2005). Policy and intervention considerations of a network analysis of street gangs. *Criminology & Public Policy*, *4*(3), 607–636.

McGloin, J. M., & Kirk, D. S. (2010a). An overview of social network analysis. *Journal of Criminal Justice Education, 21*(2), 169–181.

McGloin, J. M., & Kirk, D. S. (2010b). Social network analysis. In A. Piquero & D. Weisburd (Eds.), *Handbook of quantitative criminology* (pp. 209–224). New York, NY: Springer.

McGloin, J. M., & Piquero, A. (2010). On the relationship between co-offending network redundancy and offending versatility. *Journal of Research in Crime and Delinquency, 47*(1), 63–90.

Miller, E. (2012). Patterns of onset and decline among terrorist organizations. *Journal of Quantitative Criminology, 28*(1), 77–101.

Miller, J. (2001). *One of the guys: Girls, gangs, and gender*. New York, NY: Oxford University Press.

Miller, W. B. (1957). The impact of a community group work program on delinquent corner groups. *Social Service Review, 31*(4), 309–406.

Miller, W. B. (1958). Lower class culture as a generating milieu of gang delinquency. *Journal of Social Issues, 23*, 5–19.

Miller, W. B. (1962). The impact of a "total-community" delinquency control project. *Social Problems, 10*, 168–191.

Morselli, C. (2009). *Inside criminal networks.* New York, NY: Springer.

Morselli, C., Giguère, C., & Petit, K. (2007). The efficiency/security trade-off in criminal networks. *Social Networks, 29*(1), 143–153.

Morselli, C., Tanguay, D., & Labalette, A.-M. (2008). Criminal conflicts and collective violence: Biker-related account settlements in Quebec, 1994–2001. In D. Siegel & H. Nelen (Eds.), *Organized crime: Culture, markets and policies* (pp. 145–164). New York, NY: Springer.

Morselli, C., & Tremblay, P. (2004). Criminal achievement, offender networks, and the benefits of low self-control. *Criminology, 42*(3), 773–804.

Morselli, C., Tremblay, P., & McCarthy, B. (2006). Mentors and criminal achievement. *Criminology, 44*(1), 17–43.

Mucha, P. J., Richardson, T., Macon, K., Porter, M. A., & Onnela, J.-P. (2010). Community structure in time-dependent, multiscale, and multiplex networks. *Science, 328*, 876–878.

Newman, M. E. J. (2006). Modularity and community structure in networks. *Proceedings of the National Academy of Sciences, 103*(23), 8577–8582.

Newman, M. E. J. (2018). *Networks* (2nd ed.). Oxford: Oxford University Press.

Newman, M. E. J., & Girvan, M. (2004). Finding and evaluating community structure in networks. *Physical Review E, 69*, 026113.

Ouellet, M., & Bouchard, M. (2018). The 40 members of the Toronto 18: Group boundaries and the analysis of illicit networks. *Deviant Behavior, 39*(11), 1467–1482.

Ouellet, M., Bouchard, M., & Charette, Y. (2019). One gang dies, another gains? The network dynamics of criminal group persistence. *Criminology,* Online First. https://doi.org/10.1111/1745-9125.12194

Palla, G., Barabási, A., & Vicsek, T. (2007). Quantifying social group evolution. *Nature, 446*, 664–667.

Palla, G., Derényi, I., Farkas, I., & Vicsek, T. (2005). Uncovering the overlapping community structure of complex networks in nature and society. *Nature, 435*, 814–818.

Papachristos, A. V. (2006). Social network analysis and gang research: Theory and methods. In J. F. Short & L. A. Hughes (Eds.), *Studying youth gangs* (pp. 99–116). Lanham, MD: Altamira.

Papachristos, A. V. (2009). Murder by structure: Dominance relations and the social structure of gang homicide. *American Journal of Sociology, 115*(1), 74–128.

Papachristos, A. V. (2011). The coming of a networked criminology. In J. MacDonald (Ed.), *Advances in criminological theory* (pp. 101–140). New Brunswick, NJ: Transaction Publishers.

Papachristos, A. V. (2013). The importance of cohesion for gang research, policy, and practice. *Criminology & Public Policy, 12*(1), 49–58.

Papachristos, A. V., Hureau, D. M., & Braga, A. A. (2013). The corner and the crew: The influence of geography and social networks on gang violence. *American Sociological Review, 78*(3), 417–447.

Paoli, L. (2002). The paradoxes of organized crime. *Crime, Law and Social Change, 37*(1), 51–97.

Patton, D. U., Lane, J., Leonard, P., MacBeth, J. & Smith Lee, J. R. (2017). Gang violence on the digital street: Case study of a South Side Chicago gang member's Twitter communication. *New Media & Society, 19*(7), 1000–1018.

Pyrooz, D. C., & Mitchell, M. M. (2015). Little gang research, big gang research. In S. H. Decker & D. C. Pyrooz (Eds.), *The handbook of gangs* (pp. 28–55). West Sussex: John Wiley & Sons.

Radil, S. M., Flint, C., & Tita, G. E. (2010). Spatializing social networks: Using social network analysis to investigate geographies of gang rivalry, territoriality and violence in Los Angeles. *Annals of the Association of American Geographers*, *100*(2), 307–326.

Sanchez-Jankowski, M. (1991). *Islands in the street: Gangs and American urban society.* Los Angeles, CA: University of California Press.

Sarnecki, J. (2001). *Delinquent networks: Youth co-offending in Stockholm.* Cambridge: Cambridge University Press.

Schaefer, D. R., Bouchard, M., Young, J. T. N., & Kreager, D. A. (2017). Friends in locked places: An investigation of prison inmate network structure. *Social Networks*, *51*, 88–103.

Schmidt, L. A. (2012). Social networking and the fourth amendment: Location tracking on Facebook, Twitter, and Foursquare. *Cornell Journal of Law and Public Policy*, *22*(2), 515–536.

Shi, Y., Fedor, A. D., Genkin, M., & Brashears, M. E. (2017). A member saved is a member earned? The recruitment-retention trade-off and organizational strategies for membership growth. *American Sociological Review*, *82*(2), 407–434.

Shirkhorshidi, A. S., Aghabozorgi, S., & Wah, T. Y. (2015). A comparison study on similarity and dissimilarity measures in clustering continuous data. *PLoS One.* Retrieved from https://journals.plos.org/plosone/article?id=10.1371/journal.pone.0144059. Accessed on January 30, 2019.

Short, J. F. (1974). Youth, gangs and society: Micro- and macrosociological processes. *The Sociological Quarterly*, *15*(1), 3–19.

Short J. F. (1998). The level of explanation problem revisited. *Criminology*, *36*, 3–36.

Short, J. F., & Strodtbeck, F. L. (1965). *Group process and gang delinquency.* Chicago, IL: University of Chicago Press.

Sierra-Arévalo, M., & Papachristos, A. V. (2015). Social network analysis and gangs. In S. H. Decker & D. C. Pyrooz (Eds.), *The handbook of gangs* (pp. 157–177). West Sussex: John Wiley & Sons.

Simmel, G. (1955). *The web of group*-affiliation. New York, NY: Free Press.

Snijders, T. A. (2011). *Statistical models for social networks. Annual Review of Sociology*, *37*, 131–153.

Stevenson, R., & Crossley, N. (2014). Change in covert social movement networks: The 'inner circle' of the Provisional Irish Republican Army. *Social Movement Studies*, *13*(1), 70–91.

Sugie, N. F. (2018). Utilizing smartphones to study disadvantaged and hard-to-reach groups. *Sociological Methods & Research*, *47*(3), 458–491.

Suttles, G. D. (1968). *The social order of the slum: Ethnicity and territory in the inner city.* Chicago, IL: University of Chicago Press.

Thornberry, T., Krohn, M., Lizotte, A., & Chard-Wierschem, D. (1993). The role of juvenile gangs in facilitating delinquent behavior. *Journal of Research in Crime and Delinquency*, *30*(1), 55–87.

Thrasher, F. M. (1927). *The gang: A study of 1,313 gangs in Chicago.* Chicago, IL: University of Chicago Press.

Tita, G. E., & Radil, S. M. (2011). Spatializing the social networks of gangs to explore patterns of violence. *Journal of Quantitative Criminology*, *27*(4), 521–545.

Tremblay, P., Laisne, S., Cordeau, G., Shewshuck, A., & MacLean, B. (1989). Carrières criminelles collectives: évolution d'une population délinquante. *Criminologie*, *22*(2), 65–94.

van Gennip, Y., Hu, H., Hunter, B., & Porter, M. A. (2012). Geosocial graph-based community detection. In *IEEE 12th international conference on data mining workshops*. Retrieved from https://ieeexplore.ieee.org/abstract/document/6406515/authors. Accessed on January 30, 2019.

Vedres, B., & Stark, D. (2010). Structural folds: Generative disruption in overlapping groups. *American Journal of Sociology*, *115*(4), 1150–1190.

Vigil, J. D. (1988). *Barrio gangs: Street life and identity in Southern California*. Austin, TX: University of Texas Press.

PART II

SPECIAL GROUPS AND PROBLEMS

CHAPTER 4

INNOVATIVE METHODS OF GATHERING SURVEY DATA ON VIOLENCE AGAINST WOMEN

Walter S. DeKeseredy

ABSTRACT

Purpose – *This chapter presents some innovative ways in which researchers can collect survey data on various types of violence against women.*

Methodology/approach – *The suggestions made here are drawn from over 30 years of national, international, and local survey research.*

Findings – *The methods described in this chapter minimize underreporting, produce theoretically relevant data, and have meaningful policy consequences.*

Originality/value – *The research techniques reviewed here have made many important contributions to the field and the data they uncovered have helped raise public awareness about one of the world's most compelling social problems.*

Keywords: Violence against women; surveys; research methods; feminism; gender; questionnaires

INTRODUCTION

Over 30 years of rigorous survey research conclusively shows that women around the world are abused by men in "numbers that would numb the mind of Einstein" (Lewis cited in Vallee, 2007, p. 22). Furthermore, the rates of

Methods of Criminology and Criminal Justice Research
Sociology of Crime, Law and Deviance, Volume 24, 69–84

ISSN: 1521-6136/doi:10.1108/S1521-613620190000024008

various types of violence against women in Canada and the United States have not dropped over the past 20 years despite progressive legislative reforms, the ongoing efforts of feminist coalitions' lobbying and education initiatives, and other major steps to enhance women's health and safety (DeKeseredy, Hall-Sanchez, & Nolan, 2018; Senn et al., 2014). These two claims are buttressed by small- and large-scale surveys that used the methods suggested in this chapter. The techniques recommended here are not exhaustive, but are superior to those used in mainstream crime victimization and self-report surveys (e.g., the National Crime Victimization Survey) that are not specifically designed to capture rich quantitative and qualitative data on male-to-female physical and sexual assaults, sexual harassment, stalking, image-based sexual abuse, and other gendered harms that exist on what Kelly (1987, 1988) refers to as the "continuum of sexual violence." Perfect male-to-female violence surveys are not possible, but good ones can and should be done. The methods reviewed in this chapter are important steps toward achieving this goal.

BROAD OPERATIONAL DEFINITIONS

Defining violence against women is much more than "a matter of semantics." Major debates over definition are not trivial; they seriously affect how data are gathered and the quality and quantity of social support services for women who are beaten, sexually assaulted, and abused in other ways by current or former male partners or acquaintances (DeKeseredy, 2011). Further, definitions are used politically as tools in social struggles. Together with poverty, unemployment, terrorism, and other social problems, violence against women is a highly politicized topic of social scientific inquiry, and definitions of this harm reflect this reality (DeKeseredy & Schwartz, 2011; Ellis, 1987).

Some feminist scholars contend that only physical behaviors, such as beatings and forced vaginal penetration, that meet criminal code standards should be accurately measured because this is the way to "mainstream" gender into the measurement of violence against women (Walby et al., 2017). However, as Myhill (2017) puts it, while accurate measurement of behaviors that only involve physical contact is commendable, "such an approach will paradoxically obscure the gendered nature of abuse in other respects" (p. 38). Before addressing this point, it is first essential to focus on some additional problems by using narrow legalistic definitions.

Consider Tjaden and Thoeness' (2000) US National Violence Against Women Survey (NVAWS). It was introduced to respondents as a crime and personal safety survey, one that excluded a broad range of hurtful behaviors exempt from the purview of criminal law (DeKeseredy & Schwartz, 2011). Not surprisingly, then, the NVAWS uncovered a very low incidence rate (1.8% in the previous 12 months) of women victimized by one or more of these acts committed by an intimate partner: rape, physical assault, rape and/or physical assault, and stalking. The problem is that unless women clearly label hurtful behaviors as "criminal" in their minds they tend not to report them in a crime survey. If a researcher tells someone that they are studying criminal behavior and then asks a question about whether you were ever hit or attacked the typical person will only answer "yes" if they have in mind a hit or attack that they think was criminal. If you have defined being hit by a spouse as normal non-criminal behavior, you will no doubt tell the interviewer that you have never been attacked or you will only tell her about clearly criminal attacks, such as being assaulted by a stranger (DeKeseredy & Schwartz, 2013).

The problem is that in dealing with attacks by intimates, including forcible rape by intimate partners or dates or friends, many women who experience what the law clearly defines as assault or forcible rape do not label their assaults as criminal or sometimes even as a form of victimization. For instance, Pitts and Schwartz (1993) asked a number of women if they had ever been forced into sexual intercourse, described in a way that clearly fit the state of Ohio's definition of forcible rape. As part of an interview about their experiences, they were later asked if they ever had been raped. Although women who had just reported forced sex were asked that question, a strong majority denied that they had ever been raped. These women knew that something terrible had happened and were discussing a number of reactions to it, but they had not applied the word *rape* to their experiences. Often, this is because they believe the word *rape* only applies to violent attacks.

By comparison, when surveys are not operated in the context of criminal assault and victimization, there are major reporting differences (DeKeseredy & Schwartz, 2013). Mihalic and Elliott (1997), for example, found that up to 83% of the marital violence incidents reported in surveys of family behavior are not reported in contexts when the presentation emphasis is on criminal assault and victimization.

Most large-scale representative sample surveys that are not contextualized as crime often use modified versions of popular measures such as the Revised Conflict Tactics Scale (CTS2) developed by Straus, Hamby, Boney-McCoy, and Sugarman (1996) or Koss et al.'s (2007) Revised Sexual Experiences Survey (RSES). These studies generally show at least 11% of North American women in marital/cohabiting relationships are physically abused by their male partners in any 12-month period, and at least 25% of North American female undergraduates experience some variety of sexual assault during the same time frame (DeKeseredy, Hall-Sanchez, et al., 2018).

In other words, if we restrict our operational definitions of intimate male-to-female violence to the limited realm of the criminal law and acts that people perceive to be covered there, then we will uncover relatively less intimate violence against women. If we use broader definitions of conflict and violence, the amount of violence uncovered is much higher, and the highest rates are uncovered by surveys that broaden definitions to include injurious non-physical acts. This brings me back to Myhill's (2017) point about narrow definitions obscuring the gendered nature of abuse in other respects. Though all forms of physical abuse and touching are commonly considered more serious than non-physical forms of victimization, this obscures the reality that many women view behaviors such as stalking, cyberstalking, sexual harassment, and some social media attacks as more terrifying than some acts that the law defines as assaults (DeKeseredy, Schwartz, Nolan, Mastron, & Hall-Sanchez, 2018; Ptacek, 2016). Non-physical forms of abuse, especially sexual harassment, are much more common in many women's lives than are physically violent acts committed by male partners (Kelly, 2012), with studies showing that catcalls, harassment, and unwanted sexual attention can have important long-term psychological effects even before girls become teenagers (Castillo, 2018). These behaviors also influence many women to avoid going to public places.

As sexual assaults on college campuses and in other contexts are rampant, it is not surprising that the above and other variants of non-physical sexual assault are highly traumatic (DeKeseredy & Rennison, 2019). What Kelly and Radford (1987) stated decades ago is still relevant:

> [A]t the time women are being followed/flashed at/harassed they do not know how the event will end. It is only in retrospect that such events can be defined as "minor." (p. 242)

In sum, broad definitions enable researchers to document a wide array of painful, interrelated behaviors that thousands of women experience daily, many of which are exempt from the purview of the criminal justice system and that are trivialized or minimized by the law, general public, and the mainstream media. Researchers may analyze sexual harassment, sexual contact, beatings, forced intercourse, and other harms separately, but, for countless numbers of women, these forms of abuse "seep into one another" (Ptacek, 2016, p. 128). Broad definitions also help minimize underreporting, an issue covered in the next section.

MINIMIZING UNDERREPORTING

There are many attempts to answer the question "how much male violence against women takes place behind closed doors and elsewhere?" But there is no consensus about the extent of the problem. Yet, all survey researchers in the field are likely to agree with this point: there is no reason to believe that overreporting is a problem in this area and many reasons to believe that underreporting is a problem. Despite all of the social scientific and methodological advances made over the past 30 years, "obtaining accurate estimates of the extent of woman abuse in the population at large remains the biggest methodological challenge in survey research on this topic" (Smith, 1987, p. 18).

Abused women and male offenders might not disclose incidents for many reasons. Some people are completely embarrassed to find themselves in such a situation and do not want to let others know about it. Another common reason is fear of reprisal. Many women report that they were told that if they ever told anyone or called the police, that they would be much more severely hurt or killed. Methodologists, too, often worry about forward and backward telescoping. Here a person who has been beaten often might be unable to accurately place each event in a specific time period, such as when asked how often something happened in the past six months. Anyone who has ever felt that a series of events all ran together in their mind would understand this problem. There is also simply memory error: people who work hard to put unpleasantness out of their mind could in fact just plainly forget. Finally, of course, there is purposeful deception (Meloy & Miller, 2011).

As stated previously, an important cause of underreporting is framing a study as a crime survey. There are many other possible reasons for non-reporting, including a reluctance or inability to subject oneself to the unpleasantry of recalling traumatic behaviors or events. Also, some victims and offenders believe that violent or psychological assaults are too trivial or inconsequential to mention (Pritchard, DeKeseredy, Nolan, & Hall-Sanchez, 2018).

Some women might not yet have given up on their relationship and might be holding out hope that the violence can be stopped and it can be saved. However, they may feel that if they report the violence that might be a step that will signal the end of the relationship. As well, many batterers are involved in a complex process of attempting to remain in control of relationships (DeKeseredy, Dragiewicz, & Schwartz, 2017). They may not be ashamed of the violence because of the pain it caused, but they might be ashamed of the violence because it represents a last-ditch action needed to compensate their inability to maintain control through the use of masculine authority (DeKeseredy & Schwartz, 1998).

New technologies have their plusses and minuses. It is now easier than ever before for researchers who collect violence data to interview a random sample of people who own landline telephones. Still, that is also a problem. More and more people, and especially younger ones, only have cell phones and cannot be interviewed on land lines. Others without access to landlines might be low-income people, homeless people (including women driven from their homes because of violence), and women who are in mental health institutions or prisons (both of whom have high rates of violence victimization) (DeKeseredy & Schwartz, 2013). There are other problems that contribute to underreporting (e.g., language barriers) and all of them are difficult to overcome and are not likely to be eliminated in the near future. However, there have been some significant attempts to minimize underreporting, one of which is the use of supplementary open-ended questions.

Supplementary Open-ended Questions

We have witnessed great advances in victimization survey research over the past 30 years, due in large part to the efforts of feminist scholars. Further, many feminists today recognize that their empirical concerns can be effectively addressed by adhering to the "cannons of established social science" (Smith, 1994, p. 123). Feminist researchers also alert us to the importance of relying on closed-ended questions because they do not give respondents additional opportunities to disclose abusive experiences. At the outset, people may not report incidents for reasons described previously (e.g., memory error and fear of reprisal). Nevertheless, if respondents are probed later on by an interviewer or asked to complete self-report, supplementary open-ended questions, some silent or forgetful participants will reveal having been victimized or been abusive, or reveal other types of important information related to the topics covered in the survey (DeKeseredy, 2017).

Below is an example of such a question, which was used in DeKeseredy and Schwartz's (1998) Canadian national survey of woman abuse in university/college dating. It is a slightly modified version of the one Smith (1987) developed for his Toronto woman abuse survey and a similar rendition was recently included in the Campus Quality of Life Survey (CQLS) that conducted a large residential school located in a South Atlantic part of the United States (DeKeseredy, Burnham, Nicewarner, Nolan, & Hall-Sanchez, in press):

> We really appreciate the time you have taken to complete this survey. And we'd like to assure you that everything you have told us will remain *strictly confidential*.
>
> We realize that the topics covered in this survey are sensitive and that many women are reluctant to talk about their dating experiences. But we're also a bit worried that we haven't asked the right questions.
>
> So now that you have had a chance to think about the topics, have you had (any other) experiences in which you were physically and/or sexually harmed by your dating partners while you attended college or university? Please provide this information in the space below.

DeKeseredy and Schwartz (1998) never got around to analyze the qualitative data produced by this question, but Smith's (1987) supplementary questions were very effective. Some silent or forgetful female survivors ($n = 60$) changed their answers when asked again in different words by a telephone interviewer. Belated responses increased the overall violence prevalence rate by approximately 10% and 21 belated disclosures increased the severe violence prevalence rate. Smith defined prevalence as the percentage of women who reported ever having been physically abused.

The CQLS research team is in the process of analyzing the responses to its question and members are not finished scrutinizing the qualitative violence against women data, but DeKeseredy, Burnham, et al. (in press) discovered qualitative CQLS data indicating that there may be many angry White male students who are experiencing what Kimmel (2017) coins as *aggrieved entitlement*, which is a correlate of violence against women (DeKeseredy, Fabricius, & Hall-Sanchez, 2015):

> It is that sense that those benefits to which you believed yourself entitled have been snatched away from you by unseen forces larger and more powerful. You feel yourself to be heir to a great promise, the American Dream, which has turned into an impossible fantasy for the very people who were *supposed* to inherit it (p. 18, emphasis in original).

The "American Dream" Kimmel refers to is one where White men are superior to, and receive more privileges than, women and ethnic minorities. Their rage is expressed in many contexts and the CQLS is one venue. Before presenting some of the narratives elicited by its supplementary open-ended question, it should be noted that 13% of the 5,718 respondents answered it. The research team did not anticipate many comments reflecting aggrieved entitlement, but this was not the case. In fact, 44 participants provided statements indicative of this problem and the rich qualitative data added much texture and context to some of the following statistical findings. About 40% of the sample reported that they believed women on the campus experience discrimination and of the students who answered a question asking if they agreed with the statement "The institution tolerates a culture of sexual misconduct," 75% either agreed or strongly agreed. Their perception is well-founded because 34% of the female respondents reported experiencing at least one of five types of sexual assault (DeKeseredy, Hall-Sanchez, et al., 2018).

One of the main strategies angry white men repeatedly use to deal with "their problems" is that they are the "real victims" and that rates of male to female sexual assault on college campuses and elsewhere are greatly exaggerated (DeKeseredy, Dragiewicz, et al., 2017). This is one of the main themes found in CQLS qualitative data. A white, heterosexual, male undergraduate vividly highlights a variation of this theme:

> This survey will undoubtedly be used to show that white men are bad and don't have any of the bad experiences that "people of color" or refrigerator gendered people face .... Furthermore, the school police should not handle sexual assault cases. This is to be handled by actual law enforcement not connected to the school. That way there isn't any bias. If one did occur and the perpetrator is found guilty, the school should take whatever action it deems necessary. But we live in a country of innocent until proven guilty. The university should at least act like it. But, because I have checked "white" and "male" in your survey, none of this matters to you.

A similar student adds:

> I would be greatly happy if this school would stop perpetuating "the rape culture" meme. There is no rape culture, and faulty statistics are used when talking about sexual assault. It is nowhere the epidemic academia has made it out to be. Rape is bad, yes, and should be punished to the fullest extent of the law. This enthusiastic consent BS is a load of crap, though. Most of our language is not verbal anyway. It is very obvious if someone does not want to have sex. I think that the social justice warriors have gotten the better of us.

To the best of my knowledge, thanks to the inclusion of a supplementary open-ended question, the CQLS is the first study to uncover rich qualitative data on aggrieved entitlement on the college campus. On top of eliciting data on important issues not measured by closed-ended items and giving respondents more opportunities to disclose events, questions like the above build researcher–respondent rapport (Pritchard et al., 2018), which is central goal of feminist scholarship. In the words of Smith (1994):

> For one thing, an open format may reduce the threat of a question on violence because it allows the respondent to qualify her response, to express exact shades of meaning, rather than forcing her to choose from a number of possibly threatening alternatives. For another, open questions may reduce the power imbalance inherent in the interviewer situation (the relationship between researcher and researched parallels the hierarchical nature of traditional male–female relationships) because open questions encourage interaction and collaboration between interviewer and respondent .... The less threatening the question and the more equal the power relationship, the greater the probability of rapport, and in turn, of eliciting an honest answer to a sensitive question on violence. (p. 115)

While supplementary open-ended questions and other qualitative techniques used in surveys are effective, these approaches are typically omitted from journal articles and book chapters that offer in-depth reviews of methods used to glean woman abuse data (e.g., Jaquier, Johnson, & Fisher, 2011; Wood, Sulley,

Kammer-Kerwick, Follingstad, & Busch-Armendariz, 2017). It seems, at least in North America, that Smith's (1987, 1994) path-breaking efforts to improve the quality of survey research are used by less than a handful of woman abuse scholars who use quantitative methods. Even so, it should be noted that the US National Crime Victimization survey (NCVS) includes "incident narratives," which are open-ended responses to a final question at the end of the survey that asks participants to report what happened to them. Albeit qualitative in nature, the narratives are not the actual victims' verbatim accounts, but rather statements transcribed by NCVS interviewers (Jaquier et al., 2011). Moreover, the narratives lack rich contextual detail about events leading up to an assault or after an attack, and it is hard to determine from reading them why incidents were not reported to the police (Weiss, 2011).

Multiple Measures of Victimization

To enhance the reliability and validity of social variables, several methodologists promote the use of multiple measures (e.g., Bohrnstedt, 2010). Until recently, most violence against women surveys only used modified versions of either the CTS2 or RSES to measure various types of violence. These are reliable and valid measures, and they are widely employed around the world. Even so, they ignore many injurious acts like stalking. So, many violence against women researchers, especially those who conduct campus surveys, now recognize that it is essential to use these questions, as well as separate measures of intimate partner physical violence, sexual assault, and sexual harassment (Wood et al., 2017). Some campus surveys also include measures of hate crime and bias incidents because many women are assaulted by men because of their real or perceived race/ethnicity, national origin, religion, sex, sexual orientation, physical or mental disability, or political orientation (DeKeseredy, 2009; DeKeseredy, Nolan, & Hall-Sanchez, 2019).

Though physical and sexual violence against female college students is extensively studied, campus surveys that include measures of stalking, especially *technology-facilitated stalking*, are in short supply (DeKeseredy, Hall-Sanchez, Nolan, & Schwartz, 2017; Wood et al., 2017). This is problematic because while non-electronic forms of stalking (e.g., following a person) still exist and are extensive at institutions of higher learning, it is now possible to stalk a person through newer technology. This could include an unwanted presence on social media up through easily available spy craft techniques, such as hidden microphones or camera, or hidden GPS devices to facilitate learning the person's location (DeKeseredy, Dragiewicz, et al., 2017; Harris, 2018).

Similarly, sparse are studies of the dissemination of unwanted sexual messages and images among college students (Woodlock, 2017). However, it is estimated that there are more than 3,000 Web sites devoted just to the narrower topic of "revenge pornography" or sexual images posted by men without the permission of the women portrayed (Lamphere & Pikciunas, 2016). The best study, one of the general population rather than of college students, is Powell and Henry's (2016) national Australian survey. Nearly 3,000 people aged 18–54 participated and 1 in 10 respondents reported that someone had posted online or sent to others nude or semi-nude pictures of them without their permission and 9.6% reported that someone threatened to post such images or to send them to others. Note, too, that in a review of the extant empirical literature on the subject, Henry and Powell (2018) found very little qualitative or quantitative information about adults, such as college students, although there is growing body of research about children and younger adolescents (Powell, Henry, & Flynn, 2018). Furthermore, they found almost no reliable data on the nature, scope, or impact of technology-facilitated sexual violence.

A significant void in this arena is quantitative research on what associations might exist between victimization by electronic means of college women and their accounts of off-line sexual assaults and intimate physical violence (DeKeseredy, Schwartz, et al., 2019). The intertwining of such online and offline victimization is an example of *polyvictimization* (DeKeseredy & Rennison, 2019). This concept refers to

> the experiences of multiple victimizations of *different kinds*, such as sexual victimization, witnessing family violence, and exposure to community violence, not just multiple episodes of the same kind of victimization. (Mitchell, Segura, Jones, & Turner, 2018, p. 762; emphasis in original)

A small but expanding body of college-based research shows that many women are targets of technology-facilitated forms of abuse, and these harms are related to female students' intimate partner violence and sexual assault experiences (Marganski & Melander, 2018). For example, 14% of DeKeseredy, Schwartz, et al.'s (2019) sample of 5,718 college students were women who were watched or followed from a distance, or spied on with a listening device, camera, or GPS. About 28% were sent unwanted messages through texts, voice messages, emails, or through social media apps, and 21% received unwanted sexual messages/images, including pornography. Moreover, survivors of technology-facilitated stalking were 2.3 times more likely to report a face-to-face sexual assault than women who were not victimized. As well, female participants who reported receiving unwanted sexual messages/images were 3.4 times more likely to state being sexually assaulted offline than women who did not receive them.

DeKeseredy and his colleagues also found that women who reported being the target of technology-facilitated stalking were 2.6 times more likely to report intimate physical violence than women who did not report stalking. Furthermore, women who reported unwanted sexual messages/images were more than 2 times more likely to report intimate physical violence than respondents who were not sent these things.

Also informed by the concept of polyvictimization and using the same data set, DeKeseredy, Schwartz, et al. (2018) found that female students were victims of repeated or diverse types of abuse, ranging from obscene phone calls to stalking to harassment to penetrative sexual assault. However, studies of polyvictimization of adult women are rare. Although there is an extensive literature on polyvictimization, virtually all of it is concerned with the effect of childhood trauma and victimization on currently distressed children or adolescents (DeKeseredy, Schwartz, et al., 2018).

Arguably, this part of my chapter overemphasizes the use of multiple measures and underemphasizes what Bohrnstedt (2010) coins as "reflective thinking in the measurement process" (p. 398). When selecting items to be included in any type of survey, we should always heed his words:

> Without the techniques, one would probably never know how good or poor items are. But far too often, much too little time goes into writing items .... If a set of items is poorly written, no technique – regardless of its "fanciness" or sophistication – can salvage them once they are employed in the field. (p. 398)

SELF-REPORT SURVEYS ADMINISTERED TO ADULT MEN

There are many violence against women surveys, but the vast majority are victimization surveys and adult male perpetration data are in short supply (DeKeseredy & Rennison, 2013; Wood et al., 2017). What accounts for this? Perhaps Jacquier et al. (2011) offer the best answer:

> It is generally agreed that population surveys, in which random samples of women are interviewed about their experiences of violence using detailed, behaviorally specific questions yield more valid and reliable estimate of the prevalence of these phenomenon in the population ...." (p. 26)

Most self-report crime surveys of any sort measure delinquent activities by high school students and tend to focus on relatively minor offenses like using drugs or alcohol (Mosher, 2013). Of course, some self-report surveys have focused on the abuse of women in university/college dating and other intimate contexts (e.g., DeKeseredy & Schwartz, 1998; Straus & Gelles, 1986), but it is fair to claim that one of the largest gaps in our social scientific knowledge about male-to-female violence remains self-reported adult male abusive behaviors (DeKeseredy, 2017).

Because of social desirability effects and other factors, listening to women's voices and inviting them to complete surveys enables researchers to uncover much higher estimates of any type of woman abuse than those derived from self-report surveys administered to men (DeKeseredy & Rennison, 2013). Still, the research community is at the point where it can confidently state that a substantial number of women experience male violence. Hence, it is now time to use survey technology to yield better answers to some very important questions, such as "Why Does He Do That? (Bancroft, 2002). As Scully (1990) points out, there are problems in completely depending on females to report on male abusers because "they do not share the reality of ... violent men. Such insight is acquired through invading and critically examining ... men" (p. 4).

EXAMINING WITHIN GROUP ETHNIC DIFFERENCES

Almost every US survey of any type of crime or other social problems includes pan-ethnic group categories such as African-American White, Asian, and Hispanic/ Latina. Treating these and other ethnic groups as homogeneous is problematic because in reality they include "diverse subpopulations that have very distinct ethnic, religious, historical, philosophical and social values that may have important roles in the dynamics of violence against women" (Perilla, Lippy, Rosales, & Serrata, 2011, p. 205). Needless to say, not all Black people are the same and there are differences in rates of intimate violence among African-Americans, African-Caribbeans, and Africans (DeKeseredy & Rennison, 2013). As well, there are variations in rates of such violence among different Aboriginal groups (Aldarondo & Castro-Fernandez, 2011; DeKeseredy, Dragiewicz, & Rennison, 2012).

Additionally, the plight of immigrant and refugee women warrants better empirical scrutiny in US surveys. These women are often classified as "White," obscuring issues related to ethnicity and immigration status. Related to this pitfall is that some common types of abuse directed at immigrant and refugee women, such as using immigration status as a method of *coercive control*, are not measured by mainstream surveys and are not included in widely used violence against women measures like Straus et al.'s (1996) CTS2 (DeKeseredy & Rennison, 2013; Perilla et al., 2011). Coercive control involves psychologically and emotionally abusive behaviors that are often subtle and hard to detect and prove, and that seem more forgivable to people unfamiliar with the dynamics of violence against women (DeKeseredy, Dragiewicz, et al., 2017). The primary objective of coercive control is to restrict a woman's liberties, and common examples are stalking, threatening looks, criticism, and "microregulating a partner's behavior" (Kernsmith, 2008; Stark, 2007, p. 229). As Stark (2007) puts it, the "cumulative effect … can be a hostage-like state of physical paralysis, subjugation, and chronic fear that has no counterpart in any other crime in private or public life" (p. 244).

The points made here support Perilla et al.'s (2011) claim about "the importance of exploring within-group differences to gain a more nuanced understanding of how groups differ in their rates of DV" (p. 7). This goal can be achieved by using better measures of ethnicity. However, this is not an easy task because there is no standard, widely accepted procedure for collecting ethnic group data, and the definition of what constitutes an ethnic group is the subject of much social scientific debate (Connelly, Gayla, & Lambert, 2016). The good news, though, is that there are many measures to choose from, all of which have strengths and limitations. One of the most important points to consider is extending response categories well beyond the above narrow ones (e.g., White and Asian) and to include the category "other" with a request to specify so that respondents can provide an ethnic/cultural background that is not included among the closed-ended items.

Certainly, "sometimes it is difficult to accrue a sufficient sample for traditional designs to permit careful analyses of multiple ethnicities, especially to capture the vast differences between pan-ethnic groups" (White, Koss, & Kazdin, 2011, p. 307). Moreover, normal sampling techniques will not generate a sufficient number of ethnic minorities to allow for a complex, multivariate analysis of the patterns of woman abuse (Jones, Maclean, & Young, 1986). To overcome this problem, Jones et al. oversampled Asian and Afro-Caribbean people who lived in the London Borough of Islington. Similarly, researchers in other countries should follow Jones et al.'s (1986) effort to develop an ethnic minority "booster sample." In North American colleges, this goal could be achieved by contacting campus officials for lists of foreign students who have difficulty in speaking either French or English (note that Canada is officially bilingual).

To compensate for language problems, researchers need to translate questionnaires. This procedure is costly, but it can minimize underreporting. For instance, a substantial number of Italian women refused to be interviewed in Smith's (1986) first Toronto woman abuse survey because they claimed that his questions were unintelligible (Northrup, 1985). In response to this problem, Smith (1987) used a translated instrument in his second survey, and this approach resulted in "a somewhat improved" response rate. Unfortunately, he does not state the degree of improvement.

Returning to the issue of coercive control in the lives of immigrant and refugee women, Myhill (2017) correctly points out that, "The question of how to measure coercive control, or … the non-physically violent forms of coercion that represent its core, remains open and empirical" (p. 41). There are, of course, different measures available (see Stark & Hester, 2019), but I agree with Myhill (2017) who favors those that include a combination of the following behaviors: "isolation, intimidation, humiliation, extreme jealousy, surveillance, and financial control" (p. 41). Furthermore, in this current "high tech" era, it is essential to include measures of *technology-facilitated coercive control*, which includes monitoring emails and some of electronic means of abusing women discussed earlier, as well as other tactics identified by Dragiewicz, Woodlock, Harris, and Reid (2019).

Regardless of how we study the relationship between violence against women and ethnicity, avoid stereotyping or constructing perpetrators and survivors who belong to any ethnic minority group as "Others." A large literature shows that "there are few forms of violence that belong exclusively to any particular culture" (Aronson Fontes & McCloskey, 2011, p. 152). Many would agree that the ubiquity of patriarchy is more important in shaping woman abuse than are location and race/ethnic (DeKeseredy et al., 2012).

CONCLUSION

Babbie (1973) reminds us that "no survey fully satisfies the theoretical ideals of scientific inquiry" (p. 3). Even so, given time and budget constraints, researchers should strive to develop violence against women surveys that meet the highest disciplinary standards, overcome the limitations of mainstream crime surveys, and that take the gendered nature of woman abuse seriously. The methods suggested in this chapter help achieve these goals, but many readers can probably think of more. Undoubtedly, too, new imaginative ways of gleaning survey data on violence against women will be needed because this social problem is a "never-ending and constantly evolving issue" (Ledwitz-Rigby, 1993, p. 93). Consider the "dark side" of new technologies. Leading experts on violence against women only started to address this problem in the past few years. As Goodmark (2011) notes, "When the first domestic violence and stalking laws were passed, no one could have foreseen how technology would facilitate abuse, stalking, and harassment" (p. 195). New technological developments to be seen in the near future will facilitate such harms and survey researchers will have to modify their instruments, samples, and other techniques accordingly.

Nevertheless, it is always necessary to keep "looking backward to move forward," which means constantly revisiting past empirical contributions (DeKeseredy, 2016), such as the use of supplementary open-ended questions, multiple measures, and broad operational definitions. Maybe, then, it is best to conclude here by expanding on this point with two highly experienced survey researchers' words of wisdom:

> Amidst all of our speculation on the future – some of which will surely prove misguided – we [should] by no means lose sight of the value of continuity. We imagine that innovations … will serve to expand the range of options for survey researchers rather than to fully supplant those currently practiced …. Future investigators should judiciously balance them together with the new approaches that will inevitably emerge. (Wright & Marsden, 2010, p. 24)

REFERENCES

Aldarondo, E., & Castro-Fernandez, M. (2011). Risk and protective factors for domestic violence perpetration. In J. W. White, M. P. Koss, & A. E. Kazdin (Eds.), *Violence against women and children: Mapping the terrain* (pp. 221–242). Washington, DC: American Psychological Association.

Aronson Fontes, L., & McCloskey, K. (2011). Cultural issues in violence against women. In C. M. Renzetti & J. L. Edleson (Eds.), *Sourcebook on violence against women* (2nd ed., pp. 151–167). Thousand Oaks, CA: Sage.

Babbie, E. (1973). *Survey research methods*. Belmont, CA: Wadsworth.

Bancroft, L. (2002). *Why does he do that? Inside the minds of angry and controlling men*. New York, NY: Berkley.

Bohrnstedt, G. W. (2010). Measurement models for survey research. In P. V. Marsden & J. D. Wright (Eds.), *Handbook of survey research* (2nd ed., pp. 347–404). Bingley: Emerald.

Castillo, M. (2018). Sexual harassment starts at a young age for many girls: The effect can be lifelong. *The Lily*. Retrieved from https://www.thelily.com/sexual-harassment-starts-at-a-young-age-for-many-girls-the-effect-can-be-life-long. Accessed on January 28, 2019.

Connelly, R., Gayle, V., & Lambert, P. S. (2016). Ethnicity and ethnic group measures in social survey research. *Methodological Innovations*, *9*. https://doi.org/10.1177/2059799116642885

DeKeseredy, W. S. (2009). Male violence against women in North America as hate crime. In B. Perry (Ed.), *Hate crimes: The victims of hate* (pp. 151–172). Santa Barbara, CA: Praeger.

DeKeseredy, W. S. (2011). *Violence against women: Myths, facts, controversies*. Toronto, ON: University of Toronto Press.

DeKeseredy, W. S. (2016). Looking backward to move forward: Revisiting some past feminist contributions to the study of violence against women. *Violence and Gender*, *3*(4), 177–180.

DeKeseredy, W. S. (2017). Using crime surveys as tools of critical insight and progressive change. In M. H. Jacobson & S. Walklate (Eds.), *Liquid criminology: Doing imaginative criminological research* (pp. 31–48). London: Routledge.

DeKeseredy, W. S., Burnham, K., Nicewarner, R., Nolan, J., & Hall-Sanchez, A. (in press). Aggrieved entitlement in the ivory tower: Qualitative results from a large-scale campus climate survey. *Journal of Qualitative Criminal Justice and Criminology*.

DeKeseredy, W. S., Dragiewicz, M., & Rennison, C. M. (2012). Racial/ethnic variations in violence against women: Urban, suburban, and rural differences. *International Journal of Rural Criminology*, *1*(2), 184–202.

DeKeseredy, W. S., Dragiewicz, M., & Schwartz, M. D. (2017). *Abusive endings: Separation and divorce violence against women*. Oakland, CA: University of California Press.

DeKeseredy, W. S., Fabricius, A., & Hall-Sanchez, A. (2015). Fueling aggrieved entitlement: The contribution of women against feminism. In W. S. DeKeseredy & L. Leonard (Eds.), *Crimsoc report 4: Gender, victimology & restorative justice* (pp. 3–33). Sherfield Gables: Waterside Press.

DeKeseredy, W. S., Hall-Sanchez, A., & Nolan, J. (2018). College campus sexual assault: The contribution of peers' proabuse informational support and attachments to abusive peers. *Violence Against Women*, *24*(8), 922–935.

DeKeseredy, W. S., Nolan, J., & Hall-Sanchez, A. (2019). Hate crime and bias incidents in the ivory tower: Results from a large-scale campus survey. *American Behavioral Scientist*. DOI: 10.1177/0002764219831733.

DeKeseredy, W. S., & Rennsion, C. M. (2013). New directions in the social scientific study of separation/divorce assault. In K. Richards & J. Tauri (Eds.), *Crime, justice and social democracy: Proceedings of the second international conference* (Vol. 1, pp. 47–57). Brisbane, AU: Crime and Justice Research Center, Queensland University of Technology.

DeKeseredy, W. S., & Rennison, C. M. (2019). Key issues in the rape and sexual assault of adult women. In W. S. DeKeseredy, C. M. Rennison, & A. Hall-Sanchez (Eds.), *The Routledge international handbook of violence studies* (pp. 403–418). London: Routledge.

DeKeseredy, W. S., & Schwartz, M. D. (1998). *Woman abuse on campus: Results from the Canadian national survey*. Thousand Oaks, CA: Sage.

DeKeseredy, W. S., & Schwartz, M. D. (2011). Theoretical and definitional issues in violence against women. In C. M. Renzetti, J. L. Edleson, & R. Kennedy Bergen (Eds.), *Sourcebook on violence against women* (2nd ed., pp. 3–20). Thousand Oaks, CA: Sage.

DeKeseredy, W. S., & Schwartz, M. D. (2013). *Male peer support & violence against women: The history & verification of a theory*. Boston, MA: Northeastern University Press.

DeKeseredy, W. S., Schwartz, M. D., Nolan, J., Mastron, & Hall-Sanchez, A. (2018). Polyvictimziation and the continuum of sexual abuse at a college campus: Does negative peer support increase the likelihood of multiple victimizations? *The British Journal of Criminology*. https://doi.org/10.1093/bjc/azy036.

DeKeseredy, W. S., Schwartz, M. D., Harris, B., Woodlock, D., Nolan, J., & Hall-Sanchez, A. (2019). Technology-facilitated stalking and unwanted sexual messages/images in a college campus community: The role of negative peer support. *Sexualization, Media, & Society*. DOI: 10.1177/215824401982831.

Dragiewicz, M., Woodlock, D., Harris, B., & Reid, C. (2019). Technology-facilitated coercive control. In W. S. DeKeseredy, C. M. Rennison, & A. K. Hall-Sanchez (Eds.), *The Routledge international handbook of violence studies* (pp. 244–253). London: Routledge.

Ellis, D. (1987). *The wrong stuff: An introduction to the sociological study of deviance*. Toronto, Canada: Collier Macmillan.

Goodmark, L. (2011). State, national, and international legal initiatives to address violence against women: A survey. In C. M. Renzetti, J. L. Edleson, & R. Kennedy Bergen (Eds.), *Sourcebook on violence against women* (2nd ed., pp. 191–206). Thousand Oaks, CA: Sage.

Harris, B. (2018). Spacelessness, spatiality and intimate partner violence: Technology-facilitated abuse, stalking and justice. In K. Fitz-Gibbon, S. Walklate, J. McCulloch, & J. Maher (Eds.), *Intimate partner violence, risk and security: Securing women's lives in a global world* (pp. 52–70). London: Routledge.

Henry, N., & Powell, A. (2018). Technology-facilitated sexual violence: A literature review of empirical research. *Trauma, Violence, & Abuse*, *19*(2), 195–208.

Jaquier, V., Johnson, H., & Fisher, B. S. (2011). Research methods, measures, and ethics. In C. M. Renzetti, J. L. Edleson, & R. Kennedy Bergen (Eds.), *Sourcebook on violence against women* (2nd ed., pp. 23–45). Thousand Oaks, CA: Sage.

Jones, T., MacLean, B. D., & Young, J. (1986). *The Islington crime survey*. Aldershot: Gower.

Kelly, L. (1987). The continuum of sexual violence. In J. Hanmer & M. Maynard (Eds.), *Women, violence and social control* (pp. 46–60). Atlantic Highlands, NJ: Humanities Press International.

Kelly, L. (1988). *Surviving sexual violence*. Minneapolis, MN: University of Minnesota Press.

Kelly, L. (2012). Standing the test of time? Reflections on the concept of the continuum of violence. In J. M. Brown & S. L. Walklate (Eds.), *Handbook on sexual violence* (pp. xvii–xxvi). London: Routledge.

Kelly, L., & Radford, J. (1987). The problem of men: Feminist perspectives on sexual violence. In P. Scraton (Ed.), *Law, order and the authoritarian state: Readings in critical criminology* (pp. 237–253). Philadelphia, PA: Open University Press.

Kernsmith, P. (2008). Coercive control. In C. M. Renzetti & J. L. Edleson (Eds.), *Encyclopedia of interpersonal violence* (pp. 133–134). Thousand Oaks, CA: Sage.

Kimmel, M. (2107). *Angry white men: American masculinity at the end of an era*. New York, NY: Nation Books.

Koss, M. P. Abbey, A., Campbell, R., Cook, S., Norris, J., Testa, M., … White, J. (2007). Revising the SES: A collaborative process to improve assessment of sexual aggression and victimization. *Psychology of Women Quarterly*, *31*(4), 357–370.

Lamphere, R. D., & Pikciunas, K. T. (2016). Sexting, sextortion, and other Internet sexual offenses. In J. N. Navarro, S. Clevenger, & C. D. Marcum (Eds.), *The intersection between intimate partner abuse, technology, and cybercrime: Examining the virtual enemy* (pp. 141–165). Durham, NC: Carolina Academic Press.

Ledwitz-Rigby, F. (1993). An administrative approach to personal safety on campus: The role of a President's advisory committee on women's safety on campus. *The Journal of Human Justice*, *4*(2), 85–94.

Marganski, A., & Melander, L. (2018). Intimate partner violence victimization in the cyber and real world: Examining the extent of cyber aggression experiences and its association with in-person dating violence. *Journal of Interpersonal Violence*, *33*(7), 1071–1095.

Meloy, M. L., & Miller, S. L. (2011). *The victimization of women: Law, policies, and politics*. New York, NY: Oxford University Press.

Mihalic, S. W., & Elliott, D. (1997). If violence is domestic, does it really count? *Journal of Family Violence*, *12*(3), 293–311.

Mitchell, K. J., Segura, A., Jones, L. M., & Turner, H. A. (2018). Poly-victimization and peer harassment involvement in a technological world. *Journal of Interpersonal Violence*, *33*(5), 762–788.

Mosher, C. (2013). The myth of accurate crime measurement. In R. M. Bohm & J. T. Walker (Eds.), *Demystifying crime & criminal justice* (pp. 3–12). New York, NY: Oxford University Press.

Myhill, A. (2017). Measuring domestic violence: Context is everything. *Journal of Gender-Based Violence*, *1*(1), 33–44.

Northrup, D. (1985). *Woman abuse pilot study: Sample and field report*. Toronto, Canada: Institute for Social Research, York University.

Perilla, J. L., Lippy, C., Rosales, A., & Serrata, J. (2011). Prevalence of domestic violence. In J. W. White, M. P. Koss, & A. E. Kazdin (Eds.), *Violence against women and children: Mapping the terrain* (pp. 199–220). Washington, DC: American Psychological Association.

Pitts, V. L., & Schwartz, M. D. (1993). Promoting self-blame in hidden rape cases. *Humanity & Society*, *17*(4), 383–398.

Powell, A., & Henry, N. (2016). Technology-facilitated sexual violence victimization: Results from an online survey of Australian adults. *Journal of Interpersonal Violence*. doi:10.1177/0886260516672055.

Powell, A., Henry, N., & Flynn, A. (2018). Image-based sexual abuse. In W. S. DeKeseredy & M. Dragiewicz (Eds.), *Routledge handbook of critical criminology* (2nd ed., pp. 305–315). London: Routledge.

Pritchard, A. J., DeKeseredy, W. S., Nolan, J., & Hall-Sanchez, A. (2018). Who speaks first? Analyzing response waves in a large-scale campus climate survey. *Journal of Aggression, Maltreatment & Trauma*. doi:10.1080/10926771.2018.1468374.

Ptacek, J. (2016). Rape and the continuum of sexual abuse in intimate relationships: Interviews with U.S. women from different social classes. In K. Yllo & M. G. Torres (Eds.), *Marital rape: Consent, marriage, and social change in global context* (pp. 123–138). New York, NY: Oxford University Press.

Scully, D. (1990). *Understanding sexual violence: A study of convicted rapists*. Boston, MA: Unwin Hyman.

Senn, C. Y., Eliasziw, M., Barata, P. C., Thurston, W. E., Newby-Clark, I. R., Radtke, H. L., & SARE Study Team. (2014). Sexual violence in the lives of first-year university women in Canada: No improvements in the 21st century. *BMC Women's Health*, *14*, 3–8.

Smith, M. D. (1986). Effects of question format on the reporting of woman abuse: A telephone survey experiment. *Victimology*, *11*(2), 430–438.

Smith, M. D. (1987). The incidence and prevalence of woman abuse in Toronto. *Violence and Victims*, *2*(3), 173–187.

Smith, M. D. (1994). Enhancing the quality of survey data on violence against women: A feminist approach. *Gender & Society*, *18*(1), 109–127.

Stark, E. (2007). *Coercive control: How men entrap women in personal life*. New York, NY: Oxford University Press.

Stark, E., & Hester, M. (2019). Coercive control: Update and review. *Violence Against Women*, *25*(1), 81–104.

Straus, M. A., & Gelles, R. J. (1986). Societal change and change in family violence from 1975 to 1985 as revealed by two national surveys. *Journal of Marriage and the Family*, *48*(3), 465–479.

Straus, M. A., Hamby, S. L., Boney-McCoy, S., & Sugarman, D. B. (1996). The revised conflict tactics scales (CTS2): Development and preliminary psychometric data. *Journal of Family Issues*, *17*(3), 283–316.

Tjaden, P., & Thoennes, N. (2000). *Extent, nature, and consequences of intimate partner violence: Findings from the national violence against women survey*. Washington, D.C.: U.S. Department of Justice.

Vallee, B. (2007). *The war on women*. Toronto, Canada: Key Porter.

Walby, S., Towers, J., Balderston, S., Corradi, C., Francis, B., Heiskanen, M., Helweg, K., … Strid, S. (2017). *The concept and measurement of violence against women and men*. Bristol: Policy Press.

Weiss, K. (2011). Neutralizing sexual victimization: A typology of victims' non-reporting accounts. *Theoretical Criminology*, *15*(4), 445–467.

White, J. W., Koss, M. P., & Kazdin, A. E. (2011). Conclusions and next steps. In J. W. White, M. P. Koss, & A. E. Kazdin (Eds.), *Violence against women and children: Mapping the terrain* (pp. 287–310). Washington, DC: American Psychological Association.

Wood, L., Sulley, C., Kammer-Kerwick, M., Follingstad, D., & Busch-Armendariz, N. (2017). *Climate surveys: An inventory of understanding sexual assault and other crimes of interpersonal violence at institutions of higher education*. *Violence Against Women*, *23*(10), 1249–1267.

Woodlock, D. (2017). The abuse of technology in domestic violence and stalking. *Violence Against Women*, *23*(5), 584–602.

Wright, J. D., & Marsden, P. V. (2010). Survey research and social science: History, current practice, and future prospects. In P. V. Marsden & J. D. Wright (Eds.), *Handbook of survey research* (2nd ed., pp. 3–26). Bingley: Emerald Publishing Limited.

CHAPTER 5

METHODS OF MALE SEX WORK RESEARCH: RECOMMENDATIONS AND FUTURE RESEARCH OPPORTUNITIES

Navin Kumar

ABSTRACT

Purpose – *Exploration of the methodological aspects of male sex work is rather limited. Without a strong methodological toolkit to draw from, research in male sex work will not be able to accurately capture changes in the dynamic sex work environment. Thus, the author provides a comprehensive review of methods in male sex work along with a broad spectrum of methodological insights through which future research can be advanced.*

Methodology/approach – *Drawing from two studies that the author conducted in the male independent escorting space, this chapter provides a range of methodological insights and offers avenues for future research.*

Findings – *This chapter reviews the methods used in male sex work research over the years and details the lack of research on methodological inquiry in the field.*

Originality/value – *With the increasing normalization and dynamism of male sex work, it is necessary for the research to provide methodological guidance for the next wave of studies in the field. The recommendations and research directions proposed herein are hoped to have implications for research in the larger sex work context.*

Keywords: Male sex work; male independent escorting; criminological methods; internet men who have sex with men; online sex work

Methods of Criminology and Criminal Justice Research
Sociology of Crime, Law and Deviance, Volume 24, 85–99

ISSN: 1521-6136/doi:10.1108/S1521-613620190000024009

INTRODUCTION

Recent studies in male sex work have centered on the transitioning of the field from a paradigm of deviance and health risks to the provision of efficient and customer-centric service, at least in high income nations (Bimbi, 2007; Kumar, Minichiello, Scott, & Harrington, 2017; Minichiello, Scott, & Callander, 2013; MacPhail, Scott, & Minichiello, 2014). Given the expanding research agenda, one would expect methodological inquiry in the field to be extensive, providing guidance for further research. However, to the best of my knowledge, exploration of the methodological aspects of male sex work is rather limited. Without a strong methodological toolkit to draw from, research in male sex work will not be able to accurately capture changes in the dynamic sex work environment. Thus, a comprehensive review of methods in male sex work is needed along with a broad spectrum of methodological insights through which future research can be advanced. Drawing from two studies I conducted in the male independent escorting space, this chapter provides a range of methodological insights and offers avenues for future research. The recommendations and research directions proposed herein are hoped to have implications for research in the larger sex work context. Male sex work is defined as an occupation, legal, or otherwise, where a man engages primarily with other men in sexual activities, for which he receives money, other living necessities, or drugs (Browne, Jamieson, Minichiello, & Marino, 1998). Male independent internet-based escorting refers to a more specific form of male sex work, where men operate independently on the internet, without a manager or brothel. The structure of the chapter is as follows. First, methodologies in the male sex work arena will be detailed. I then give a brief overview of my research and provide methodological suggestions and avenues for future studies.

METHODS OF MALE SEX WORK RESEARCH

The purpose of this section is not to chart male sex work research over the years, which has already been done (Bimbi, 2007; MacPhail et al., 2014), nor to provide an extensive review of methods used in male sex work. This section instead will provide a broad overview of topics and methods in male sex work research over the years. Though a critical evaluation of the methodological research, I advance that the understandings of methods in male independent escorting research are limited, thus calling for more extensive scholarship into methodological concerns and consequent recommendations for future research. Likely due to ease of access (Scott et al., 2005), early male sex work scholarship mostly focused on street workers, sometimes with only a few respondents (Harris, 1973), and institutionalized samples (Ginsburg, 1967; Humphreys, 1970; Luckenbill, 1985; Reiss, 1961). Some research gained access to participants through a contact familiar with the community (Allen, 1980; Luckenbill, 1985, 1986) or approached male sex workers in areas they frequented (Gandy & Deisher, 1970). Semi-structured interviews were conducted at settings convenient to participants (Allen, 1980; Coombs, 1974). Some early research was brief about the methods used (Caukins & Coombs, 1976; Craft, 1966; MacNamara, 1965; Reiss, 1961;

Sagarin & MacNamara, 1975), unethical (Humphreys, 1970), or pathologized male sex workers (Gandy & Deisher, 1970).

In more recent times, with the rise of male independent escorting as the main mode of male sex work, at least in high income nations (McLean, 2013), there has been an increase in studies focused on this variant of sex work. Research has focused on a variety of issues, such as sexual compulsivity (Parsons, Bimbi, & Halkitis, 2001), sex education (Parsons, Koken, & Bimbi, 2004), stigma (Koken, Bimbi, Parsons, & Halkitis, 2004; Morrison & Whitehead, 2007), and even the use of social media (Ryan, 2016). Some researchers contacted participants through adverts placed in gay publications, online services (craigslist), online profiles (America Online), escort sites (rentmen.com, boys2rent.com, etc.), chat rooms, and sex worker review sites (Bar-Johnson & Weiss, 2014; Grov, Koken, Smith, & Parsons, 2016; McLean, 2013; Mimiaga, Reisner, Tinsley, Mayer, & Safren, 2009; Morrison & Whitehead, 2007). In several studies, researchers emailed escorts about the project and asked participants to call a university number if interested (Parsons et al., 2004; Parsons, Koken, & Bimbi, 2007; Uy, Parsons, Bimbi, Koken, & Halkitis, 2004). Other researchers utilized venue–day–time sampling (Zhao et al., 2011) or used a banner on an escort site and escort site e-newsletter to advertise for participants (Grov, Rodríguez-Díaz, Jovet-Toledo, & Parsons, 2015; Grov, Starks, et al., 2015), among other methods.

Apart from the more common methods of interviews, surveys, and ethnographic observations (Bar-Johnson & Weiss, 2014; Grov, Rodríguez-Díaz, Ditmore, Restar, & Parsons, 2014; Walby, 2012), several other data collection techniques have been used to explore a range of research questions. In order to understand the drivers of independent escort pricing, hedonic regression has been applied (Logan, 2010, 2016), content analysis to detail the global scope of escorting (Kumar, Minichiello, et al., 2017) and the difference in escort ads based on the gender of clientele the adverts targeted (Pruitt, 2016). Other techniques have also been used, such as, mathematical modeling to understand HIV incidence (Monteiro et al., 2015), deviant case analysis to understand instances of escorts acting counter to the behavior of their colleagues (Oselin, 2016), latent class analysis to delve into client behavior with their most recent male escort (Grov, Starks, et al., 2015), and diaries to chart sexual practices (Minichiello et al., 2000). Scholars have also designed preliminary interventions to mitigate the risks of male sex work (Kumar, Minichiello, et al., 2017; Thomas et al., 2017). Some researchers did not pay participants for their time (Grov et al., 2014; Grov, Rodríguez-Díaz, et al., 2015), while others provided a spectrum of recompense amounts, such as USD12 (Jamel, 2011), USD20 (Bar-Johnson & Weiss, 2014; Oselin, 2016), and USD 75 (Parsons, Bimbi, Koken, & Halkitis, 2005). Apart from male independent escorting, recent research has also explored other variants of male sex work, such as street and agency workers. Researchers have detailed substance use (Yu, Clatts, Goldsamt, & Giang, 2015), HIV/AIDS-relevant concerns (Sosa-Rubí, Salinas-Rodríguez, Montoya-Rodríguez, & Galárraga, 2018; Zhao et al., 2011), mental health (McCabe et al., 2011), social ecology (Ellison & Weitzer, 2016), and diversity of experience (Nureña et al., 2011) in street-based sex worker samples. Regarding recent research on agency-based male sex workers, scholars have explored the social and emotional contexts of agency life (Smith, Grov, & Seal, 2008; Smith, Grov, Seal, Bernhardt, & McCall, 2015) and sexual behavior (Smith & Seal, 2008) among other topics.

However, despite the range of topics that have been explored in male sex work, to the best of my knowledge, there still exist very few papers that review the methodological concerns that arise in the field, proposing areas of future research. Pruitt (2007) detailed whether male independent escorts were more likely to respond to emails from a researcher or a *client*. He indicated that deception was necessary as escorts were not likely to reply to inquiries from social scientists. Pruitt (2007) sent two sets of emails. The first set of emails stated that the sender was a professor researching internet escorts. The second wave of emails was sent from an anonymous account, asking escort rates. The response rate for the *client* emails was far higher than the sociologist variant. Pruitt (2007) then advanced that deception is useful for gaining access to those engaged in deviant behavior and who also have formed communal internet groups. He then further states that the unwillingness of scholars to use deception will mar understandings on societal machinations. It is possible that since Pruitt's (2007) study, which was conducted a decade ago at the time of writing, the difference in response rates between identifying as a sociologist or a client may have narrowed, due to increasing normalization and professionalization of the field (MacPhail et al., 2014). While Pruitt (2007) provided insight on a specific aspect of male sex work research, his research does not explore the multiplicity of methods in male sex work, nor extend paths to future scholarship. Clearly, a more comprehensive review of methods is needed, with recommendations for future research advanced in a range of areas.

Drawing from interviews of 30 male independent escorts in Ottawa, Montreal, and New York, Walby (2010) detailed the methodological concerns arising from men interviewing other men about sex work. Unlike Pruitt (2007), Walby (2010) did not use deception as he did not want escorts to confuse him for a client. Before the interview commenced, multiple participants questioned whether Walby (2010) was gay. When Walby (2010) did not provide the answer participants were expecting, some respondents became upset. By providing a response in the affirmative, a sexualized rapport may occur. Walby (2010) proposed that a vague answer to questions on researcher sexuality either created avenues for broader queries on sexuality, or positioned the scholar as a sexuality *outsider*. Sexualization was a common thread throughout the research process, with multiple propositions for sexual favors. The sexualization often continued during and after the interviews, with escorts propositioning the researcher. Walby (2010) attempted to prevent sexualization by wearing business attire and taking an unfriendly tone when participants made inappropriate requests. While some scholars encouraged sexual activity with respondents (Lambevski, 1999), Walby (2010) suggested a professional persona to craft rigorous research. He also cautioned that when men research men, almost any gesture can be interpreted as sexual. As with Pruitt (2007), Walby (2010) provided insight into an area of methodological consideration in the field. While useful for improving interview-based studies, Walby (2010) did not detail broader methodological concerns in the field, from which a spectrum of research questions can be drawn to chart the next arc of research. Scott,

Callander, and Minichiello (2014) detailed the recruitment of clients of male sex workers and the associated challenges. While such work is integral to those who research this population, the bulk of scholarship in male sex work targets male sex workers. Thus, a broader spectrum of methodological concerns in male sex work needs to be reviewed to guide the evolving research agenda.

Apart from literature focused on the methodological issues of male sex work research, scholars often detailed methodological concerns in their studies. Logan (2010), in his study on the factors that affected escort pricing, noted that a larger data source could have been drawn upon, and the possible biases with self-reported escort data. Wang et al. (2015), in their paper on the condom usage of male sex workers, recommended that smartphones could be used for disseminating information on safer sex behaviors. While such points are useful when conducting research in the field, these methodological recommendations and concerns tend to be a side note to a larger study. To guide researchers on conducting rigorous research in the area, a deeper exploration of methods is needed, along with areas of future research stemming from these techniques. The next sections will detail methodological insights that arose from my studies, along with the consequent recommendations and avenues for future research.

INTERVIEWING MALE ESCORTS

In the arena of the occupational features of male sex work, scholarship has been successful at aiding legitimization (Logan, 2010). However, research focusing on specific facets of the occupational area is minimal, despite male sex work swiftly moving toward a liberalized model in the Global North (Kumar, Minichiello, Scott, & Harrington, 2016). Scholarship on the occupational environment of male sex work is integral to shed light on the rapidly shifting constitution of the field. I thus conducted a study, drawing from 20 interviews with escorts in Brisbane, Australia. I explored the aspect of job success within the occupational environment, advancing that male escorting was an occupation demarcated by established markers of success, with certain characteristics needed to attain these markers. I proposed that independent escorting may be moving toward professionalization, away from modes of stigma (Kumar & Grov, 2017; Kumar, Scott, & Minichiello, 2017).

Following approval from the IRB Committee, 150 potential participants were contacted through email addresses listed on escort sites (rentmen.com, squirt.org, etc.), and the project was also advertised to male independent escorts on Respect Inc's mailing list. Respect Inc is a non-profit community-based organization for sex workers of all genders, centered on the rights and welfare of sex workers in Queensland, Australia (Respect Inc, 2015). The email provided a link to a survey form, and participants gave their contact details. After participant details had been collected, I called interested respondents to set an interview time and location. Interviews were conducted at cafes or participant homes and averaged 45 minutes. Escorts reviewed an information sheet and signed a consent form in line with IRB guidelines. All details were kept confidential and pseudonyms used. Participants were asked whether they considered sex work an occupation, and about the role of masculinity in the occupational experience. The interviews were recorded via electronic recording devices, or only notes taken if the participant preferred. At the completion of the interview, reimbursement of AUD50 was provided. Participants were then thanked and asked if they could refer suitable friends to the study (Sanders, 2006a). Interviews were transcribed and uploaded into NVivo10 for coding and subsequent analysis.

University Administrative Issues

Most Australian universities have a two-tiered system for IRB: high-risk and low-risk (National Health and Medical Research Council, 2014). Upon recommendation of the faculty IRB officer, a low-risk application was submitted. However, the IRB deemed the project unsuitable for a low-risk classification. It was then pointed out to the IRB that male independent escorting was legal in the context and would not involve any illegal activity, and the project was then reviewed under the low-risk classification, and subsequently approved. While the IRB deliberations were not as significant as those reported by scholars of female sex work (Hammond & Kingston, 2014; Sanders, 2006b), there was still some level of delay because sex work was viewed as too risky for a low-risk classification. Although male independent escorting is becoming increasingly normalized, some IRB members either do not believe so or are completely unaware of the transition.

Although not focused on male independent escorting, Mustanski (2011) detailed the various ethical and regulatory issues that arose when conducting research on lesbian, gay, bisexual, and transgender (LGBT) youth. To mitigate the impression institutional review board (IRB) members had of male escorting being a risky occupation, several recommendations made by Mustanski (2011) are highly relevant. By attending the meetings where the project will be reviewed, serving on the committee, publishing on participant experiences, and clarifying unclear IRB questions, researchers in the field of male independent escorting can also put forth that the field is not as dangerous as perceived, and participants are not vulnerable or in need of protection. Future research in the methodological arena can thus explore the processes by which participants are recruited, and contrast the research recruitment processes with similar case studies in more commonplace occupations such as hairdressing, and deviant ones such as street gang membership. Such research may demonstrate that the male escorting research process is more like researching a service occupation rather than a highly stigmatized activity. Such research would not only allow for greater methodological understanding, but also demonstrate to IRBs that male independent escorting is not as dangerous and maligned as originally believed.

Working with Sex Workers' Community Organizations

I originally believed that Brisbane, population of 2.3 million, would not yield sufficient participants for the planned study. Thus, a sex workers' community-based organization based in Sydney, population of 4.9 million, was contacted. However, the Sydney-based group stated that the research capacity had been met for the period, and they would not be able to assist. I then contacted Respect Inc, based in Brisbane, who almost immediately offered to meet us to discuss the project. Not only did they provide advice on the study, staff members present also requested to be interviewed and offered to contact those in their network to advertise the study. Male escorts interviewed expressed approval of my study, given the endorsement by Respect Inc, possibly enhancing the quality of data. Especially given that some members of sex workers' organizations in Australia believe that recent research in the field is not reflective of the realities of escorting (Cox, 2015), it may be necessary to work with such organizations closely in order to accurately depict male escorting (Argento et al., 2016; Goldring, Westall, & Cain, 2016), as well as to create stronger links between researchers and sex workers' organizations.

Future research can focus on developing a scale to determine whether the organization in a city will be willing to assist with male independent escorting research; based on the city size, size of the gay/bisexual population, among other factors. The next stage of scholarship can also guide scholars on how to effectively develop contact materials and overall study design in partnership with sex workers' organizations. The possible ethical implications that may arise when interviewing escorts who, in their capacity as sex workers' organization staff members, assisted with the project design, may also be a pertinent future study. Also, in situations where large samples are not needed, it may be more sensible for researchers to select second tier cities, in which sex workers' community-based organizations are not overloaded with research requests and possibly more interested in assisting with the study. The male escort population in the United States is strongly correlated with the sizes of the metropolitan statistical area (Logan, 2010), and thus areas with a large population, even if they are second tier cities, can be the subject of rigorous research.

Interview Process

Some researchers wore business attire during interviews to discourage sexualization (Hammond, 2010; Walby, 2010). On the other hand, I wore casual attire, but did not receive any sexual advances. Given how the researcher presents oneself can affect the study outcome (Fowler & Mangione, 1990; Houtkoop-Steenstra, 1997), future research can be conducted where the attire of the researcher is varied (formal vs casual), to shed light on what is the most apt means of presentation when conducting male sex work research in the increasingly normalized environment.

Participants did not query my sexuality during the interviews. Only a single escort asked me a personal question; regarding whether I was nervous when conducting interviews, but this may have been an attempt to make conversation, as the participant seemed uninterested in the response. Unlike the innuendo-laden outcomes in other research (Walby, 2010), participants described their services in rather businesslike terms, such as when speaking about the skills required to be an escort:

> You need time management; I know what I'm doing for the next three weeks right at this point. (Jacob, bisexual)

> You need to understand social media very well; you have to have people helping you in terms of driving you or possibly even people entering your messages. (Charles, bisexual)

Some scholars (Hammond & Kingston, 2014; Walby, 2010) received suggestive messages from some participants after interviews had been conducted. However, after completing my interviews, I did not receive any unsolicited messages, except for emails from a single participant who wanted to further develop on the points he had made, regarding how escorts attempt to undermine each other's business:

> Hi, I remembered another key way that competing escorts employ underhanded tactics against each other. Sometimes they will masquerade as clients to find out unpublished information about your rates and things you do in order to make themselves more attractive to clients. It's hard to think of relevant examples in an interview situation!
>
> Cheers, Philip

The lack of sexualization may be due to several possibilities. Firstly, I am South Asian by ethnicity, although not by nationality. Perhaps the perceived lack of sexual attractiveness in the Australian context may have prevented sexualization (Callander, Holt, & Newman, 2015; Raj, 2011). The participant contact emails indicated the study concerned the occupational experience, perhaps only those who viewed male independent escorting as a serious occupation were interested in participating, possibly precluding those who would be more likely to sexualize the researcher from signing up. It could also be that the sample I reached was more familiar with research projects, and perhaps knew how to conduct themselves appropriately during research studies. However, given the paucity of methodological exploration in male sex work research, I cannot provide sound reasons for my interview experiences. A possible study could explore different interview styles, and the subsequent differences in sexualization and depth of data. Another study could explore how the researcher's ethnicity affects participant responses, given that ethnicity plays a role in sexual attractiveness in the gay/bisexual male community (Callander, Newman, & Holt, 2015).

MALE ESCORT WEBSITES

Backed by the internet, male escorting is far more visible globally, with an increasing demand for paid male sexual intercourse (MacPhail et al., 2014). The world wide web provides an excellent venue for sex work to transition from streets to the web (McLean, 2013). The move to the internet allows for a far more competitive marketplace, where service, accountability, and protection are paramount (Kumar et al., 2016). Scholarship is needed on the worldwide distribution of male sex work to provide greater insight into the professionalization of male escorting and to shed light on the pathway to decriminalization. Give the progressive move to web-based services, I conducted a study, assembling a dataset of worldwide male escorting sites to elucidate the size, scale, and scope of internet-based male escorting. Results indicated that most websites are independent and not linked to escort agencies. Also, most of the sites cater to male escorts seeking to engage with male clientele, with many sites for female clients and couples. Escort sites are spread globally. Most websites are in Asia, Europe, and South America, with a few huge sites in the United States and Europe catering to a global customer base. I advanced that, while subject to significant regulation globally, male escorting is becoming more visible in a range of cultural contexts, as indicated by websites emerging in public sites (Kumar et al., 2016).

Where feasible, residents of nations where I was cataloging escort sites, were asked for slang terms to be used as keywords on Google. In situations where I was not able to engage local contacts, a fixed set of terms were utilized as search keywords. The terms were as follows: male sex work, male escort, male prostitute, gay for pay, rent boy, and call boy. Using Google Translate, I translated these terms into the major languages of each nation. The name of each country was also added to the indicated search terms, such as *call boy Nederland*. A total of 534 websites were identified, but some were excluded as upon closer inspection, they were not actually escort sites, but online forums for gay or bisexual men. The remaining 499 sites were analyzed for the following variables: agency affiliation, clientele gender, number of escorts, original nation of operation, cities covered, years of operation, language of website, site traffic, legality of sex work in nations of operation, legality of same-sex intercourse in nations of operation, search functionality, and existence of review system.

Site traffic was measured through Alexa Traffic Ranks. Alexa compiles internet traffic by logging user data. Traffic ranks are determined using the following: average daily visitors and page views over past three months (Alexa Internet, 2015). Previous scholarship has applied traffic ranks (Gomadam, Ranabahu, Nagarajan, Sheth, & Verma, 2008; Ihm & Pai, 2011) and the technique was deemed applicable for my study. About 70% of the sites I cataloged had traffic ranks. To determine whether sex work was legal in a nation, I used the United States Department of Human Rights Reports or the nation's penal code (Department Of State, 2015). Based on this data, I put forth the following categories of legality: illegal, legal, legality varies by state, varying legality, and no laws. For legality of same-sex intercourse, data were obtained from the International Lesbian, Gay, Bisexual, Trans, and Intersex Association (IGLA) reports (Carroll & Mendos, 2017) or the country's penal code. I demarcated legality into the following categories: illegal, legal, legality varies by state, and varying legality. The search functions I observed were organized into the following categories: age, sexual orientation, sexual position, penis size, circumcision, willingness to travel, and height. Similarly, the spectrum of review functions was categorized into the following groups: no review function, function available but not used, *star* rating system, *star* rating system with dropdown comment list, *star* rating system and full-text review, *star* rating system with dropdown comment list, and full-text review. The *star* rating system refers to a feature where users can select out of five stars to review escort services. I ensured data validity with multiple coders, who inspected data against the above indicated categories. If variations were observed between rates, discussion would take place until agreement was reached, and the variable recoded as necessary.

Accessing Websites

I cataloged escort sites on a university computer, and an IT technician, conducting routine servicing, filed a complaint. The technician felt university resources were being used inappropriately and was offended by the content. I was instructed to explain the situation to university upper management. After several conversations with the management, the complaint was eventually rescinded. While the outcome of the situation was not overly damaging, these experiences indicated that there is stigma against researching content of a sexual nature, even in a department which is known for such research. Not only did administrative staff find the research inappropriate, the university considered the complaint to be a serious one, until argued otherwise. Administrative resources were wasted, despite no serious ramifications.

Given the increasing representation of male sex work on the internet, it is essential for scholars to know whether researching this area is likely to create any administrative issues. Universities generally have systems in place to prevent access of purportedly inappropriate material, but it is not always clear whether such policies disallow researchers from collecting such data on university computers. I recommend that scholars who may view purportedly inappropriate material for their research, speak to the relevant administrative department before conducting such studies. If such research is likely to contravene IT department policy, it is advised that the researcher speak with other scholars in a similar research area at the university, to submit a formal request to change or modify IT department policy as necessary. Future studies in the methodological vein can provide guidance in this area, with a listing of scholars' experiences with such administrative issues, and their responses to these concerns. On a broader arc, my experiences draw parallels with perceptions of the discipline as frivolous and a farce (Hammond & Kingston, 2014). Not only is it important to ensure favorable administrative policies, an attitudinal change around sex work scholarship is necessary. I suggest that researchers call for new students and hires at the university to be briefed about various areas of scholarship at the institution, with a special focus on research that can be perceived as unorthodox. Such a program would mitigate complaints about inappropriate research, and perceptions of some variants of scholarship being worthier than others.

Cataloging Techniques

The large number of male sex work websites presents some methodological concerns. I conducted a single sweep of male sex work sites, and I advise that future scholarship seeking to catalog websites engage in multiple rounds of indexing. Multiple researchers simultaneously detailing websites could be advantageous, where lists assembled by each researcher could be compared. Several nations still exist where sex work and same sex relations are illegal. In such cases, sex work websites may be purposely difficult to locate, password protected, or on the darknet. To identify such sites, local contacts in each nation is likely necessary. Developing a worldwide network of contacts is time consuming, but may be necessary if one wants to identify online male sex work in jurisdictions where the field is illegal. I suggest working with sex workers' non-governmental organizations which have global reach. Not only would partnering with such organizations aid in cataloging low visibility online sex work, but also strengthen relationships between researchers and sex workers, improving the rigor of scholarship (Cox, 2015). Due to my limited network of contacts in the sex work space, I was also not able to identify all slang terms for male sex work globally. In nations where sex work is illegal, such slang terms may only be known to persons in the space, and not easily available online. Thus, establishing a global network of contacts would aid in identifying culturally specific terms for sex work as well.

Building on the possibility of sex work sites being on the darknet, scholarship indicates that sex trafficking may proliferate on the darknet (Hoyer, 2017; Kushubekova, Bahar, & Freeman, 2016). I am not suggesting that sex trafficking is equivalent to sex work, but that given the possible prevalence of sex trafficking sites on the darknet, sex work sites may also exist in the same space, especially in nations where the activity is illegal. In my study, preliminary searches did not yield any sites on the darknet, but with specialized tools, and collaborating with computer scientists (Yang, Liu, Kizza, & Ege, 2009), future work may do a more thorough job of indexing such sites. More sophisticated techniques of site cataloging would be useful to ensure replicability and depth. A range of web crawlers is available to catalog websites, and these can be used in future scholarship (Menczer, Pant, & Srinivasan, 2004). I made the decision not to include classified advertising sites like Backpage and Craiglist, as they are not venues primarily for listing sex work. However, recent research has indicated that a significant amount of sex work is advertised on these sites (Raphael, 2017). Thus, a means of cataloging escort adverts on classified advertising sites should be developed. As mentioned, web crawlers may be efficacious for such purposes. My analysis provided a snapshot of websites for a particular year. While cross-sectional data have their advantages (Sedgwick, 2014), I suggest adding a longitudinal study element to future research. The change in metrics over time, such as, number of escorts listed, traffic ranks, and level of service, could shed light on how male sex work markets are changing and adapting.

CONCLUSION

Male sex work research has focused on changing themes over the years and utilized a host of novel techniques to explore various research questions. However, male sex work scholars have rarely engaged in critical methodological review, advancing areas for future research. With the increasing normalization and dynamism of male sex work, it is necessary for research to provide methodological guidance for the next wave of studies in the field. To this end, this chapter reviewed the methods used in male sex work research over the years, and detailed the lack of research on methodological inquiry in the field. Drawing on two studies, I proposed several recommendations and avenues for future research. It is hoped that these suggestions will advance male sex work research, in line with the rapidly shifting sex work environment.

REFERENCES

Alexa Internet. (2015). How are Alexa's traffic rankings determined? Retrieved from http://support.alexa.com/hc/en-us/articles/200449744-How-are-Alexa-s-traffic-rankings-determined-. Accessed on October 24, 2015.

Allen, D. M. (1980). Young male prostitutes: A psychosocial study. *Archives of Sexual Behavior*, *9*(5), 399–426. https://doi.org/10.1007/BF02115941

Argento, E., Taylor, M., Jollimore, J., Taylor, C., Jennex, J., Krusi, A., & Shannon, K. (2016). The loss of Boystown and transition to online sex work: Strategies and barriers to increase safety among men sex workers and clients of men. *American Journal of Men's Health, 12*(6), 1994–2005. https://doi.org/10.1177/1557988316655785

Bar-Johnson, M. D., & Weiss, P. (2014). A comparison of male sex workers in Prague: Internet escorts versus men who work in specialized bars and clubs. *The Journal of Sex Research, 52*(3), 1–9.

Bimbi, D. S. (2007). Male prostitution: Pathology, paradigms and progress in research. *Journal of Homosexuality, 53*(1–2), 7–35.

Browne, J., Jamieson, M., Minichiello, V., & Marino, R. (1998). A review of male to male commercial sex encounters. *Venereology, 11*(4), 32.

Callander, D., Holt, M., & Newman, C. E. (2015). 'Not everyone's gonna like me': Accounting for race and racism in sex and dating web services for gay and bisexual men. *Ethnicities, 16*(1), 3–21. https://doi.org/10.1177/1468796815581428

Callander, D., Newman, C. E., & Holt, M. (2015). Is sexual racism really racism? Distinguishing attitudes toward sexual racism and generic racism among gay and bisexual men. *Archives of Sexual Behavior, 44*(7), 1991–2000.

Carroll, A., & Mendos, L. R. (2017). *State-sponsored homophobia 2017: A world survey of sexual orientation laws: Criminalisation, protection and recognition*. Geneva, Switzerland: ILGA.

Caukins, S. E., & Coombs, N. R. (1976). The psychodynamics of male prostitution. *American Journal of Psychotherapy, 30*(3), 441–451.

Coombs, N. R. (1974). Male prostitution: A psychosocial view of behavior. *American Journal of Orthopsychiatry, 44*(5), 782.

Cox, C. (2015). Male sex work and society [Book Review]. *HIV Australia, 13*(1).

Craft, M. (1966). Boy prostitutes and their fate. *The British Journal of Psychiatry, 112*(492), 1111–1114.

Department of State. (2015). Human Rights Reports. Retrieved from http://www.state.gov/j/drl/rls/hrrpt/index.htm. Accessed on May 10, 2016.

Ellison, G., & Weitzer, R. (2016). The dynamics of male and female street prostitution in Manchester, England. *Men and Masculinities, 20*(2), 181–203. https://doi.org/10.1177/1097184X15625318

Fowler, F. J., & Mangione, T. W. (1990). *Standardized survey interviewing: Minimizing interviewer-related error* (Vol. 18). Newbury Park, CA: SAGE Publications.

Gandy, P., & Deisher, R. (1970). Young male prostitutes: The physician's role in social rehabilitation. *JAMA, 212*(10), 1661–1666.

Ginsburg, K. N. (1967). The "meat-rack": A study of the male homosexual prostitute. *American Journal of Psychotherapy, 21*(2), 170–185.

Goldring, J., Westall, A., & Cain, L. (2016). *An exploratory study of the growth of online male sex work in Manchester*. Manchester: Manchester Metropolitan University.

Gomadam, K., Ranabahu, A., Nagarajan, M., Sheth, A. P., & Verma, K. (2008). A faceted classification based approach to search and rank web apis (pp. 177–184). Presented at the 2008 IEEE international conference on web services, ICWS'08. IEEE. Beijing, China.

Grov, C., Koken, J., Smith, M., & Parsons, J. T. (2016). How do male sex workers on Craigslist differ from those on Rentboy? A comparison of two samples. *Culture, Health & Sexuality, 19*(4), 405–421.

Grov, C., Rodríguez-Díaz, C. E., Ditmore, M. H., Restar, A., & Parsons, J. T. (2014). What kinds of workshops do internet-based male escorts want? Implications for prevention and health promotion. *Sexuality Research and Social Policy, 11*(2), 176–185.

Grov, C., Rodríguez-Díaz, C. E., Jovet-Toledo, G. G., & Parsons, J. T. (2015). Comparing male escorts' sexual behaviour with their last male client versus non-commercial male partner. *Culture, Health & Sexuality, 17*(2), 194–207.

Grov, C., Starks, T. J., Wolff, M., Smith, M. D., Koken, J. A., & Parsons, J. T. (2015). Patterns of client behavior with their most recent male escort: An application of latent class analysis. *Archives of Sexual Behavior, 44*(4), 1035–1045.

Hammond, N. (2010). Tackling taboos: Men who pay for sex and the emotional researcher. In K. Hardy, S. Kingston, & T. Sanders (Eds.), *New sociologies of sex work* (pp. 59–74). *Aldershot: Ashgate*.

Hammond, N., & Kingston, S. (2014). Experiencing stigma as sex work researchers in professional and personal lives. *Sexualities, 17*(3), 329–347. https://doi.org/10.1177/1363460713516333

Harris, M. (1973). The Dilly boys: The game of male prostitution in Piccadilly. *Journal of Contemporary Ethnography, 6*(3), 382–383.

Houtkoop-Steenstra, H. (1997). Being friendly in survey interviews. *Journal of Pragmatics*, *28*(5), 591–623. https://doi.org/10.1016/S0378-2166(97)00018-0

Hoyer, J. (2017). Sex trafficking in the digital age: The role of virtual currency-specific legislation in keeping pace with technology. *Wayne Law Review*, *63*, 83.

Humphreys, L. (1970). *Tearoom trade: impersonal sex in public places*. Chicago, IL: Aldine.

Ihm, S., & Pai, V. S. (2011). Towards understanding modern web traffic (pp. 295–312). Presented at the proceedings of the 2011 ACM SIGCOMM conference on Internet measurement conference. ACM. Toronto, Ontario, Canada.

Jamel, J. (2011). An investigation of the incidence of client-perpetrated sexual violence against male sex workers. *International Journal of Sexual Health*, *23*(1), 63–78.

Koken, J. A., Bimbi, D. S., Parsons, J. T., & Halkitis, P. N. (2004). The experience of stigma in the lives of male Internet escorts. *Journal of Psychology & Human Sexuality*, *16*(1), 13–32.

Kumar, N., & Grov, C. (2017). Exploring the occupational context of independent male escorts who seek male clients: The case of job success. *American Journal of Men's Health*, *12*(4), 877–883. https://doi.org/10.1177/1557988317746836

Kumar, N., Minichiello, V., Scott, J., & Harrington, T. (2016). A global overview of male escort websites. *Journal of Homosexuality*, *64*(12), 1731–1744. https://doi.org/10.1080/00918369.2016.1265356

Kumar, N., Minichiello, V., Scott, J., & Harrington, T. (2017). A global overview of male escort websites. *Journal of Homosexuality*, *64*(12), 1731–1744. https://doi.org/10.1080/00918369.2016.1265356

Kumar, N., Scott, J., & Minichiello, V. (2017). Masculinity and the occupational experience of male independent escorts who seek male clients. *Social Sciences*, *6*(2), 58. https://doi.org/10.3390/socsci6020058

Kushubekova, S., Bahar, E. D., & Freeman, I. (2016). Sexual marketing of women: Sex trafficking from former Soviet Union to Turkey. In *The 2016 WEI International Academic Conference Proceedings*, Boston, USA.

Lambevski, S. A. (1999). Suck my nation-masculinity, ethnicity and the politics of (Homo) sex. *Sexualities*, *2*(4), 397–419.

Logan, T. D. (2010). Personal characteristics, sexual behaviors, and male sex work: A quantitative approach. *American Sociological Review*, *75*(5), 679–704. https://doi.org/10.1177/0003122410379581

Logan, T. D. (2016). *Economics, sexuality, and male sex work*. Cambridge: Cambridge University Press.

Luckenbill, D. F. (1985). Entering male prostitution. *Journal of Contemporary Ethnography*, *14*(2), 131–153. https://doi.org/10.1177/089124168501400201

Luckenbill, D. F. (1986). Deviant career mobility: The case of male prostitutes. *Social Problems*, *33*(4), 283–296. https://doi.org/10.2307/800720

MacNamara, D. E. (1965). Male prostitution in American-cities—A socioeconomic or pathological phenomenon. *American Journal of Orthopsychiatry*, *35*(2), 204–204.

MacPhail, C., Scott, J., & Minichiello, V. (2014). Technology, normalisation and male sex work. *Culture, Health & Sexuality*, *17*(4), 483–495. https://doi.org/10.1080/13691058.2014.951396

McCabe, I., Acree, M., O'Mahony, F., McCabe, J., Kenny, J., Twyford, J., … McGlanaghy, E. (2011). Male street prostitution in Dublin: A psychological analysis. *Journal of Homosexuality*, *58*(8), 998–1021.

McLean, A. (2013). 'You can do it from your sofa': The increasing popularity of the internet as a working site amongst male sex workers in Melbourne. *Journal of Sociology*, *51*(4), 887–902. https://doi.org/10.1177/1440783313480416

Menczer, F., Pant, G., & Srinivasan, P. (2004). Topical web crawlers: Evaluating adaptive algorithms. *ACM Transactions on Internet Technology*, *4*(4), 378–419. https://doi.org/10.1145/1031114.1031117

Mimiaga, M. J., Reisner, S. L., Tinsley, J. P., Mayer, K. H., & Safren, S. A. (2009). Street workers and internet escorts: contextual and psychosocial factors surrounding HIV risk behavior among men who engage in sex work with other men. *Journal of Urban Health*, *86*(1), 54–66.

Minichiello, V., Marino, R., Browne, J., Jamieson, M., Peterson, K., Reuter, B., & Robinson, K. (2000). Commercial sex between men: A prospective diary-based study. *Journal of Sex Research*, *37*(2), 151–160.

Minichiello, V., Scott, J., & Callander, D. (2013). New pleasures and old dangers: Reinventing male sex work. *Journal of Sex Research*, *50*(3–4), 263–275.

Monteiro, J. F. G., Marshall, B. D., Escudero, D., Sosa-Rubí, S. G., González, A., Flanigan, T., ... Galárraga, O. (2015). Preventing HIV transmission among partners of HIV-positive male sex workers in Mexico City: A modeling study. *AIDS and Behavior*, *19*(9), 1579–1588.

Morrison, T. G., & Whitehead, B. W. (2007). Nobody's ever going to make a fag pretty woman: Stigma awareness and the putative effects of stigma among a sample of Canadian male sex workers. *Journal of Homosexuality*, *53*(1–2), 201–217.

Mustanski, B. (2011). Ethical and Regulatory Issues with Conducting Sexuality Research with LGBT Adolescents: A Call to Action for a Scientifically Informed Approach. *Archives of Sexual Behavior*, *40*(673). Retrieved from https://doi.org/10.1007/s10508-011-9745-1.

National Health and Medical Research Council. (2014). Chapter 2.1. Risk and benefit. Retrieved from https://www.nhmrc.gov.au/book/chapter-2-1-risk-and-benefit. Accessed on September 29, 2015.

Nureña, C. R., Zúñiga, M., Zunt, J., Mejía, C., Montano, S., & Sánchez, J. L. (2011). Diversity of commercial sex among men and male-born trans people in three Peruvian cities. *Culture, Health & Sexuality*, *13*(10), 1207–1221.

Oselin, S. S. (2016). You catch more flies with honey: Sex work, violence, and masculinity on the streets.. Presented at the Sociological Forum (Vol. 31, pp. 203–222), Wiley Online Library.

Parsons, J. T., Bimbi, D., & Halkitis, P. N. (2001). Sexual compulsivity among gay/bisexual male escorts who advertise on the internet. *Sexual Addiction & Compulsivity*, *8*(2), 101–112. https://doi.org/10.1080/10720160127562

Parsons, J. T., Bimbi, D. S., Koken, J. A., & Halkitis, P. N. (2005). Factors related to childhood sexual abuse among gay/bisexual male internet escorts. *Journal of Child Sexual Abuse*, *14*(2), 1–23. https://doi.org/10.1300/J070v14n02_01

Parsons, J. T., Koken, J. A., & Bimbi, D. S. (2004). The use of the Internet by gay and bisexual male escorts: sex workers as sex educators. *AIDS Care*, *16*(8), 1021–1035.

Parsons, J. T., Koken, J. A., & Bimbi, D. S. (2007). Looking beyond HIV: Eliciting individual and community needs of male Internet escorts. *Journal of Homosexuality*, *53*(1–2), 219–240.

Pruitt, M. V. (2007). Deviant Research: Deception, Male Internet Escorts, and Response Rates. *Deviant Behavior*, *29*(1), 70–82. DOI: 10.1080/01639620701457782

Pruitt, M. V. (2016). "Just a Gigolo": Differences in advertisements of male-for-female and male-for-male online escorts. *Deviant Behavior*, *39*(1), 64–79.

Raj, S. (2011). Grindring bodies: Racial and affective economies of online queer desire. *Critical Race and Whiteness Studies*, *7*(2), 1–12.

Raphael, J. (2017). Denial of harm: Sex trafficking, backpage, and free speech absolutism. *Dignity: A Journal on Sexual Exploitation and Violence*, *2*(1), 8.

Reiss, A. J. J. (1961). The social integration of queers and peers. *Social Problems*, *9*(2), 102–120. https://doi.org/10.2307/799006

Respect Inc. (2015). Home page — Respect Inc, Queensland [Page]. Retrieved from http://www.respectqld.org.au/. Accessed on June 17, 2015.

Ryan, P. (2016). # Follow: Exploring the role of social media in the online construction of male sex worker lives in Dublin, Ireland. *Gender, Place & Culture*, *23*(12), 1713–1724.

Sagarin, E., & MacNamara, D. E. (1975). The homosexual as a crime victim. *International Journal of Criminology and Penology*, *3*, 13–25.

Sanders, T. (2006a). Female sex workers as health educators with men who buy sex: Utilising narratives of rationalisations. *Social Science & Medicine*, *62*(10), 2434–2444.

Sanders, T. (2006b). Researching sex work: Dynamics, difficulties, and decisions. In D. Hobbs & R. Wright. (Eds.), *The SAGE handbook of fieldwork* (pp. 201–221). Newbury Park, California: SAGE Publications Inc.

Scott, J., Callander, D. & Minichiello, V. (2014). Clients of Male Sex Workers. In V. Minichiello & J. Scott (Eds.), *Male sex work and society* (pp. 150–177). New York, NY: Harrington Park Press.

Scott, J., Minichiello, V., Marino, R., Harvey, G. P., Jamieson, M., & Browne, J. (2005). Understanding the new context of the male sex work industry. *Journal of Interpersonal Violence*, *20*(3), 320–342.

Sedgwick, P. (2014). Cross sectional studies: Advantages and disadvantages. *BMJ: British Medical Journal*, *348*.

Smith, M. D., Grov, C., & Seal, D. W. (2008). Agency-based male sex work: A descriptive focus on physical, personal, and social space. *The Journal of Men's Studies*, *16*(2), 193–210.

Smith, M. D., Grov, C., Seal, D. W., Bernhardt, N., & McCall, P. (2015). Social–emotional aspects of male escorting: Experiences of men working for an agency. *Archives of Sexual Behavior*, *44*(4), 1047–1058.

Smith, M. D., & Seal, D. W. (2008). Sexual behavior, mental health, substance use, and HIV risk among agency-based male escorts in a small US city. *International Journal of Sexual Health*, *19*(4), 27–39.

Sosa-Rubí, S. G., Salinas-Rodríguez, A., Montoya-Rodríguez, A. A., & Galárraga, O. (2018). The relationship between psychological temporal perspective and HIV/STI risk behaviors among male sex workers in Mexico city. *Archives of Sexual Behavior*, *47*(5), 1551–1563.

Thomas, B., Closson, E. F., Biello, K., Menon, S., Navakodi, P., Dhanalakshmi, A., … Mimiaga, M. J. (2017). Development and open pilot trial of an HIV-prevention intervention integrating mobile-phone technology for male sex workers in Chennai, India. *Archives of Sexual Behavior*, *46*(4), 1035–1046.

Uy, J. M., Parsons, J. T., Bimbi, D. S., Koken, J. A., & Halkitis, P. N. (2004). Gay and bisexual male escorts who advertise on the Internet: Understanding reasons for and effects of involvement in commercial sex. *International Journal of Men's Health*, *3*(1), 11–26.

Walby, K. (2010). Interviews as encounters: issues of sexuality and reflexivity when men interview men about commercial same sex relations. *Qualitative Research*, *10*(6), 639–657. https://doi.org/10.1177/1468794110380525

Walby, K. (2012). *Touching encounters: Sex, work, and male-for-male Internet escorting*. Chicago, Ill: University of Chicago Press.

Wang, L.-H., Yan, J., Yang, G.-L., Long, S., Yu, Y., Wu, X.-L. (2015). Prevalence of Consistent Condom Use with Various Types of Sex Partners and Associated Factors among Money Boys in Changsha, China. *The Journal of Sexual Medicine*, *12*(4), 936–945.

Yang, L., Liu, F., Kizza, J. M., & Ege, R. K. (2009). Discovering topics from dark websites. In *2009 IEEE symposium on computational intelligence in cyber security* (pp. 175–179). Nashville, Tennessee, USA. https://doi.org/10.1109/CICYBS.2009.4925106

Yu, G., Clatts, M. C., Goldsamt, L. A., & Giang, L. M. (2015). Substance use among male sex workers in Vietnam: Prevalence, onset, and interactions with sexual risk. *International Journal of Drug Policy*, *26*(5), 516–521.

Zhao, J., Cai, W.-D., Chen, L., Zhao, J.-K., Gan, Y.-X., Zi, Y.-Y., … Wang, X.-R. (2011). A comparison of HIV infection and related risks among male sex workers in different venues in Shenzhen, China. *AIDS and Behavior*, *15*(3), 635–642.

CHAPTER 6

EMPLOYING MIXED METHODS: THE CASE OF ELDER FINANCIAL EXPLOITATION

Julie Brancale and Thomas G. Blomberg

ABSTRACT

Purpose – *This chapter will demonstrate the usefulness of mixed methods research in an understudied area of criminology and criminal justice, namely elder financial exploitation.*

Methodology/approach – *The data and research methodology described in this chapter come from a recently completed comprehensive case study of elder financial exploitation in Florida.*

Findings – *Elder financial exploitation is a growing social problem in the United States and there is little theoretical or empirical research available regarding the prevalence, risk factors, protective factors, and consequences. Given that the current status of the research literature is largely fragmented and discontinuous, conducting a survey aimed at validation was not possible. Through the mixed method case study involving a literature review, focus group discussions, and interview questions, the authors have developed a theoretical framework for elder financial exploitation that can be quantitatively validated.*

Originality/value – *This chapter provides justification for the expanded use of mixed methods research for other understudied topic areas within criminology and criminal justice and provides the foundation for the development of a comprehensive theoretical framework for explaining elder financial exploitation.*

Keywords: Case study; elder financial exploitation; mixed methods research; qualitative research methods; theoretical development; elder financial fraud

Methods of Criminology and Criminal Justice Research
Sociology of Crime, Law and Deviance, Volume 24, 101–114

ISSN: 1521-6136/doi:10.1108/S1521-613620190000024010

INTRODUCTION

The discipline of criminology is dominated by quantitative research studies that often involve large datasets and rigorous statistical analyses. Many topic areas, such as theory testing of crime causation, have strong empirical traditions in which hypotheses can be developed and validated. However, this is not the case in the study of a number of timely and important areas within criminology and criminal justice, including the subject of this chapter. For example, little is known about financial exploitation of the elderly, including the prevalence, risk factors, protective factors, and consequences. Moreover, as the elderly population continues to grow, there are concerns that this problem will only intensify in its frequency and the severity of negative consequences to victims. Elder financial exploitation has not been given systematic attention from researchers or policymakers and is underreported by victims to authorities. Differences in research designs and other methodological problems have resulted in discontinuous and largely fragmented findings that have limited our understanding of this social problem. Consequently, the available research knowledge cannot be drawn upon to develop testable hypotheses from which findings can be used to inform policy decisions.

Given these challenges, the use of quantitative research methods and hypothesis testing, was not appropriate for the study of elder financial exploitation. Rather, the use of qualitative research methods, namely a case study research design, was employed to build an empirical base from which hypotheses could be drawn and causal inferences tested quantitatively. In the sections that follow, we will discuss the challenges of conducting research on an understudied criminological topic area. We will also demonstrate how we confronted the voids in the relevant literature and developed a research strategy that provided a foundation for future research. The methodological approach used in this study can be employed by researchers to explore other understudied topic areas within criminology and criminal justice.

LITERATURE REVIEW

Elder financial exploitation encompasses a broad spectrum of conduct perpetrated against elderly citizens with the goal of defrauding them financially. While not specific to elders, Titus, Heinzelmann, and Boyle (1995, p. 54) define financial exploitation as "the deliberate intent to deceive with the promise of goods, services, or other financial benefits that in fact do not exist or that were never intended to be provided."

Research has produced conflicting findings about whether elders are more likely to be victims of financial exploitation than younger adults. Some studies have found that the elderly are more likely to be victims (AARP, 1996, 1999; Struck, 2006), while others have found that they are not (Muscat, James, & Graycar, 2002; Pak & Shadel, 2005; Policastro & Payne, 2015). However, there are certain types of financial exploitation for which the elderly do appear to be more frequently targeted and victimized as compared to their younger counterparts, including telemarketing scams, charitable donation fraud, lottery/sweepstakes fraud, healthcare fraud, caretaker fraud, and home repair fraud (AARP, 1996; National Adult Protective Services Association, 2016; National Council on Aging, 2017). Empirical evidence on why elders may be targeted more frequently for certain types of financial exploitation is not conclusive.

It is difficult to estimate the national prevalence of elder financial exploitation because numerous cases go unreported, the definition of "elderly" varies across studies, and there are many forms of exploitation, not all of which are criminal but rather constitute civil or consumer protection matters that are unethical and inappropriate (Curtis, 2006). In a study of elderly Arizona and Florida residents, it was found that over two-thirds of the respondents had experienced an attempted fraud in the two years prior to the survey (Holtfreter, Reisig, Mears, & Wolfe, 2014). In addition, during the same time period, the researchers found that one-in-five respondents reported being the victim of financial fraud.

Further, there are methodological differences in the available self-report surveys that have resulted in variation in reported prevalence rates. Advocacy groups and consumer protection agencies, with the primary focus of developing national prevalence estimates, have conducted most of the large national-level surveys and academics have relied on smaller and more local-level samples to identify common risk factors (Holtfreter et al., 2014). For example, the Federal Trade Commission (FTC) and AARP have each conducted nationally representative surveys of 2,000–3,000 citizens to gauge the national prevalence of financial exploitation (these surveys were of the general population and estimates for the elderly citizens were extrapolated). Academics have not focused on generating national estimates but rather have conducted smaller-scale surveys aimed at identifying victim characteristics and risk factors. For example, Policastro and Payne (2015) conducted a study of 746 elderly Virginia residents to obtain a better understanding of the differing types of crimes impacting elders based on varying lifestyle characteristics. Former Attorney General Eric Holder indicated that approximately 25% of elders experience an incident of financial exploitation annually; True Link (2015) reported that 36.9% of elders had experienced financial abuse in the previous five years; and the FTC (Anderson, 2010) reported prevalence rates to be between 6.5% and 9.1% in the prior year. Thus, the currently available prevalence estimates range from 6.5% to 36.9%. However, these percentages likely underestimate the true extent of the problem because researchers agree that financial exploitation of the elderly citizens is underreported both to officials and in self-report surveys (AARP Foundation, 2003; FINRA/WISE, 2006; Johnson, 2002). Surveys have indicated that between 20% and 50% of victims do not report financial fraud or exploitation to authorities. Given these limitations of prior surveys, researchers, government officials, and practitioners agree that available prevalence estimates are incomplete.

In addition to the incomplete prevalence estimates, research on risk factors and protective factors is also limited and not conclusive. There is also very little theoretical explanation for the causes of financial exploitation, and criminal victimization more broadly, among members of the elderly population. Complicating research on elder financial exploitation is that prevalence rates, circumstances, risk factors, protective factors, and reporting behavior appear to vary significantly depending on the type of financial exploitation.

As social bonds change during late-adulthood, individuals may become susceptible to financial exploitation. Many older adults experience changes in their social networks as a result of divorce, retirement, relocation, the death of a spouse, death of friends, and changing physical and cognitive abilities (Brancale, 2017). Research has suggested that both divorce and the death of a spouse are risk factors for financial exploitation (AARP, 2003; Alves & Wilson, 2008; Anderson, 2007, 2010; Hafemeister, 2003; Rabiner et al., 2004). Holtfreter et al. (2014) found that being unmarried increases the likelihood of experiencing the improper or illegal management of funds, assets or property, and forgery. However, other research has produced contradictory results. True Link (2015) reported that the loss of a spouse was not a risk factor for any form of elder financial fraud or exploitation. AARP (2011) found that being married made those over 50 years old more likely to be victims of exploitation related to investments, although those elders who were not married were at an increased risk of exploitation through lottery scams.

Employment status may also impact the elderly citizen's vulnerability for financial exploitation. For example, Holtfreter et al. (2014) found that elders who are employed were at greater risk for financial exploitation through the improper or illegal management of funds, assets, or property, and forgery, but that retirement put the individual at greater risk for financial exploitation from shopping fraud. Acierno, Hernandez-Tejada, Muzzy, and Steve (2009) found that unemployment put elderly individuals at a slightly greater risk for financial exploitation by family members and employed elders are at greater risk for financial exploitation by strangers. While a correlation between employment and financial exploitation has been identified, it is unclear why.

The daily activities and routines of an elderly individual may also influence their risk of financial exploitation. Prior studies have included both daily social activities outside the home and Internet shopping behavior as measures of routine activities. However, adequate attention has not been given to the specific types of activities that may influence risk. Muscat et al. (2002) found that elderly individuals who left their home at least once a week were more likely to be victims of financial exploitation than those who stayed at home. It is not clear from this study which type(s) of financial exploitation elderly individuals are more susceptible as a result of their routine activities or how and why there was an increased vulnerability for exploitation. Research has also found that frequent Internet shopping increases the likelihood of financial exploitation (AARP, 1999, 2011; Holtfreter et al., 2014). However, similar to the prior research on routine activities, it is unclear how or why Internet shopping increases an elder's risk for financial exploitation.

Many of the articles, studies, and reports identified in the prior literature do not provide theoretical explanations or empirical cause–effect tests of risk factors; rather they provide descriptive accounts compiled from summary statistics that are incomplete. Additionally, the studies used different definitions and measurements of age and financial exploitation and were not guided by theoretical frameworks. Therefore, it is unknown whether and to what degree certain behaviors or characteristics are risk factors, protective factors, predictors, or correlates of elder financial exploitation. Consequently, the prior research does not yield conclusive generalizations regarding the causes, prevalence, and importantly, effective methods of prevention. Rather, the prior research is largely descriptive with often-conflicting findings and interpretations.

In sum, the existing literature on financial exploitation of the elderly is fragmented and inconclusive. Moreover, the available research is devoid of theoretical frameworks and there are no datasets currently available to provide needed tests of theories or causal explanations. Because financial exploitation is drastically underreported among the elderly, secondary analysis derived from law enforcement data is not possible and research in this area must rely largely on self-report studies. Inconsistent definitions of financial exploitation in survey and interview instruments have also complicated the ability of researchers and policymakers to develop sound conclusions and policy and practice recommendations.

CHRONOLOGY OF STUDY AND METHODS

As demonstrated by the review of the prior literature, the knowledge base regarding the prevalence, risk factors, protective factors, and reporting behavior associated with elder financial exploitation is limited, often contradictory, and largely without theory. As a result, comprehensive description, explanation, and prediction of elder financial exploitation have yet to be provided. Following, our literature review, it was decided that the foundation of knowledge was not adequately established to develop meaningful and testable hypotheses to be addressed through a survey and subsequent quantitative data analyses. Rather, we determined that to move our understanding of this topic forward, it was necessary to establish a grounded empirical foundation through a mixed method case study approach.

Case study research is an appropriate research method when little is known about the topic and the goal is to provide in-depth discovery and description of a problem to advance knowledge (Cousin, 2005). Much of the criticism leveled against case study research has been that the findings are not generalizable, are arbitrary, and biased (Flyvbjerg, 2006). However, we contend that this claim is misleading and can be detrimental to the fundamental goals of science and advancing our understanding of critical issues. Case study research can be and is a necessary method of scientific inquiry in the social sciences (Ragin & Becker, 1992).

Ultimately, a mixed method case study approach was selected for our study of elder financial exploitation because in determining what to ask respondents in survey questions, a significant amount of prior research and understanding on the topic is required. If we proceeded with the initial plan of conducting a national survey, the research team would have developed survey questions based on questionable assumptions rather than established scientific evidence. Glaser and Strauss (1967) argued that the intimate connection with empirical reality (as provided by an in-depth case study) guides the development of testable, relevant, and valid theories. In sum, we found it to be more valuable to begin with the discovery and building of an empirically grounded knowledge base rather than trying to immediately test questionable hypotheses.

The research design for our study emerged entirely from the problem itself and after the research plan was changed to a case-study approach, we began by identifying areas of the country with a large population of elderly citizens. Through this process, we chose to conduct the study in the largest active-living retirement community in the United States. The retirement community occupies parts of three counties in Florida. According to US Census estimates, the population of the retirement community surpassed 100,000 residents in 2013 and continues to grow at a steady pace. The median age is 66 and 98% of the residents are white. Income and housing costs vary widely. To maintain its status as an official retirement community, at least 80% of the homes must be occupied with at least one person over the age of 54. The community is designed for active-living elderly adults, with numerous town squares, sports and recreation centers, and restaurants. This area was chosen for our case study because of the large concentration of elderly citizens, which presented a logistically feasible way to contact and seek volunteers for participation in focus groups and interviews.

The study site was also chosen because of a very active presence from Seniors vs Crime (SvC). SvC is a primarily volunteer-based organization that is affiliated with the Florida Attorney General's Office. The organization employs one executive director, five region directors, and the remaining staff members are volunteers. A majority of the volunteers are over the age of 50 and act as advocates and mediators with the mission of helping to protect elders from consumer fraud and helping individuals recoup losses from financial exploitation or fraud incidents. SvC is well known, trusted, and respected among residents of the retirement community, which was beneficial for our study because SvC staff were used as gate-keepers and provided the research team with legitimacy and access to the retirement community.

As in our study, most case study research does not begin with hypotheses, but rather general research questions with the focus upon discovery rather than validation/rejection of hypotheses. The research questions guiding our study were: (1) What are the most common types of elder financial exploitation? (2) What factors influence the reporting decisions victims? (3) What is the role of age-graded life events on the risk of elder financial exploitation? (4) What are the consequences of elder financial exploitation on the quality of life, physical health, and emotional health of victims? (5) What are protective factors against elder financial exploitation?

The study was completed between February 2015 and June 2016 and included the collection and analysis of data from a variety of sources. The study's design used a mixed methods approach that included: (1) an extensive review of the literature, (2) the collection of national survey data on elder financial exploitation and identify theft from the National Crime Victimization Survey-Identity Theft Supplement (NCVS-ITS), and the National Public Survey on White Collar Crime, (3) town hall meetings, (4) the collection of incident data from SvC and the local sheriff's office, and (5) focus groups with SvC volunteers and residents, and (6) individual interviews with residents.

The review of literature served several purposes. First, it was used to review the prevalence of elder exploitation, identify the various definitions and measures used by the prior studies, and develop a preliminary typology of elder exploitation that considers the type of exploitation, perpetrator characteristics, and the risk factors associated with the victims. Finally, the review of prior studies was used to inform the development of the focus group and interview questions.

The National White Collar Crime Center provided data from the National Public Survey on White Collar Crime for 2010. The analysis of the data was limited to those 55 and over to serve as a comparison and to examine whether the findings in the retirement community were similar to those that were observed across the nation. Specifically, the analysis was intended to identify the most common forms of exploitation and assess whether the prevalence and types of elder financial exploitation in the retirement community were similar to those seen nationally. Other national victimization data came from the 2012 NCVS-ITS, which was collected by the National Institute of Justice. The NCVS-ITS was exploratory and focused on the circumstances surrounding financial exploitation including physical and mental health problems suffered as a result of victimization. These national data were used to compare results with the case study findings.

SvC provided local data on the cases that were reported to their organization by residents from 2003 to 2015. We worked closely with SvC representatives to better understand their data system and gain greater insight into the data. The analysis included the identification of the most common forms of financial exploitation, the amount of money lost and recovered, and characteristics of the perpetrators. We also collected data from the local county sheriff's office to complement the SvC data. These two sources were combined to provide a more complete picture of elder financial exploitation in the retirement community. These data provided insight into the extent of exploitation within the retirement community and helped to inform the focus groups and interviews.

The first step in the process of recruiting volunteers to participate in focus groups and interviews was to host two town hall meetings in the retirement community. Participants were recruited through newspaper advertisements and information about the study left at the SvC offices. The town hall presentations were given in November 2015 at two local locations on consecutive days. The presentations included a description of the study, an introduction of the research team, a summary of prior research, and preliminary findings from the analyses of the national, SvC, and sheriff data. The meetings lasted for approximately two hours. In order to assist the hearing impaired, a sign language translator was used during one of the meetings. Attendees were asked to answer a 10 question survey, and provide contact information if they wished to participate in later focus groups or interviews.

An important objective of the town hall meetings was to familiarize residents with the research team members, the goals, and the intentions of the research project. Because we sought to obtain personal and potentially embarrassing information from elderly residents, we found it best to introduce the research team and study prior to asking for their participation. We received positive feedback from many of the individuals who participated in the study regarding the town-hall meetings. The residents indicated they believed that they could trust the research team and felt more comfortable discussing important and personal information after meeting us at the town hall meetings and learning more about the study, the intentions of the researchers, and elder financial exploitation in general.

Following the town hall meetings, in February 2016, focus groups were conducted with SvC staff and retirement community residents. The focus groups centered on six topics: financial exploitation incidents, financial exploitation methods and perpetrators, risk and protective factors, the role of financial planners/advisors, reporting behavior, and policy issues related to financial exploitation against the elderly citizens. In total, five focus groups were conducted. The focus group meetings were recorded and later transcribed.

Individual interviews were conducted either in-person at the local SvC office or the local public library. Where in-person interviews were not possible, interviews were conducted via telephone. Four members of the research team attended the first two interviews in order to identify the most successful strategies for the interviews. Following the initial interviews, two members of the research team, one interviewer and one note-taker, attended each interview. Each interview was recorded and later transcribed.

The data analysis portion of the project involved constant comparison between data, constructs, and prior literature. Researchers identified themes across the interviews in order to draw inferences about the relationships between various risk factors, protective factors, and elder financial exploitation. Through this process, we accumulated evidence from diverse sources which converged on a single-well defined construct and theory. This method of data collection was particularly useful for understanding why certain emergent relationships held together (Eisenhardt, 1989). Specifically, case study research often provides a good understanding of the dynamics underlying the relationship of why things are happening. The likelihood of generating a novel theory increases as the attempts to reconcile evidence across cases, types of data, different investigators, and existing literature. Through this research design, the theory emerged from the data itself rather than being led by pre-determined hypotheses and prior research.

SELECT FINDINGS FROM OUR MIXED METHODS APPROACH

The five research questions we addressed in our study are presented below with a brief summary overview of the corresponding findings. In addition, a discussion of how our findings can be situated within the available literature on elder financial exploitation is presented.

What are the Most Common Types of Elder Financial Exploitation?

The national survey data revealed that credit card theft, misrepresentation of the price of a product or service, and unnecessary repairs to one's home, vehicle, or appliances, were the most frequent forms of household victimization.

SvC data revealed that nearly three-fourths of complaints in the retirement community are filed against contractors and landscapers for issues such as incomplete work, unsatisfactory performance, and contract disputes. Identity theft, credit/debit card fraud, and check forgery were among the least-frequently reported incidents of exploitation to SvC and no cases of exploitation perpetrated by family members were reported to SvC. However, cases of exploitation perpetrated by family members did appear in several of the individual interviews that we conducted. This further illustrates that prevalence rates for elder financial exploitation depend greatly on the source of the data being analyzed.

As presented in the literature review, a reliable and comprehensive prevalence rate of elder financial exploitation is not currently available. Studies vary in their reporting of prevalence based upon the data used, definitions of exploitation employed, and the population surveyed. This is consistent with our findings across the four data sources that we examined; namely, national survey data, local law enforcement arrests rates, SvC case files, and interview responses from retirement community residents.

What Factors Influence the Reporting Decisions of Victims?

Exploring the reporting patterns and trends of elder financial exploitation is a critical component in attempting to establish prevalence rates. Specifically, it is important to develop an understanding of the types of exploitation that are most and least likely to be reported and if there are certain characteristics of individuals who may be more or less likely to report their experiences. Through our study, we found that individuals were much less likely to report targeting attempts than they were to report completed victimizations to law enforcement. However, interviewed participants did indicate that they would "probably" alert their friends and neighbors about various targeting attempts, especially telephone attempts and door-to-door sales.

When asked why individuals did not report their victimization experience, the most frequently cited reasons were that they did not know the appropriate agency or organization to report to and that if they did report, they did not believe that anything could or would be done. If victims did choose to report their victimization, they were most likely to report to the company that perpetrated the exploitation; most frequently this involved financial institutions, insurances companies, or home service repair/contracting companies and much less likely to law enforcement. Despite reporting, most indicated that they were unsuccessful at recovering money and victims tended to be frustrated and unhappy with the reporting process.

What is the Role of Age-graded Life Events on the Risk of Elder Financial Exploitation?

Significant life-altering events such as the death or incapacitation of a spouse due to illness (which frequently results in the other spouse become a caregiver), divorce, or serious health diagnoses were found to be major precursors for exploitation. In some cases, the victim required someone else to perform household, automobile, or other services because they were no longer able to do so due to illness or aging. Significant pain, injury, or a serious health diagnosis were noted as critical turning points that many respondents believed made them vulnerable to experiencing financial exploitation.

Moving to the retirement community also emerged as a salient age-graded life event that many respondents believed was predictive of an increased risk of experiencing financial exploitation. Specifically, the move resulted in a change to the social support networks of many respondents. Most reported living in their prior place of residence for over 10 years. In that time, they built substantial social networks including family, friends, doctors, and service providers. Smaller social networks coupled with the frequent financial exploitation targeting of the retirement community resulted in victimization for many of the residents we interviewed. A majority of residents reported that they felt rarely, if ever, targeted for financial exploitation in their prior home. However, since moving to the retirement community they were inundated with exploitation targeting attempts via telephone calls, postal mailing, advertisements in the newspapers, and requests to attend "free lunch" seminars. The "free lunch" seminars were typically hosted by doctors, financial planners, insurance salespeople, and travel agents seeking to sell "too good to be true" products or services involving pressure sale tactics or misleading advertisements. Moreover, little, if any, vetting or screening of presenters appears to be completed by the owners of the retirement community to determine the legitimacy of those hosting seminars.

The turning points listed above may be associated with financial exploitation in several ways, first, if the spouse who handled the financial decisions is no longer able to do so because of divorce, death, or a serious illness the other spouse may not know how to properly manage finances. Second, particular changing life events are likely to create a significant amount of distress and/or distraction leaving the individual vulnerable to financial exploitation because they are too busy dealing with bereavement, care giving, pain, or an illness to think about possible exploitation. Third, the turning points may result in an individual being physically or mentally unable to handle daily housework or decisions that they were previously able to do. For example, chronic pain, injuries, or serious illnesses likely limit the amount of housework an individual is able to do making it necessary to hire an outsider. Fourth, changing social support networks as a result of the aging process (i.e., individuals passing away, illness, or relocation) resulted in many respondents being without people they could trust. The identification of these turning points helped to develop a theory of victimization using tenants from life course theory (Brancale, 2017).

What are the Consequences of Elder Financial Exploitation on the Quality of Life, Physical Health, and Emotional Health of Victims?

Regardless of the type of exploitation experienced or the amount of money lost, a common theme that emerged was that exploitation had profound impacts on the victims' quality of life, physical health, emotional health and self-concept, financial decisions, and interactions with others. As a result of being defrauded, respondents indicated that they lost trust in strangers, service providers, financial planners, and medical doctors. A majority of victims reported feelings of lasting "anger," "frustration," and "disgust," others indicated that they are "constantly stressed out," "nervous," "sleep deprived," and feel as though they have "lost control" of their finances and livelihoods. Individuals who experienced multiple victimizations were more likely to report that they feel "lost," "hopeless," and "helpless" in all aspects of their life, from managing their finances to their interactions with others.

What are Protective Factors Against Elder Financial Exploitation?

Education was the most commonly recommended means of prevention. Residents repeatedly said they needed more information and education on financial exploitation scams occurring in their neighborhood, suggestions on who to report to, and options for recovering any money lost. Large meetings providing a lot of information in a short amount of time were thought to be less effective than information printed in the newspaper or through small group sessions. There are 2,400 clubs registered with the community's recreation department and many of them encourage guest speakers at their monthly meetings. Residents noted these meetings would be ideal for spreading important information on financial exploitation prevention strategies.

CONCLUSION

The available research on the growing social problem of elder financial exploitation is inconclusive. Therefore, to further explore the risk factors, protective factors, and consequences of this crime, traditional and solely quantitative criminological methods of inquiry were deemed to be inappropriate. In our study, we employed a mixed method case study that enabled us to gain an in-depth understanding through the constant comparison and analysis of data obtained from multiple sources. Through this process, we were able to develop a testable theory of elder financial exploitation using tenants from life course theory. The theory was developed using an interactive approach between the problem at hand and the research design. Using the theory developed from the data collection and analysis phase of the research project, we can now more responsibly develop hypotheses for quantitative validation and develop survey questions that are informed from evidence.

Case study and qualitative research are not the most common research designs employed in current criminological studies. This style of research has also suffered from largely unnecessary criticism because of the limited applicability to validation studies. However, Clark (1968, p. 167) noted that:

> the lack of immediate validation is defensible in that the ultimate validity of all research rests not in the tests of significance of the moment but upon whether the findings hang together with findings from other studies to produce a theoretical structure.

Further, Clark argued more generally that qualitative and context-driven research, or research-for-use and research-for-understanding, results in the most dependable analyses.

Four significant case study examples in criminology that can clearly show the relevance of Clark's arguments and illustrate the importance of mixed method research designs in advancing knowledge bases are Sykes' (1958) Society of Captives, Sudnow's (1965) Normal Crimes, Skolnick's (1966) Justice Without Trial, and Blomberg's (1977) Diversion and Accelerated Social Control. These four studies were aimed not at validation but discovery in areas where little was known and theory validation was not possible. Sykes found that prisons are not places of rehabilitation but rather are places of deprivation where survival becomes the inmate code. In his study, Sudnow concluded that courts do not operate under a due process model but rather a crime control model through the extensive plea-bargaining of "normal crimes." Skolnick found that police in the United States do not maintain order under the rule of law but rather provide order by administering justice without trial. In his study, Blomberg concluded that the use of diversion did not reduce the number of clients or scope of the juvenile justice system but rather resulted in an unintended expansion of the system, which "widened the net." All these case studies resulted in the identification of outcomes that have since been validated.

Scientific advancement is often incremental and should not be rushed by the desire to prematurely conduct large-scale statistical analyses. The overarching goal of scientific advancement should be knowledge building and oftentimes that begins with case studies and qualitative analyses that provide a foundation for additional empirical studies. Crime, victimization, and criminal justice system responses are complex phenomena and so very often no single research method will suffice in providing a complete understanding. Our qualitative case study of elder financial exploitation has shed light on a growing social problem in the United States and has contributed to the development of a theory with testable hypotheses for addressing this issue, which we are currently pursuing.

Examples of other criminological areas that could benefit from mixed method research designs include topics in which specific decision-making mechanisms, motivations, and individual thought processes are in question. For example, in the study of desistance, quantitative datasets are available and can help identify if and when a person stops offending. However, the datasets are unable to provide insight into the turning points and reasons why offending behavior stops. Namely, what were the individual internal cognitive processes that led people away from crime? These factors are difficult to capture through the use of survey questions. Another area that would benefit from increased mixed methods research is the impact of parental incarceration on children. A significant gap in this line of research is the limited amount of available information on the children's own perspectives about the impact their parents' incarceration has had on their lives and development. Further, the relationship dynamics is associated with cases of inter-personal violence and domestic violence. Quantitative datasets are available that provide information on the specific offense, relationship between the victim and offender, and criminal justice system response. However, missing from these datasets are the context and motivations surrounding the behaviors. Other areas that would benefit from mixed methods research involve understanding the motivations of judges' pretrial release and sentencing decisions, the reporting decisions of victims, consequences of victimization, and victimization patterns among difficult to reach populations, such as the elderly citizens who live in assisted living facilities and the homeless people. Ultimately, criminological researchers need to tailor their research methodology to the problem at hand and what is known and not known about the problem rather than embracing a particular research methodology. Such research methodology that is grounded in the research problem is fundamental to discovery and eventual validation.

REFERENCES

AARP. (1996). *Telemarketing fraud and older Americans: An AARP survey*. Washington, DC: AARP.

AARP. (1999). *Princeton survey research associates, consumer behavior, experiences, and attitudes: A comparison by age groups*. Princeton, NJ: AARP.

AARP. (2011). *AARP foundation national fraud victim study*. Washington, DC.

AARP Foundation. (2003). *Off the hook: Reducing participation in telemarketing fraud*. Washington, DC.

Acierno, R., Hernandez-Tejada, M., Muzzy, W., & Steve, K. (2009). *The national elder mistreatment study*. Washington, DC: U.S. Department of Justice.

Alves, L., & Wilson, S. (2008). The effects of loneliness on telemarketing fraud vulnerability among older adults. *Journal of Elder Abuse & Neglect*, *20*(1), 63–85.

Anderson, K. (2007). *Consumer fraud in the united states: The second FTC survey*. Washington, DC: Federal Trade Commission.

Anderson, K. (2010). *Consumer fraud in the united states: The third FTC survey*. Washington, DC: Federal Trade Commission.

Blomberg, T. (1977). Diversion and accelerated social control. *Journal of Criminal Law and Criminology*, *68*(2), 274–282.

Brancale, J. (2017). *Exploring the influence of life course turning points on elder financial exploitation*. Unpublished doctoral dissertation. Florida State University, Tallahassee, FL.

Clark, B. (1968). *Adult education in transition: A study of institutional insecurity*. Berkeley, CA: University of California Press.

Cousin, G. (2005). Case study research. *Journal of Geography in Higher Education*, *29*(3), 421–427.

Curtis, L. (2006). Partnering with faith communities to provide elder fraud prevention, intervention, and victim services. *OVC Bulletin*, Office of Victims of Crime, Washington, DC. Retrieved from https://www.ovc.gov/publications/bulletins/elderfraud_case/welcome.html

Eisenhardt, K. (1989). Building theories from case study research. *Academy of Management Review*, *14*(4), 532–550.

Flyvbjerg, B. (2006). Five misunderstandings about case-study research. *Qualitative Inquiry*, *12*(2), 219–245.

Glaser, B., & Strauss, A. (1967). *The discovery of grounded theory: Strategies of qualitative research*. London: Wiedenfeld and Nicholson.

Hafemeister, T. (2003). Financial abuse of the elderly in domestic settings. In R. Bonnie & R. Wallace (Eds.), *Elder mistreatment: Abuse, neglect, and exploitation in an aging America* (pp. 382–445). Washington, DC: The National Academies Press.

Holtfreter, K., Reisig, M., Mears, D., & Wolfe, S. (2014). *Financial exploitation of the elderly in a consumer context*. Washington, DC: U.S. Department of Justice.

Johnson, K. (2002). *Financial crimes against the elderly*. Problem-oriented Guides for Police, No. 20. Washington, DC: U.S. Department of Justice.

Muscat, G., Graycar, A., & James, M. (2002). *Older people and consumer fraud*. Trends and Issues in Crime and Criminal Justice, No. 220. Canberra: Australian Institute of Criminology.

National Adult Protective Services Association. (2016). *Elder financial exploitation*. Retrieved from http://www.napsa-now.org/policy-advocacy/exploitation/

National Council on Aging. (2017). *Top 10 financial scams targeting seniors.* Retrieved from https://www.ncoa.org/economic-security/money-management/scams-security/top-10-scamstargeting-seniors/

Pak, K., & Shadel, D. (2005). *The psychology of consumer fraud.* Unpublished doctoral dissertation. Tilburg University, Tilburg, Netherlands.

Policastro, C., & Payne, B. (2015). Can you hear me now? Telemarketing fraud victimization and lifestyles. *American Journal of Criminal Justice*, *40*, 620–638.

Rabiner, D., Brown D., & O'Keeffe, J. (2004). Financial exploitation of older persons: Policy issues and recommendations for addressing them. *Journal of Elder Abuse & Neglect*, *16*(1), 65–84.

Ragin, C., & Becker, H. (1992). *What is a case? Exploring the foundations of social inquiry*. Cambridge: Cambridge University Press.

Skolnick, J. (1966). *Justice without trial: Law enforcement in democratic society*. New York, NY: John Wiley & Sons.

Sudnow, D. (1965). Normal crimes: Sociological features of the penal code in the public defender office. *Social Problems*, *12*(3), 255–276.

Sykes, G. (1958). *The society of captives: A study of a maximum security prison*. Princeton, NJ: Princeton University Press.

Titus, R., Heinzelmann, F., & Boyle J. (1995). Victimizations of persons by fraud. *Crime & Delinquency*, *41*(1), 54–72.

True Link. (2015). *The true link report on elder financial abuse*. Retrieved from https://truelink-wordpress-assets.s3.amazonaws.com/wp-content/uploads/True-Link-Report-OnElder-Financial-Abuse-012815.pdf

CHAPTER 7

PERCEPTIONS OF SCHOOL SAFETY IN THE AFTERMATH OF A SHOOTING: CHALLENGE TO INTERNAL VALIDITY?

Jennifer O'Neill, Timothy McCuddy and Finn-Aage Esbensen

ABSTRACT

Purpose – *In the midst of the second wave of data collection for a Comprehensive School Safety Initiative (CSSI) research project, a mass shooting occurred at Marjory Stoneman Douglas High School in Parkland, Florida. This tragic incident provoked responses across the United States, including intense political discourse, organized student protests, and active shooter drills. In order to assess the potential influence of a major threat to school safety on the perceptions of adolescents, this chapter analyzes the survey responses of middle and high school students in St. Louis County.*

Methodology/approach – *Approximately one-third of the sample was surveyed prior to the shooting and the remaining students completed surveys within three months after the shooting. The authors examines the potential influence of the shooting on students' reports on a number of school safety issues, including fear and perceived risk of victimization, likelihood of reporting guns on campus, and engaging in avoidance behaviors.*

Findings – *Results indicate that the shooting significantly influenced students' perceptions of school disorder and likelihood of reporting a weapon at school,*

Methods of Criminology and Criminal Justice Research
Sociology of Crime, Law and Deviance, Volume 24, 115–132

ISSN: 1521-6136/doi:10.1108/S1521-613620190000024011

especially in white, less disadvantaged schools. The results also reflect meaningful effects based on the timing of data collection post-shooting, with many of the significant changes appearing within three weeks after February 14, 2018.

Originality/value – *This study explores how external events may influence student perceptions of school safety. Moreover, this study offers a methodological contribution by demonstrating an assessment of the Parkland shooting as a potential threat to internal validity.*

Keywords: History effect; school shooting; perceptions of school safety; internal validity; fear of crime; indirect victimization

INTRODUCTION

School safety research and programing have gained increased attention following highly publicized mass shootings on school properties. In response to the 2012 shooting at Sandy Hook Elementary School, the US Congress allocated approximately $250 million over the course of four years to the National Institution of Justice to oversee the Comprehensive School Safety Initiative (CSSI). This initiative aims to examine the causes and consequences of school violence and evaluate or implement strategies and programs to enhance school safety. In the midst of one CSSI project's data collection, what has been characterized as the "deadliest school shooting since Sandy Hook" occurred at Marjory Stoneman Douglas High School in Parkland, Florida (Sanchez, 2018). The shooting resulted in 17 deaths, a surge of media coverage, re-ignition of the political debate over gun policies and school security measures, and a student-led movement for national gun control (Bromwich, 2018; Siegel, 2018). Research continually documents that fatalities in schools, especially casualties at the level of the Parkland shooting, are statistically rare (Dinkes, Cataldi, Kena, & Baum, 2006). Fox and Fridel (2019, p. 8) note, "Without minimizing the pain and anguish resulting from the shootings," national responses to shootings may be disproportionate considering they are statistically rare. Of the more than 50 million students enrolled in schools in the five years preceding the Parkland shooting, 13 were shot and killed, thus indicating that the risk of victimization in a school shooting is relatively low. That said, responses to these rare shootings in schools and broader society ensure students are made aware of the threat of these violent events, and there is substantial evidence that indirect exposure to violent events can influence fear and broader perceptions of the environment (see Skogan & Maxfield, 1981; Smolej & Kivivuori, 2006; Warr, 2000).

Media attention to events such as school shootings may increase individuals' fear, or draw attention to problems in schools, making issues more salient to even those individuals removed from the specific event. Due to these potential effects, it is worthwhile to explore how the Parkland shooting may influence student perceptions. Moreover, because the shooting occurred during the second wave of an ongoing school safety study (one in which the same students are followed for three years), the incident could pose a threat to the internal validity of the study (e.g., Campbell & Stanley, 1963). Any potential history effects should be explored to assess if the shooting exerts external influence on changes in students' fear and other perceptions of school safety. The current study examines the timing of the Parkland shooting in relation to middle and high school students' self-reports of fear, perceived risk, school avoidance behaviors, and specific perceptions related to guns in schools. The analyses contribute to our understanding of how external events influence student perceptions. Additionally, this study offers a methodological contribution by demonstrating an assessment of the Parkland shooting as a potential threat to the internal validity of the University of Missouri – St. Louis Comprehensive School Safety Initiative (UMSL CSSI) project, focusing on the extent to which the shooting influenced changes in perceptions from 2017 to 2018.

UMSL CSSI is a school-based survey research project examining a variety of factors related to school safety including school climate, school and neighborhood disorder, fear of victimization, perceptions of risk, experiences with offending, and experiences with victimization. The research design includes three waves of data collection and began in January 2017 with surveys of 1,840 7th grade and 1,800 8th grade students (3,640 total – 99.4% of the active consent sample). These two cohorts (i.e., the same students) were administered the survey again a year later, from January through May of 2018 (N=3,165). Due to the timeline of data collection, the Parkland shooting on February 14, 2018 created conditions for a "natural experiment": approximately one-third of the wave two sample completed the survey prior to the shooting, and the other two-thirds completed the survey at varying time intervals following the shooting so that changes in responses could be observed pre- and post-event. Because wave one data includes responses from the same individuals, we can explore within individual changes in responses, and compare the changes of those who completed the wave two survey before the shooting to those who completed the survey after the shooting. Extant criminological literature suggests that exposure to the shooting could influence students' perceptions; therefore, the event should be assessed in order to examine the internal validity of the UMSL CSSI project and dutifully document history effects on meaningful outcomes.

This chapter addresses this threat to internal validity by first reviewing the literature on exposure to violence and fear, as well as research on the effects of mass shootings on individual perceptions of safety. Considering past findings, we hypothesize the potential effects of the shooting on student perceptions and empirically test for this threat to internal validity by examining changes in perceptions across waves. Results are interpreted within the context of established literature on the relationship between exposure to violence and perceptions of safety, as well as with a methodological focus on how the Parkland shooting influences UMSL CSSI.

LITERATURE REVIEW

The shooting at Marjory Stoneman Douglas High School in Parkland, Florida resulted in 17 deaths, including 14 students and 3 staff members, and had a substantive residual impact across the nation (Galea et al., 2018; Sanchez, 2018). Analyses of digital publications demonstrate that the shooting received more news coverage than other mass shootings, thus illustrating the highly public nature of the event (Siegel, 2018). The volume of news coverage, resulting discussion involving school safety, and specific student involvement in marches and protests (Bromwich, 2018) all suggest that the Parkland shooting could potentially impact the internal validity of the UMSL CSSI data through what Campbell and Stanley (1963) identified as a "history" effect. For a study to have internal validity the study design must rule out external influences (i.e., history effects) (Campbell & Stanley, 1963; Schutt, 2018). History effects occur when events outside the scope of the research project influence the outcomes of a study. They can be especially problematic in experimental studies where only one study group is affected or in longitudinal studies that seek to document changes over time (Campbell & Stanley, 1963). UMSL CSSI is a longitudinal project following cohorts of 7th and 8th grade students over three years. The panel design provides the opportunity to conduct analyses with the necessary temporal ordering for causal claims, but the Parkland shooting may result in external influence on students' survey reports. Therefore, we review relevant literature to guide our investigation of the Parkland shooting and its potential effect on the internal validity of the UMSL CSSI project.

There are two related relationships supported in criminological literature that suggest the Parkland shooting might influence student perceptions. First, the literature on fear of crime finds that indirect victimization can increase fear of violence, safety-related perceptions, and behavior. Second, intense media coverage of violent events can increase individuals' fear of crime, as well as perceived risk of victimization. Considering these relationships, the Parkland shooting has specific characteristics that could increase student fear and have negative consequences for perceptions of the school environment.

Violence and Fear

Garofalo (1981) critically explores fear of crime and explains that individuals are exposed to a variety of sources regarding crime or violence – including their own direct experiences. He creates a model of fear of crime that identifies how processing information about violence can inform responses to this information. To simplify, Garofalo (1981) argues that one's social position determines exposure to information about violence and how s/he perceives this information. An individual considers this information in their perceptions of risk (i.e., how vulnerable they feel to certain types of crime) and their fear. Considering this model, individuals may experience increases in fear and perceived risk, and decreases in feelings of safety after hearing about incidents of violence involving people they know or occurring in their neighborhood (see Ferraro, 1995; Skogan & Maxfield, 1981). Melde and Esbensen (2009, p. 517) proposed an extension of earlier fear models by incorporating risky lifestyle and victimization as predictors of fear of crime. They found that although victimization was greater among those involved in a delinquent lifestyle, these youth reported experiencing less fear of victimization relative to those not involved in delinquent lifestyles. Given the limited research explaining fear of crime through vicarious exposure, we hope our research may inform such theoretical advancement.

Media Effects

Media coverage plays an important role in indirect victimization by increasing individuals' exposure to information about violence and focusing on particularly extreme incidents (Warr, 2000). Various media types (e.g., televised news, radio, and newspaper) have been studied in order to determine how coverage of violent incidents influences viewers/readers. Evidence suggests that some individuals experience increases in fear and perceptions of risk after being exposed to news accounts of violence (Chiricos, Eschols, & Gertz, 1997; Smolej & Kivivuori, 2006).

The potential media effects on perceptions of crime may be more salient among the emerging generation of adolescents who grew up with the ubiquity of social media and electronic devices (Palfrey & Gasser, 2008). According to a national study, around 95% of adolescents have access to smartphones (PEW Research Center, 2018) and youth may be more receptive of news made available through social media (Madden, Lenhart, & Fontaine, 2017). In fact, prior studies have found social media can more strongly influence perceptions of crime relative to television-based media. For example, Jones (2017) found that users of social media perceived crime as occurring more frequently compared to those who watched the news on television. Moreover, Intravia, Wolff, Paez, and Gibbs (2017) found that time spent on social media was associated with increased fear of crime, and these effects were strongest among those who felt safe in their neighborhood. This latter finding is especially important given that the current study examines the notion that violence in Parkland, Florida may influence student perceptions in a study taking place in St. Louis, Missouri. It is reasonable to assume the majority (if not all) of the students in our sample were exposed to information about the shooting, and therefore may have experienced indirect victimization.

Shootings and Student Reactions

Within the broader focus of indirect victimization and fear of crime literature, there is a limited amount of work specifically examining student reactions to school shootings. However, due to the timing of national data collection efforts, such as the School Crime Supplement to the National Crime Victimization Survey (NCVS-SCS), scholars have been able to examine student responses pre- and post-school shootings that garnered national attention. For example, the shooting at Columbine High School in 1999 took place during the NCVS-SCS, which uses a rotating panel design where seven groups are each surveyed once a month. Around two-thirds of the sample was surveyed prior to the shooting and the remaining third were surveyed after. Other studies utilize college samples that were surveyed prior to the Virginia Tech shooting in 2007, such as the work by Kaminski, Koons-Witt, Thompson, and Weiss (2010). In this study, students were surveyed about their fear of crime in March of 2007 with two follow-up surveys taking place later that year. While the first example more closely aligns with the natural experiment that took place within the UMSL CSSI, the latter represents a guided effort to assess changes in the perception of fear.

The findings of this body of research are mixed, with most evidence suggesting influence on perceptions rather than actual behaviors. Some studies document small increases in fear of victimization following the shootings at Columbine (Addington, 2003; Brener, Simon, Anderson, Barrios, & Small, 2002; Stretesky & Hogan, 2001), Northern Illinois University, and Virginia Tech (Kaminski et al., 2010). Brener et al. (2002) also find an increase in students' reports that they avoid school because they feel unsafe after the Columbine shooting, although no change in avoidance behaviors is documented in similar research (Addington, 2003). This prior research provides some provisional indication that the Parkland shooting may influence student outcomes related to fear, feelings of safety, and, among other behaviors, school attendance.

Characteristics of Parkland

In consideration of the Parkland shooting's potential to pose a threat to the internal validity of the UMSL CSSI study, it is important to understand the specific characteristics of the event that could influence student perceptions of safety. The prior literature on fear and indirect victimization suggests that certain aspects of the shooting may affect students in the UMSL CSSI sample. Broadly speaking, a highly publicized event in which a shooter kills 17 students and staff members in a school has the potential to affect the way students think about their school. Furthermore, the literature suggests that an important facet of individuals' reactions to violence involves perceived social distance between the individual and the victims (Chiricos et al., 1997; Skogan & Maxfield, 1981). When individuals feel an affinity with victims, they are more likely to experience increases in fear of victimization, perceived risk, or other effects. For example, white women watching news accounts regarding the violent victimization of white women are more likely to experience effects of this exposure than individuals who do not share demographic characteristics with victims (Chiricos et al., 1997). Responses to the Parkland shooting involved students across the nation in ways that could decrease UMSL CSSI respondents' perceived social distance between themselves and the victims. The students at Marjory Stoneman Douglas High School have been deeply involved in responses to the shooting in terms of social activism and engaging with the media. The students are adept social media users and continuously share information about their experiences with broad audiences (Bromwich, 2018). They have also helped organize national protests such as the National School Walkout on March 14, 2018 (Yee & Blinder, 2018) and the March for Our Lives on March 24, 2018 (Sanchez, 2018). These events involved students across the nation and potentially increased affinity between UMSL CSSI respondents and the victims, consequently allowing the shooting to play a larger role in their considerations of school safety.

Considering the Parkland shooting in the context of broader literature constitutes an important first step in exploring the event as a challenge to the internal validity of the UMSL CSSI study. Past research identifies outcomes potentially affected by the shooting: namely, student fear of victimization, perceptions of risk, avoidance behaviors, and general ideas of safety in the school environment. Moving forward with research on perceptions of school safety requires identifying challenges such as history effects to ensure that sound methods inform any conclusions. The following sections describe a series of steps taken to assess potential effects of the Parkland shooting on the internal validity of the study.

DATA AND METHODS

The UMSL CSSI project is designed to investigate the causes and consequences of school violence using a three-wave longitudinal panel design. In 2016, six districts in St. Louis County agreed to participate in the study – including 12 middle schools. There were approximately 4,700 7th and 8th grade students enrolled in the schools, parental consent was obtained from 3,663 (78%) and of these, 3,640 (99.4%) students were surveyed at wave one. The second wave of data collection occurred in spring of 2018, during which 3,165 (86.4% of active consent sample) students were retained and were now in 8th and 9th grades. Table 1 presents descriptive statistics for the two waves of data. It is important to note that all of the 9th grade students had transitioned from middle to high school.

The racial distribution of study participants should be considered within the context of St. Louis County as race becomes relevant in subsequent analyses assessing the influence of the Parkland shooting. In wave two, 40% of surveyed students are black, 40% are white, and 20% are some other race. This even representation of black and white students corresponds to differences in the sampled

Table 1. Sample Characteristics.

	Wave One (*N*=3,640), %	Wave Two (*N*=3,165), %
Sex		
Male	47	46
Female	53	54
Race/ethnicity		
White	38	40
Black	42	40
Other	20	20
Age		
12 and younger	20	0
13	48	20
14	30	48
15 and older	2	32
Grade level		
7th	51	–
8th	49	52
9th	–	48

schools. Half of the participating schools are located in what is called North County while the other half are in South County. St. Louis County is considerably segregated by race and socioeconomic disadvantage, so that North County is majority black and includes areas with higher concentrated disadvantage. Conversely, South County has a majority white population with lower levels of disadvantage. These sample characteristics inform steps taken during analyses, so that changes in respondent outcomes can be observed while acknowledging school and student characteristics.

Measures

The following analyses focus on seven measures capturing self-reported perceptions and behaviors that may have been influenced by the Parkland shooting. *School disorder* consists of a six-item scale ($\alpha = 0.80$) that asks students "how much of a problem each of the following is in your school?" Specific items include kids bullying or teasing other children, students beating up or threatening other students, kids of different racial or cultural groups not getting along with each other, students bringing guns to school, having things stolen at school, and gangs in your school. Responses range from 1 to 3 and capture if respondents felt these issues were not a problem, somewhat of a problem, or a big problem. To capture attitudes specific to guns, the "bringing guns to school" item is also examined independent of the larger scale.

Perceived risk comprises three items ($\alpha = 0.70$) that asks students "how likely do you think it is that the following things will happen to you?" The individual items refer to having things stolen at school, being attacked or threatened at school, and being bullied at school. Response categories range from "1. Not at all likely" to "5. Very likely." *Fear* refers to the same three items ($\alpha = 0.76$) but asks respondents "how afraid are you of the following things happening to you?" with responses ranging from "1. Not at all afraid" to "5. Very Afraid." Given the focus of this inquiry, responses to the single items assessing risk and fear of attack were also examined. A single item – *Can't concentrate* – captures students' feelings of not being safe at school (i.e., "I sometimes can't concentrate at school because I just don't feel safe"). Response categories ranged from "1. Strongly disagree" to "5. Strongly agree."

Two single-item measures assess the potential effect of the Parkland shooting on behavioral outcomes. *School avoidance* refers to how often the student did not attend school "because you were afraid that someone might harm you or be mean to you." Response categories include "1. Never 2. Rarely 3. Sometimes 4. Often." *Gun reporting* measures students' likelihood of reporting someone bringing a gun to school. Response categories again ranged from "1. Not at all likely" to "5. Very likely."

The second wave of surveys was administered to 979 students prior to the shooting on February 14, 2018, and the remaining 2,186 surveys were collected in the weeks following. After cases with missing data on relevant variables were excluded (158), the analytical sample includes data from 3,007 students – 947 pre-Parkland and 2,060 post-Parkland. A series of comparisons between pre- and post-Parkland samples demonstrate how respondents' perceptions changed following the shooting. Change scores were calculated by subtracting individual students' wave one scores from their wave two scores, resulting in values that indicate changes in perceptions from wave one to wave two. Analysis of change scores show how changes between waves differ based on whether the students' wave two responses were collected before or after the Parkland shooting.

RESULTS

Cross-sectional Comparison in Wave Two

Table 2 presents a cross-sectional comparison of the data pre- and post-Parkland shooting for sample characteristics and outcome measures. Significant differences between pre- and post-shooting are found for: perceptions of school disorder, kids bringing guns to school, avoiding school, reporting guns, and not being able to concentrate due to feeling unsafe. These differences, however, should be interpreted with caution because there are significant differences between the pre- and post-samples. The post-shooting sample includes fewer white students and subsequently more black students, compared to the pre-shooting sample. This differential representation is apparent in the North and South County measures as well; the average number of North County students is significantly higher post-shooting and the average number of South County students is significantly lower. In addition, the post-shooting sample is slightly older. The changes in demographic characteristics could account for the changes in student outcomes; therefore, subsequent analyses must take racial and age differences into account.

Differences in Change Scores Pre- and Post-Parkland

The next progression in exploring student responses is to compare change scores in outcomes based on timing of wave two data collection. Change scores provide more information about the potential influence of the shooting by allowing students' wave one responses to act as a control on their wave two outcomes. Rather than simply assessing if, for instance, average fear values are greater in wave two,

Table 2. Cross-sectional Sample Characteristics Pre- and Post-parkland Shooting (N=3,007).

	Full Sample (n=3,007)	Pre-shooting (n=947)	Post-shooting (n=2,060)
Perceived school disorder	1.64	1.57	1.67*
Kids bringing guns	1.26	1.17	1.30*
Fear of school victimization	1.82	1.79	1.83
Risk of school victimization	1.92	1.90	1.93
Avoid going to school	24%	21%	25%*
Can't concentrate because unsafe	1.92	1.79	1.98*

Notes: A total of 158 respondents did not provide valid information on all items and are excluded.
* Refers to a mean value significantly different than the referent group at $p < 0.05$.

change scores represent how an *individual's* fear changed from wave one to wave two. A positive change score indicates that scores increased in wave two, while negative scores reflect a decrease. These changes are compared between those who were surveyed before Parkland in the second wave to those surveyed after Parkland to determine whether timing of wave two data collection (i.e., exposure to Parkland) influences change scores. Table 3 reports change scores for the full pre- and post-shooting samples, as well as change scores for mutually exclusive groups surveyed one week through six weeks after the shooting.

Beginning with the pre- and post-Parkland comparisons, the change scores reflect some meaningful findings regarding perceptions of school disorder, fear of being attacked or threatened with a weapon, likelihood of reporting a gun, and issues concentrating due to feeling unsafe. Students' perceptions of disorder generally decrease from wave one to wave two; however, they decrease significantly *less* if the students' wave two surveys were collected after they were exposed to Parkland. This suggests that those students surveyed after the Parkland shooting are reporting more disorder, or safety threats, in their school than those surveyed prior to the shooting. This relationship is especially pronounced when examining the "Kids bringing guns to school" item independently.

A similar pattern occurs for students' fear of being attacked or threatened at school. Fear generally decreases in the second wave, but decreases less for those surveyed after Parkland at a marginally significant level. There are also marginally significant differences in the pre- and post-Parkland change scores for problems concentrating due to feeling unsafe, with those surveyed post-Parkland reporting increased scores in wave two compared to wave one, and those surveyed pre-Parkland reporting decreased scores. Lastly, the differences in change scores reflect an unexpected pattern concerning students' likelihood for reporting a gun on campus. Students indicated a reduced likelihood for reporting someone bringing a gun to school if they were surveyed after the Parkland shooting, indicating that students are generally less likely to report guns in wave two and that exposure to Parkland decreases reporting likelihood even more. Interestingly, these results suggest that the shooting does not influence students' perceptions of risk of victimization or avoidance behaviors.

These findings garner some support for Parkland's observable influence on student outcomes, but it is also worth exploring the temporal nature of effects in order to understand when the influence appears, and if it diminishes over time. Very little research documents the duration of fear or other outcomes following influential violent events (Warr, 2000). The few studies investigating the influence of shootings on student perceptions vary in timing of data collection so that it is difficult to draw conclusions regarding when students experience effects and for how long. There is some evidence, however, of decayed effects. For instance, Kaminski et al. (2010) find a decay in increased fear several weeks after the Virginia Tech shooting. Recognizing these patterns allows for greater understanding of how the Parkland shooting posed external influence on student outcomes; therefore, we attempt to document timing by dividing the post-shooting sample into the seven mutually exclusive groups presented in Table 3. The first group encompasses all students surveyed in the seven days following the

Table 3. Change Scores Between Wave Two and Wave One.

	Full Sample (n=3,007)	Pre-shooting (n=947)	Post-shooting (n=2,060)	Post-shooting Samples						
				1 week (n=206)	2 weeks (n=521)	3 weeks (n=319)	4 weeks (n=405)	5 weeks (n=107)	6 weeks (n=262)	>6 weeks (n=240)
Perceived school disorder (1–3)	−0.057	−0.102	−0.036*	−0.082	0.002*	0.129*	−0.051†	−0.116	−0.140	−0.124
Kids bringing guns (1–3)	−0.031	−0.091	−0.004*	−0.078	0.006*	0.139*	0.008*	−0.160	0.004	−0.111
Fear of school victimization (1–5)	−0.107	−0.117	−0.102	−0.126	−0.042	0.098*	−0.094	−0.135	−0.364*	−0.193
Attacked/threatened (1–5)	−0.143	−0.199	−0.117†	−0.141	−0.023†	0.092*	−0.052*	−0.142	−0.502*	−0.261
Risk of school victimization (1–5)	−0.115	−0.114	−0.116	−0.133	−0.065	−0.025	−0.115	−0.025	−0.245†	−0.238†
Attacked/threatened (1–5)	−0.094	−0.130	−0.078	−0.054	−0.031†	−0.016	−0.056	0.047	−0.197	−0.244
Avoid going to school										
Any avoidance (0–1)	0.007	−0.005	0.013	0.000	0.010	0.032	0.030	0.085†	−0.035	−0.004
Sometimes/often avoid (0–1)	0	−0.009	0.004	0.024	−0.008	0.013	0.005	0.019	0.000	−0.004
Report gun at school (1–5)	−0.198	0.006	−0.292*	−0.180	−0.118	−0.297*	−0.267*	−0.264†	−0.588*	−0.494*
Can't concentrate b/c unsafe (1–5)	0.045	−0.012	0.071†	0.000	0.101†	0.115†	0.120*	0.231*	−0.051	−0.013

Notes: A total of 158 respondents did not provide valid information on all items and are excluded.
Change score calculated by subtracting wave one from wave two, so positive values indicate a higher value at wave two.
*Refers to a mean value significantly different than the referent group (pre-shooting) at $p < 0.05$ and † refers to $p < 0.10$.

shooting, with subsequent groups capturing the weeks after. Change scores were examined for each group and compared to the pre-shooting sample's change scores. The week-to-week changes for the substantive significant effects are illustrated in Fig. 1.

Plotting the change scores over time identifies some meaningful patterns in perceptions of school disorder and kids bringing guns to school. As mentioned previously, students generally perceive less disorder in wave two than wave one, indicated by the line's starting position below zero. This decrease is reduced in the first week after the shooting, then change scores indicate that students' perceived disorder increases significantly in weeks two and three. The kids bringing guns to school item follows this pattern. Both measures indicate some evidence of a diminishing Parkland influence, with change scores falling below zero five weeks after the shooting. This suggests that the events of Parkland affected the way that students perceive their environment, potentially leading them to take greater notice of safety threats or characterize school issues as a greater problem than they had previously. It is important to highlight that the "Parkland effect" appears to be transient; that is, after peaking during week 3, there is a decaying effect that results in virtually no effect of those surveyed more than four weeks after the shooting. It is also worth noting that the shooting had no statistically significant effect on students' avoidance behaviors or their perceived risk of victimization. With respect to the greatest impact of the shooting being in the third week after the shooting, it is possible that the subsequent events and extensive media (both mass and social media) coverage confounded the effect of the shooting itself.

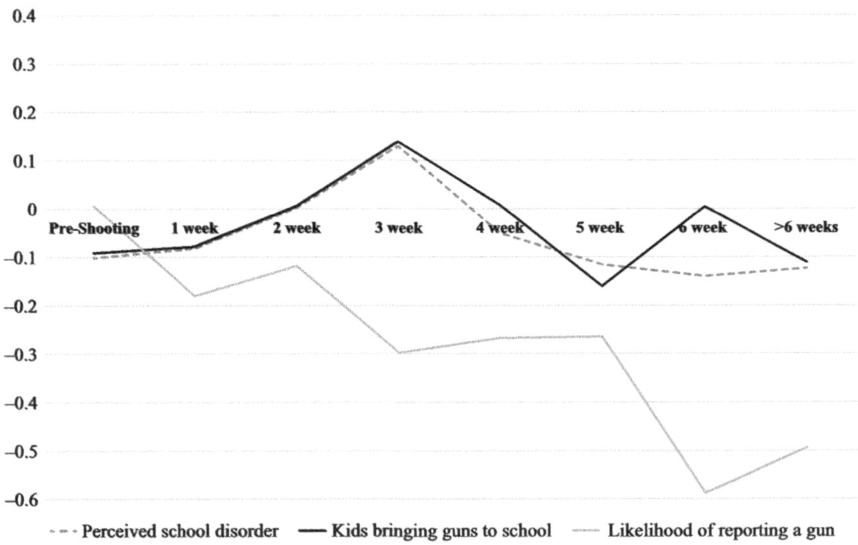

Fig. 1. Change Scores from Wave One to Wave Two: Items with Significant Differences Pre-shooting and Post-shooting.

The figure also illustrates the downward trend of students' likelihood of reporting a gun on campus. In the pre-shooting group, students' likelihood of reporting a gun in wave two is very similar to responses from wave one (i.e., the change score is close to zero). After the shooting, students' wave two responses indicate they are less likely to report a gun than they were in wave one with overall increasing magnitude in the six weeks following the shooting. It appears that students are less likely to report a gun on campus after they are exposed to information about the Parkland shooting. Speculating about this relationship, students may be more fearful of reporting a gun in the context of a recent school shooting because they fear retaliation. Conversely, students may personally know other students who carry guns on campus and feel protected against the threat of unknown shooters so that they are unlikely to report. Regardless of the explanation, this relationship demonstrates a substantive difference in student reports pre- and post-Parkland shooting.

Considering Sample Differences in Examination of Change Scores

The initial mapping of change scores provides some support that the Parkland shooting influenced student outcomes; however, as the cross-sectional wave two data describes, there were important demographic differences in the pre- and post-Parkland samples. These samples showed differential representation by North and South County students, and therefore differences in black and white populations. Evidence of changes in perceptions of school disorder and likelihood of reporting a gun may be driven by these sample differences, which would suggest that the external event did not disrupt student outcomes. To move forward in identifying potential influences of the Parkland shooting on student responses, the sample is partitioned into South County and North County groups. Then, change scores are again assessed according to the initial process: *t*-tests are conducted to examine significant differences between the pre- and post-shooting groups, and five groups are created according to the week of wave two data collection in order to assess patterns after the shooting. Fig. 2 displays significant differences in change-scores for the South County sample compared to the North County sample.

This comparison illustrates a stark difference in the influence of Parkland on South County student responses compared to those in North County. In the South County sample, change scores differ significantly pre- and post-Parkland for the majority of outcomes examined, including the three outcomes with demonstrated changes in the overall sample: perceptions of school disorder, kids bringing guns to school, and likelihood of reporting a gun. There are also significant changes in students' fear of victimization, and specifically fear of being attacked or threatened. The pattern for changes in fear resembles the patterns described previously: overall, students report less fear in wave two than in wave one, but this decrease lessens post-Parkland. The week-to-week trends illustrate that students' fear increases in wave two relative to wave one starting two weeks after the shooting, the change peaks in week three, and then diminishes. Additional significant differences in change scores are observed for perceptions of risk of being attacked or threatened and reports of not being able to concentrate due to feeling unsafe at

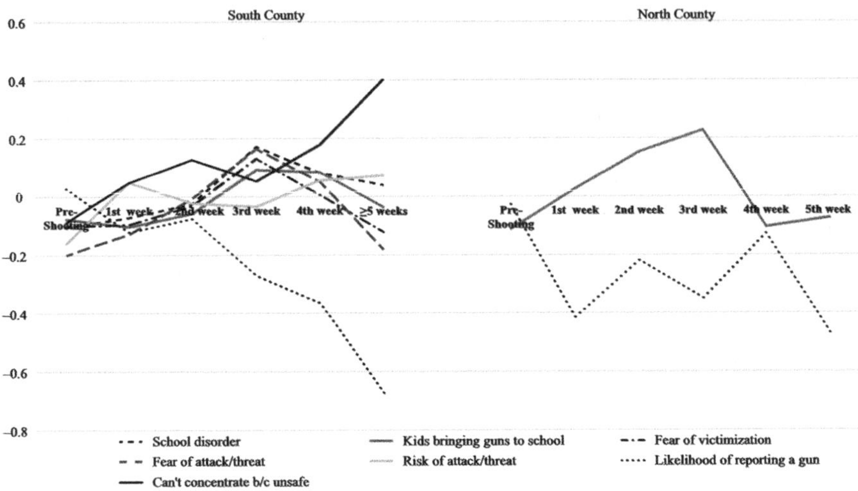

Fig. 2. Change Scores from Wave One to Wave Two by County,
Notes: Four observations were excluded in this figure due to students moving out of St. Louis County between waves. Contact author for a colored copy of figures.

school. Perceptions of risk increase in wave two in the first week after Parkland, and then return to levels slightly lower than wave one risk, before increasing again. Regarding the "Can't concentrate because unsafe" item, students report more agreement with this statement in the weeks following Parkland.

Interpretation of these patterns suggests that, in addition to recognizing greater disorder and being less likely to report guns at school following the shooting, South County students are experiencing effects on fear and risk after being exposed to the Parkland shooting. Conversely, only two relationships remain significant in the North County sample; students' change scores reflect an increase in perceptions that kids bringing guns to school is a problem and decrease in likelihood of reporting a gun after Parkland.

The apparent contrast in the Parkland influence suggests that students in majority white schools in areas with less disadvantage experience news about Parkland differently than their North County counterparts. The fear of crime literature helps illuminate the reasoning behind these differences. Despite the limited research on how highly publicized violent events impact individuals who are removed from the incident (Warr, 2000), theoretical work suggests that individuals are less likely to draw on these events in their perceptions of safety if they already experience high levels of fear or victimization in their immediate environment (Liska, Lawrence, & Sanchirico, 1982; Tyler & Cook, 1984). For individuals who have been victimized or are aware of the victimization of someone close to them, these personal experiences influence their perceptions of crime and victimization. On the other hand, those without personal experiences of victimization may consider the media more heavily (Skogan & Maxfield, 1981). These different sources may explain divergent responses as Melde and Esbensen explain (2009, p. 518):

> Given the media's tendency to overstate the actual frequency and severity of criminal offenses, those who rely on this source of information may fear victimization more than individuals who have experienced such events.

Considering the different characteristics of North and South County schools, this offers a plausible explanation for the differential influence of Parkland on student perceptions. Not only is there more concentrated disadvantage in North County, but the students in these schools report greater victimization, perceptions of disorder, and fear of crime on average than students in South County. North County students may react to the Parkland shooting differently, as they are more likely to draw on their immediate experiences and environment when they evaluate perceptions of safety, whereas South County students may not have acknowledged violence as a major threat until thinking about the Parkland shooting.

Another important difference in the pre- and post-Parkland samples concerns age. The post-Parkland sample is significantly older than the pre-Parkland sample. In addition to the age difference, evidence of a Parkland influence on responses must consider that approximately 48% of the sample moved from middle schools to high schools in wave two. This change could drive differences in change scores if individuals' reports are different in wave two because they are in a different school, and not because the Parkland shooting influenced outcomes. To address this issue, differences in middle school students' change scores are examined independently from those who transitioned to high school. Significant differences in change scores pre- and post-Parkland are displayed in Fig. 3.

Three of the previously discussed relationships between Parkland and student outcomes hold for the middle school sample. First, perceptions of kids bringing guns to school as a problem decrease less for students who were surveyed after

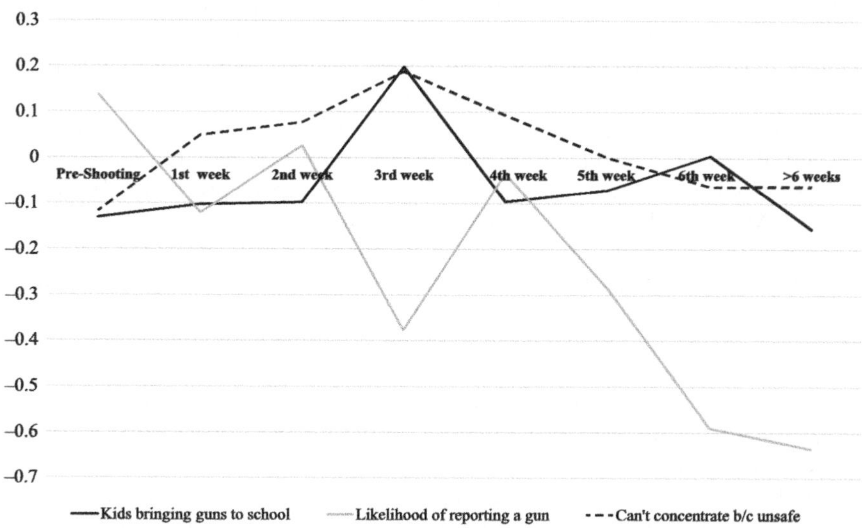

Fig. 3. Change Scores from Wave One to Wave Two: Significant Differences for Middle School Students.

the shooting, and increase in the third week, which is consistent with the pattern observed for the overall sample. Second, the likelihood of reporting a gun change scores follow the previously observed downward trend. Lastly, there is a significant change in students' reports that they cannot concentrate because they feel unsafe in school. Students' wave two responses indicate decreased agreement with the item compared to wave one. Post-shooting, students' change scores are positive, meaning they reported more agreement with the item than they had in wave one. Change scores peak in the third week before decreasing to below zero again by the sixth week. These results underscore evidence of a Parkland influence by demonstrating trends consistent with those reflected from other comparisons of pre- and post-measures.

CONCLUSION

The research reported in this chapter was guided by two main interests: (1) to assess the extent to which a highly publicized school shooting might affect students' perceptions of school safety and (2) the extent to which any such effect of a school shooting would pose a threat to the internal validity of a study. The UMSL CSSI provided an opportunity to address these interests due to the research design and fortuitous timing of the surveying of students. During January through April 2017, the research team surveyed approximately 3,600 students enrolled in the 7th and 8th grades in 12 middle schools in St. Louis County, Missouri. These same students were surveyed again in 2018. On February 14, 2018, the mass shooting occurred in Marjory Stoneman Douglas High School in Parkland, Florida, resulting in 17 deaths. To what extent, if any, does such a deadly shooting affect the attitudes and behaviors of students 1,000 miles away?

The Parkland shooting received considerable media attention associated with the initial shooting. Unlike other mass shootings, victims of the Parkland shooting took to social media to express their horror, sadness, and frustration with the frequency of such events in the US. Students organized protests with the intent of raising awareness and concern about gun violence. These efforts resulted in substantial sustained media coverage of the shooting. Our research examined the extent to which exposure to this event affected student perceptions and behaviors.

The UMSL CSSI research design provided a natural experimental situation to conduct this research. Student survey responses in 2017 provided a baseline with which the "Parkland Effect" could be examined. In 2018, approximately one-third of students were surveyed prior to February 14 and the remainder were surveyed in the weeks following the shooting. Creating individual change scores resulted in measures that controlled for prior attitudes and behaviors. The effect of the shooting was examined by using the dates of survey administration to assign students to pre- and post-shooting status and assess differences in change scores among groups.

Based upon the analyses reported in this chapter, a highly publicized shooting such as the Parkland shooting can have statistically and substantively important effects on students' responses to questions about school safety. Researchers, school officials, and policy makers should be attentive to such potentially biasing effects.

Two caveats, however, should be provided. First, school and student socio-demographic characteristics need to be considered. In this study, the differences in responses for students attending predominantly black and more disadvantaged schools and those enrolled in mostly white and not disadvantaged schools are striking. There was virtually no effect in the former but pronounced effects in the latter. Second, there appears to be a decaying effect of the shooting. Even in the white, less disadvantaged schools, the Parkland Effect was largely absent by five weeks post-shooting. Even with the heightened social and mass media coverage after the shooting, the effect on student attitudes appears transient.

With respect to the threat to internal validity, researchers should exercise caution if they are conducting program or policy evaluations involving experimental research designs. Events external to the study (i.e., history effects) may undermine outcomes. For school-based research assessing school safety, a school shooting such as that at Marjory Stoneman Douglas may well compromise the study's internal validity. Likewise, in longitudinal research in schools in which changes in attitudes and behavior are the subject of interest, attention should be given to external events that could bias student responses to survey items. To summarize, threats to external validity were found in the current study. However, the effects were temporary and context specific. By five weeks after the shooting, significant effects had subsided and, in schools characterized by socioeconomic disadvantage, the effects of the school shooting were minimal.

REFERENCES

Addington, L. A. (2003). Students' fear after Columbine: Findings from a randomized experiment. *Journal of Quantitative Criminology, 19*(4), 367–387.

Brener, N. D., Simon, T. R., Anderson, M., Barrios, L. C., & Small, M. L. (2002). Effect of the incident at Columbine on students' violence-and suicide-related behaviors. *American Journal of Preventive Medicine, 22*(3), 146–150.

Bromwich, J. E. (2018). How the Parkland students got so good at social media. *The New York Times*, March 7. Retrieved from https://www.nytimes.com/2018/03/07/us/ parkland-students-social-media.html. Assessed on November 2018.

Campbell, D. T., & Stanley, J. C. (1963). Experimental and quasi-experimental designs for research. In N. L. Gage (Ed.), *Handbook of research on teaching* (pp. 171–246). Chicago, IL: Rand McNally.

Chiricos, T., Escholz, S., & Gertz, M. (1997). Crime, news and fear of crime: Toward an identification of audience effects. *Social Problems, 44*(3), 342–357.

Dinkes, R., Cataldi E. F., Kena, G., & Baum, K. (2006). *Indicators of school crime and safety (NCES 2007-003)*. Washington, DC: U.S. Departments of Education and Justice.

Ferraro, K. F. (1995). *Fear of crime: Interpreting victimization risk.* Albany, NY: State University of New York Press.

Fox, J. A., & Fridel, E. E. (2019). School-day perils: More than just mass shootings. *The Criminologist, 44*(1), 8–11.

Galea, S., Branas, C. C., Flescher, A., Formica, M. K., Hennig, N., Liller, K.D., … Ying, J. (2018). Priorities in recovering from a lost generation of firearms research. *AJPH Gun Violence Prevention*, 858–860.

Garofalo, J. (1981). The fear of crime: Causes and consequences. *Journal of Criminal Law & Criminology, 72*(2), 839–857.

Intravia, J., Wolff, K. T., Paez, R., & Gibbs, B. R. (2017). Investigating the relationship between social media consumption and fear of crime: A partial analysis of mostly young adults. *Computers in Human Behavior*, *77*, 158–168.

Jones, J. (2017). Media and social media's impact on citizens' perception of the frequency of crime occurrence in the United States. *American International Journal of Social Science*, *6*(3), 97–102.

Kaminski, R. J., Koons-Witt, B. A., Stewart Thompson, N., & Weiss, D. (2010). The impacts of the Virginia Tech and Northern Illinois University shootings on fear of crime on campus. *Journal of Criminal Justice, 38*(1), 88–98.

Liska, A. E., Lawrence, J. J., & Sanchirico, A. (1982). Fear of crime as a social fact. *Social Forces*, *60*(3), 760–770.

Madden, M., Lenhart, A., & Fontaine, C. (2017). *How youth navigate the news landscape.* Data and Society Research Institute. Retrieved from https://kf-siteproduction.s3.amazonaws.com/publications/pdfs/000/000/230/original/Youth_News.pdf. Accessed on November 2018.

Melde, C., & Esbensen, F. (2009). The victim–offender overlap and fear of in-school victimization: A longitudinal examination of risk assessment models. *Crime & Delinquency 55*(4), 499–525.

Palfrey, J., & Gasser, U., (2008). *Born digital: Understanding the first generation of digita natives.* New York, NY: Basic Books.

Pew Research Center. (2018). *Teens, social media, & technology 2018.* Washington, DC: PEW Research Center. Retrieved from http://www.pewinternet.org/2018/05/31/teens-socialmedia-technology-2018. Accessed on November 2018.

Sanchez, R. (2018). Student marchers call Washington's inaction on gun violence unacceptable. *CNN,* March 24. Retrieved from https://www.cnn.com/2018/03/24/us/march-for-our-lives/index.html. Accessed on November 2018

Schutt, R. K. (2018). *Investigating the social world: The process and practice of research.* Thousand Oaks, CA: Pine Forge Press.

Siegel, R. (2018). The Parkland shooting is different. The news coverage proves it. *The Washington Post,* March 2. Retrieved from https://www.washingtonpost.com/ news/wonk/wp/2018/03/02/the-parkland-shooting-is-different-the-news-coverage-proves-it/?utm_term=.c4aff9aebf54. Accessed on November 2018.

Skogan, W. G., & Maxfield, M. G. (1981). *Coping with crime: Individual and neighborhood reactions.* Beverly Hills, CA: Sage Publications.

Smolej, M., & Kivivuori, J. (2006). The relation between crime news and fear of violence. *Journal of Scandinavian Studies in Criminology and Crime Prevention*, *7*(2), 211–227.

Stretesky, P. B., & Hogan, M. J. (2001). Columbine and student perceptions of safety: A quasi-experimental study. *Journal of Criminal Justice*, *29*(5), 429–443.

Tyler, T. R., & Cook, F. L. (1984). The mass media and judgments of risk: Distinguishing impact on personal and societal level judgments. *Journal of Personality and Social Psychology*, *47*(4), 693–708.

Warr, M. (2000). Fear of crime in the United States: Avenues for research and policy. *Criminal Justice, 4*(4), 451–489.

Yee, V., & Blinder, A. (2018). National school walkout: Thousands protest against gun violence across the U.S. *The New York Times*, March 14. Retrieved from https://www.nytimes.com/2018/03/14/us/school-walkout.html. Accessed on November 2018.

PART III

CROSSING BOUNDARIES

CHAPTER 8

METHODOLOGICAL CHALLENGES IN COLLABORATIVE RESEARCH WITH IMMIGRANT WOMEN EXPERIENCING INTIMATE PARTNER VIOLENCE IN CANADA

Nawal Ammar and Arshia U. Zaidi

ABSTRACT

Purpose – *The chapter explores the methodological challenges in doing community-based participatory research (CBPR) in social science investigations with immigrant women experiencing intimate partner violence (IPV) in Canada.*

Methodology/approach – *The methodological comments, observations, and challenges discussed in this chapter result from research funded by the Social Science and Humanities Council, a branch of the Canadian Federal Tri-Council. The research that the authors conducted was both quantitative and qualitative in nature. The sample consisted of three groups of women: (1) immigrant women in Canada >10 years, (2) immigrant women in Canada <10 years, and (3) visible minority women born in Canada.*

Findings – *The chapter highlights some of the lessons learned in conducting CBPR research in the context of immigrant survivors of IPV. This discussion can be relevant to both academics and non-profit/advocacy agencies interested in pursuing community partnership research on interpersonal violence.*

Methods of Criminology and Criminal Justice Research
Sociology of Crime, Law and Deviance, Volume 24, 135–149

ISSN: 1521-6136/doi:10.1108/S1521-613620190000024013

Originality/value – *There is a paucity of writings on CBPR research in the social science and the challenges. This chapter reveals the methodological challenges that the researchers experienced in doing CBPR with racialized immigrant women who are survivors of IPV. This discussion can be relevant to both academics and non-profit/advocacy agencies interested in pursuing community partnership research on interpersonal violence.*

Keywords: Collaborative; participant and advocacy research; intimate partner violence; immigrant racialized women; methodological challenges; lessons learned; community partnerships

INTRODUCTION

In this chapter, we reflect on the challenging field experiences of this community-based participatory research (CBPR) research teamwork in the context of battered-immigrant women and community partnerships. We argue that the nuances of this research method need to be discussed openly in the literature to enable more partnerships to succeed in conducting this policy impactful research. We expect that such methodological reporting will help those interested in conducting research with battered immigrant women as well as contribute to the larger body of work on CBPR. We present both a summary of the challenges we encountered and lessons learned.

The aim of this chapter is to advance understanding of the methodological and epistemological challenges that may be encountered when undertaking CBPR research with advocates of or service providers to immigrant women survivors of intimate partner violence (IPV) in the Canadian context. More particularly, this chapter focuses on the challenges of CBPR research exploring battered immigrant and non-immigrant ethnic minority women. CBPR research supports an ontology that self-consciously centers on "doing 'with' rather than doing 'for' stakeholders" (Greenwood & Levine, 2006, p. 15). This kind of research democratizes the process, acknowledges the subjective construction of reality, and provides the richness of experiences in complex situations (Greenwood & Levine, 2006; Hill-Bailey, 1997; Snelgrove, 2014). This chapter draws on the authors personal experiences of conducting CBPR on issues related to violence against immigrant women in the Canadian context. The account begins with an overview of CBPR generally and CBPR as it related to violence against women in particular. A brief discussion of the research we conducted, and on which the experiences we discuss are based, is presented before exploring the two levels of challenges we encountered.

COMMUNITY-BASED PARTICIPATORY RESEARCH

There is a long tradition of CBPR research in both Canada and the United States (Freir, 1982; Godin & Gingras, 2000; Horowitz, Robinson, & Seifer,

2009; Stringer, 2013; Schensul, 1987). Central to the CBPR research approach is a relationship between the advocates, the community being researched, and university researchers. The nature of this relationship has been examined by a number of authors (Barreteau, Bots, & Daniell, 2010; Benneworth Conway, Charles, Humphrey, & Younger, 2009; Cahill, 2007; Campbell, Dienemann, Kub, Wurmser, & Loy 1999; Christopher, Watts, McCormick, & Young, 2008; John-Steiner, 2000; Kilpatrick, Resick, & Williams, 2001; Macpherson et al., 2017; Schensul et al., 2006; Weaver & Ammar, 1991). Some authors have addressed the question about how to develop CBPR research relationships and the importance of building it over time, like the ethnographer who spends time getting to know the community (Campbell et al., 1999; Haviland, Frye, & Rajah, 2008; Schensul, 1987). Others (Facer & Enright, 2016; John-Steiner, 2000) argue that the relationship can range from short-term exchange of ideas to long-term committed activities among partners. Additionally some have focused on what the academy has done with participatory research results (Hall, 1992; Wright, Williams, Wright, & Gedjeyan, 2011, Wynne, 2006). Finally, many have addressed the status of knowledge generated in the process (Rynes, Bartunek, & Daft, 2001; Warren, Calderón, Kupscznk, Squires, & Su, 2018). Regardless, all authors agree that the essence of participatory collaborative/participatory research is not the length of the relationship, or the outcome of the research or the status of the knowledge. Rather, the importance of participatory/collaborative research is the transformative power generated in the process as well as the overall knowledge (both scientific and relational) it produces (Borda & Orlando-Rahman, 1991; Hall 1992; Weaver & Ammar, 1991).

In this chapter, we define CBPR research as Greenwood and Levine (2006, p. 15) put it:

> CBPR research is a set of self-consciously collaborative and democratic strategies for generating knowledge and designing action in which trained experts in social
>
> In addition, other forms of research and local stakeholders work together. The research focus is chosen collaboratively among the local stakeholders and the action researchers, and the relationships among the participants are organized as joint learning processes. CBPR centers on doing "with" rather than doing "for" stakeholders and credits local stakeholders with the richness of experience and reflective possibilities that the long experience of living in complex situations brings with it.

CBPR research is growing in the area of violence against women. However, it remains at an early stage of development (Campbell et al., 1999; Chalk & King, 1998; Edelson & Bible, 2001; Gondolf, Yllo, & Campbell, 1997; Haviland et al., 2008; Kilpatrick et al., 2001; Lennett & Colten, 1999; Macpherson et al., 2017; Minkler, 2000, 2005; Riger, 1999; Sullivan, Bhuyan, Senturia, Shiu-Thornton, & Ciske, 2005). The literature largely revolves around issues of establishing trust between researchers and non-researchers, establishing harmonious research priorities between the researchers and non-researchers, and involving non-researchers throughout the research process (Buchanan, 1996, Gondolf et al., 1997; Haviland et al., 2008; Kindon & Elwood, 2009; Lennett & Colten, 1999; Reinharz, 1992; Riger, 1999; Sullivan et al., 2005). This focus emerges out of real life experiences of community partners who after facilitating data collection find out those researchers used the findings in a way that undermines their clients and the needs of the community or unwittingly exposed the women to unsafe situations (Haviland et al., 2008; Kone et al., 2000; Minkler, 2000). Many community partners have had experiences with "drive-by" researchers whose focus is on their own individual advancement within the academy and who collect the data and leave (Haviland et al., 2008; Ponic & Jategaonkar, 2012; Williams, 2004). The issues of trust also dominate in violence against women collaborative research because community partners still don't own the outcome of the research and hence, they are often concerned about the potential negative impact of the results on the work they do and the dangers of exposing their clients who are survivors (Haviland et al., 2008; Perkins & Wandersman, 1990; Riger, 1999).

Collaborative/Participatory/Action (CBPR) Research and Battered Immigrant Women

Discussions of CBPR research is very scant in the research with immigrant-racialized women experiencing IPV. In the Canadian context more particularly, while the research on battered immigrant women mostly utilizes the CBPR methodology, it rarely addresses the methodology in and of itself or its challenges (Ahmad, Driver, McNally, & Stewart, 2009; Alaggia, Regehr, & Rishchynski, 2009; Hyman, Forte, Mont, Romans, & Cohen, 2006; Hyman, Mason, Guruge, Berman, Kanagaratnam, & Manuel, 2011; Torres & Fine, 2004). Within the Canadian and US works available in English there are few studies to date published in English that explore the challenges of CBPR as a methodology (e.g., Campbell et al., 1999; Dutton, Ammar, Orloff, & Terrell, 2006; Erez & Ammar, 2003; Sullivan et al., 2005; Vaughan et al., 2015; White, Yuan, Cook, & Abbey, 2013). In this chapter, we (as authors) attempt to fill such a void in the literature by being reflexive on our almost three year CBPR research with the battered immigrant women community in Ontario. More particularly, we will assess the methodological challenges of CBPR research in terms of creating and maintaining the collaborative/participatory relationship and at the same time fulfilling the research requirements on time.

OVERVIEW OF THE RESEARCH PROCESS

The Research Requirements

The research we conducted was both quantitative and qualitative in nature. Its basic data collection instrument was a survey research instrument (with both open and close-ended questions). The survey instrument included five sections. These were respondent's background, client and IPV experiences, encounters with the police, family and community support, and finally service delivery. Each survey was coded for the community organization they were from and the client *id* number assigned to them. No names were used. In this study, interpreters were available to conduct interviews in the language in which the participating women were comfortable. The sample consisted of three groups of women: (1) immigrant women in Canada >10 years, (2) immigrant women in Canada <10 years, and (3) visible minority women born in Canada. The women participants in the research were compensated $35 for the time they spent answering the questions. Data collection did not begin until ethical clearance was obtained by the university's ethics board.

The goal of this community partnership was to recruit 200 immigrant battered women for in-depth interviews about the way they experienced violence at the *client* (i.e., their individual level), within their *community* (i.e., their experiences as part of their communities), and *service* delivery levels (i.e., their experiences in accessing and using services). The collaborative research team initially at the proposal level consisted of two organizations that delivered services to immigrant and visible minority women experiencing IPV and the university researchers. Within those two organizations, the team consisted of both members who have known and worked with each other on other projects and of members who have known each other superficially. We refer to this CBPR research phase as the *concentrated partner's recruitment stage*. This is because we "concentrated" on working with two partner organizations with the assumption that they will facilitate connecting us with others as the research project developed. The challenges of this approach are discussed in the following section.

CHALLENGES AND CONSEQUENCES

We were very enthusiastic upon receiving the funding from Social Science and Humanities Council (SSHRC) to conduct this CBPR research with our supporting community partners.

No research is void of methodological challenges and shortcomings. However, This CBPR research encountered a number of short- and long-term issues directly related to its collaborative and participatory methodology. Developing new partnerships within the community working with and providing service to battered immigrant women within the region of our study seemed to present a number of challenges. Two levels of challenges will be discussed. The first level relates to the research process challenges and the second refers to the complexity and intersectionality of the matter of battered immigrant women. The challenges discussed are not necessarily specific to research on violence against battered immigrant women and many researchers using the CBPR research method have probably encountered similar challenges. However, the objective of this discussion is to highlight how such a design when applied to work with battered immigrant women includes additional tensions and challenges that are often overlooked.

Research Process Challenges

We encountered three *process challenges:*

(1) withdrawal of our initial community-based partner organizations partner resulting in our inability to recruit women and complete the allocated surveys;

(2) unexpected change in funding by the government within the community partner organization that resulted in frontline staff, leadership and service orientation changes which completely side-tracked the project; and
(3) the lack of continuity in community organizations.

The original approach of the CBPR research design, the "concentrated" approach," was to work with two community partner organizations that had access to diverse groups of immigrant battered women clients who could be recruited as survey participants for this grant. However, due to changes in both organizations the powers who agreed to participate in September were no longer able to carry out their commitment in April. Less than two months of receiving the grant one of the organizations had bowed out because they themselves have not received enough funding to hire an Executive Director. The second organization withdrew from the project because of disagreements within their board about the research, few months after the first organization was unable to work with us due to personnel matters. As a result, we had to develop an alternative collaborative team and approach.

During this phase of the research, we conducted many meetings and trips to the community partners in the initial stages of data collection that resulted in a one-sided discussion, with little hope.

The second major challenge for this research was the unexpected change in funding by the government within the community partner organization that resulted in staff and service orientation changes. The person who directed this community partner and showed a great interest in the research was no longer employed by the organization due to funding problems. This organization was a coalition of sexual assault, IPV, law enforcement, and health care agencies, and was unable to get funding from provincial sources to keep the director employed. This staff change created drawbacks, making our research a difficult task to support given the staff shortage the organization was experiencing. Like Benoit et al. (2005,p. 277) states, "political changes at municipal and provincial levels are also likely to affect the resources the community partners could contribute to the research and the data collection process." These changes indeed have the impact of changing the CBPR approach we had initially developed in the SSHRC proposal.

The third major challenge that affected this research is the change in the internal leadership of the other community partner organization. After a number of meetings with our contact person in the organization, she told us in at our final meeting "this [research] has become an issue with certain board members, and that they no longer are committed to collaborating on the research." We asked if we could meet with the board members to discuss the proposal with them and see if we could build new relationships. The new leadership, however, was not enthusiastic about the research collaboration. Their lack of enthusiasm was so strong that we were unable to secure a meeting with them to discuss our research and our approach to CBPR. We encountered this change a few months after the SSHRC funding was approved.

After several attempts to work out the challenges with our initial community partners failed, we needed to make dramatic research shifts and begin to develop a new CBPR approach in order to recruit participants for the research, keeping the grant lifecycle in mind. As a result, the university research team had to seek help from other community partners. We refer to this stage of recruiting as the *multiple-site configuration*. New community partners were identified and committed to be included as part of the collaborative research team that would assist in the recruitment of participants. This new multiple-site configuration of organizations seemed to have the advantage of collecting data that are more representative of the experiences of battered immigrant women throughout the Province.

In an effort to bring as many community organizations, we invited 10 organizations to working meetings at an accessible (in terms of parking and ease of finding) location of the university. We refer to this stage of recruiting as the *multiple-site configuration*. This new collaborative research team consisted initially of members who have worked with each other on other projects and with their help added more members who the researchers knew more superficially. A number of face-to-face meetings were conducted with these new partner organizations including directors of domestic violence shelters, representatives from the regional police services, the John Howard Society, homeless shelters, an intercultural counseling organization, the regional community council, and other practitioners who are members of violence against immigrant women organizations in Southern Ontario. In those meetings, the discussion revolved around the interest in and commitment to the project, research problems, research design, sample size, sampling procedures, data collection instrument, and dissemination of findings and other multicultural service providers. Each collaborating sector of the partnership contributed to the data collection instrument based on their areas of expertise and suggested ways of recruiting respondents.

We also collaboratively prepared flyers for recruiting women for the interviews, purchased special cell numbers (i.e., magic jack), and created new email addresses for the project in order for women to contact the research team, and gave a number of presentations to community groups about the project. The new multiple-site configuration of organizations seemed to increase our ability to collect data from a more diverse group of immigrant survivors of IPV from around the Province.

As we progressed through this multiple-site configuration of recruitment, we still were having problems recruiting enough participants. At this point, that is, two years into the project, we still had only completed 60 interviews that fit within the sampling design. While the proposal suggested a sample of 200 participants. According to our partner organizations in the multiple-site recruitment process, our slow progress in recruiting participants was due to three main reasons. The first is that organizations did not have enough immigrant or minority women survivors in their programs who qualified for the research. The second was that organizations whose clients were eligible to participate in the survey, were reluctant to participate fearing that their abuser would find out that they are discussing their abuse. The most significant barrier to recruiting participants, however, was that the agency staff who were committed to this kind of research were too busy to have our project take priority over other daily issues they were dealing with. These organizations were committed to high-quality client services, which is why we chose them as partners. However, this placed staff in the position of either choosing to provide services to more immigrant victims or taking that time away from service provision to spend referring other clients to our research. Only one of the organizations was able to provide us with a significant number of participants. This was the agency where management level staff were directly involved in the data collection and could make the arrangements needed for staff to set aside the time to conduct the surveys.

At this point and after the passage of more than two years on the research funding, we developed a new strategy, which included building on successes and an independent and stronger coordination outside the partnership organizations. As a result, we contracted with the director of the organization that provided us with the largest number of participants. We also hired a project coordinator to manage the requirements of the interviewing sessions (including making paper surveys available, checking on the eligibility of the participant, having cash available to pay participants, and being the connection between the partner organization and the researchers). This process enabled the team, the director of this one organization, and the coordinator of the project to work together to identify participants from the director's organization and from other organizations to interview. Within a year (and after a cost neutral extension of the grant) we were able to reach a close enough sample to the suggested number in the proposal. We refer to this stage of the process of participant recruiting as "Eureka."

Process Consequences

Some of the consequences of repeated changes of community partners and the development of new strategies of recruiting participants maybe recognizable to many CBPR researchers. However, some consequences are either not readily discernible or are often, for a variety of reasons, not discussed by the researchers. For example, the delay that such a change causes is one of the recognizable consequences. However, the time it takes to adjust the methodology and data collection to reflect the ideas and contributions of the new partners was not something we thought of until we started having meetings with our new partners. For example, new partners had new ideas about the wording and sequence of some questions on the survey, and different notions about recruiting participants, how to advertise, where to advertise, and the safety protocols to be followed. Additionally, the shift – from the intended concentrated – recruiting of women respondents from two sites to multi-site recruiting is probably common, but its consequences are rarely identified. In addition to the unanticipated added time and work, the shift to multi-site recruiting involved more coordination than planned for and more opportunistic interviewing than planned to match the ideal of methodical data collection we learn and teach in the classroom setting. Another consequence of changes in partnerships included not meeting timelines (funders, publications, and ethics board). We have had to ask for cost-neutral renewal from our funders twice. This request is not always granted easily, but we were grateful for their flexibility in this area. We also have had to renew our REB/IRB clearance in order to continue conducting the research beyond the anticipated two-year time-line.

The various reasons for delay in CBPR also have an impact beyond the research process itself. It sometimes can influence the reputation of the researchers involved. To many colleagues whose research is based in laboratories, or on large secondary data sets, or with students, the delay in completing research is often perceived as a researcher problem. The notion that conducting research is not under the full control of the researcher is a "foreign" and often a sign of weaker methodological rigor. In addition, the delay in completing the research has consequences on junior faculty involved in the work because – due to no fault of their own – they are unable to present the results of the research at professional conferences or publish the results of the research on time. We see this often in the quantity of the papers published by junior faculty who engage in CBPR and how their peers at tenure and promotion time negatively assess their productivity. There is little understanding of the idea that researchers engaged in CBPR research generally work harder at recruiting participants than other researchers.

LESSONS LEARNED

If some of the issues concerning CBPR research and partner organizations were openly discussed in the literature, we (and many other CBPR researchers) would write proposals that are more realistic and would work differently with community partners and perhaps have a more successful outcome with continuing the partnerships in place. It is thus important to reflect on "Lessons Learned" from a community and academic collaboration perspective. These lessons learned are even more important since there is little published work on CBPR research among battered immigrant women. The following section elaborates on three lessons learned worthy of discussion.

The first lesson the team learned is that knowing the individuals working in community organizations (however long or however close) is not sufficient. Both the community partners and the researchers in the team assumed that there was homogeneity of values and leadership in community organizations. However, the relationship is not a one-on-one between researchers and advocates in the organization. The relationship is between researchers and an entire organization. Our academic research team thought that they understood the complex structure and process of the organizations they were collaborating with because they knew and were working with individuals in the partner organizations. However, that is not sufficient, because organizations are more than the collection of individuals that work in them. As such, a collaborative team not only needs to have an in-depth understanding of the people working at the community-based organization but there is a need to have a knowledge of where the people fit in the larger makeup of their organizations (especially in the decision making process). This is especially important, given the turnover rate of leadership in non-profit community-based organizations. It is unlikely that such an experience is unique only to advocacy-research with battered immigrant women. Campbell et al. (1999) explicitly show the importance of understanding organizational structure of partners internally within the context of mainstream segments of the population. They recommended that visits and interactions with partners in their own organizations is an important component of advocacy research in violence against women.

The second lesson we learned was that simply trust among advocates and researchers was not sufficient to determine the success of CBPR research. A commitment to a common cause as a priority as well was as important. Most collaborative research literature (Ammar &Weaver, 1992; Campbell et al., 1999; Koss & White, 2008; Perilla Serrata, Weinberg, & Lippy, 2012; Schensul & Stull, 1987, Small & Uttal, 2005; Stoecker & Beckwith, 1992; Vaughan et al., 2015; White et al., 2013) strongly emphasizes the coming together of the researchers, practitioners, and advocates developing the research ideas. This same literature underscores the importance of maintaining such relationships on continuous basis (even if the team is not working on a project). The research under discussion in this chapter would have failed had the collaborative framework been dependent only on trust that results from a continuous research partnership and individualistic connections with advocates. The research team's solid commitment and continuous connection with the battered immigrant community via a long-standing prominent community organization played a significant role in assuring the success of the research project. After the withdrawal of the initial two organizations from the project, the solid commitment and continuous connection of the team to other practitioners and advocates in the communities across the region serving diverse populations of immigrant women facilitated the design of the multi-site collaborative research. However, the continual relationship with the most active community organization in the region was the key to our ability to complete the research. This relationship does not imply being in direct contact with the organization and advocates all the time. Nor is such a relationship one of "trust" only. Rather it is more of a relationship of "accessibility." In other words, researchers' relationship with the community working with battered immigrant women is one, more or less, of kinship. Just as in traditional familial connections, one can always count on their kin to provide them with help, support, and answers to difficult questions regardless of the fact that they have not talked, or seen each other for some time. This kind of "I can count on you" relationship between researchers and advocates in the context of collaborative research with battered immigrant women is what we mean by "continuous" and "accessible."

This "I can count on you" relationship was built through a history of a decade of collaborative, multidisciplinary work between the advocates in this organization and the academic team. They worked together on boards, in organizing conferences, in teaching, and in fundraising. A number of feminist researchers (Cook, 2003; Fonnow & Cook, 1991; Kwan, 2001; Naples, 2003; Reiharz, 1992; Shields, 2002) have emphasized this kind of feminist methodology as the "ethic of care," with research on women in general and in research among ethnic minority women, and women with disabilities in particular.

The third lesson we learned from doing this research was that it is not enough to be flexible when doing advocacy research, but that it is necessary to have resources to support change that results from such flexibility. Most discussion of collaborative research emphasizes the need for flexibility (Curtis, 2002; Korten,1980; Mog, 2006). There is no question that this project was successful because the advocates, the researchers, and the funders were very flexible. However, this project was completed successfully because of the intensive coordination and follow-up when the team encountered challenges. The large number of organizations involved in this research required coordination of multiple trainings, writing of contractual agreements, repeated distribution of questionnaires, implementation of different quality control efforts, more complicated follow-up on completed questionnaires, and payments to multiple interviewers who were sometimes individuals and sometimes agencies. Careful and persistent coordination of the research was carried out by our newly introduced project coordinator and the director who was a manager of a community organization. Both those positions required financial commitments that were not identified in the original budget. If the project did not have the ability to support these positions financially, we may not have been able to fulfill our suggested number of participants.

CONCLUSION

While CBPR research has a long history in the United States and Canada (see Schensul, 1987), writings on doing this kind of research with interpersonal violence in general, and battered immigrant women in particular, is just emerging in the literature. The basics required for doing CBPR- research were important to complete this study (i.e., the team members trusted each other, had worked together in the past, respect each other's contribution to research, and had a reputation as advocates and as respected researchers in the battered immigrant community). However, the team faced numerous challenges. These included the inability to gauge the various leadership and decision-making roles within the various organizations, workload conflicts, which made this research a low priority for the advocates working in the front lines of agencies, the high demand of coordination required when dealing with a multiple site CBPR research and the need to be flexible and act fast. Finally, it is not enough to understand the idea of the need for flexibility in CBPR research. Such an understanding must be supported with structures, mechanisms, finance, and personnel to transition the plans as they change.

It is difficult to conclude that these are problems particular only to CBPR research with battered immigrant women. However, it seems that agencies working with battered immigrant women in our region are under-resourced and overworked to the point of making CBPR a very low priority in their planned activities. This makes CBPR research partnerships difficult to maintain and in turn makes this form of research difficult to conduct. Because of this problem, we have little up-to-date data about battered immigrant women in Canada generally and in our region in particular to base policy, and allocate resources to serve this population of women. Hence, it is important for both researchers, advocates, policy makers, and funders to understand some of the challenges encountered in conducting this kind of research so we are able to get the data needed for service providers, policy makers, and others to promote improvements in legislation, funding, and service delivery for such social issues.

REFERENCES

Ahmad, F., Driver, N., McNally, M. J., & Stewart, D. E. (2009). "Why doesn't she seek help for partner abuse?" An exploratory study with South Asian immigrant women. *Social Science & Medicine, 69*, 613–622.

Alaggia, R., Regehr, C., & Rishchynski, G. (2009). Intimate partner violence and immigration laws in Canada: How far have we come? *International Journal of Law and Psychiatry, 32*, 335–341.

Ammar, N., & Orloff, L. (2006). "Battered immigrant women's domestic violence dynamics and legal protections." In R. Muraskin (Ed.), *It's a crime: Women and justice* (pp. 430–443). Upper Saddle River, NJ: Prentice Hall.

Ammar, N., & Weaver, R. (1992). A collaborative approach to applied survey research: The interview process. *Sociological Practice Review, 3*, 32–36.

Barreteau, O., Bots, P. W. G., & Daniell, K. A. (2010). A framework for clarifying "participation" in participatory research to prevent its rejection for the wrong reasons. *Ecology and Society, 15*, 1. [online] Retrieved from http://www.ecologyandsociety.org/vol15/iss2/art1/

Benneworth, P., Conway, C., Charles, D., Humphrey, L., & Younger, P. (2009). Characterizing modes of university engagement with wider society: A literature review and survey of best practice. Retrieved from http://talloiresnetwork.tufts.edu/wpcontent/uploads/Characterisingmodesof universityengagementwithwidersociety.pdf. Accessed on November 2018.

Borda, F., & Orlando-Rahman, M. A. (1991). *Action and knowledge breaking the monopoly with participatory action-research* (No. 300.720172 A2).

Buchanan, D. R. (1996). Building academic–community linkages for health promotion: A case study of Massachusetts. *American Journal of Health Promotion, 10*, 262–269.

Cahill, C. (2007). Doing research with young people: Participatory research and the rituals of collective work. *Children's Geographies, 5*, 297–312.

Campbell, J. C., Dienemann, J., Kub, J., Wurmser, T., & Loy, E. (1999). Collaboration as partnership. *Violence against Women, 5*, 1140–1157.

Chalk, R., & King, P. A. (1998). *Violence in families: Assessing intervention and treatment programs*. Washington, D.C.: National Academy Press.

Christopher, S., Watts, V., McCormick, A. K. H. G., & Young, S. (2008). Building and maintaining trust in a community-based participatory research partnership. *American Journal of Public Health, 98*, 1398–1406.

Cook, J. A. (2003). Depression, disability, and rehabilitation services for women. *Psychology of Women Quarterly, 27*, 121–129.

Curtis, R. (2002). Coexisting in the real world: The problems, surprises, and delights of being an ethnographer on a multidisciplinary research project. *International Journal of Drug Policy, 13*, 297–310.

Dutton, M. A., Ammar, N., Orloff, L., & Terrell, D. (2006). *Use and outcomes of protection orders by battered immigrant women*. Revised Final Technical Report #2003-WG-BX-1004. Prepared for National Institute of Justice Office of Justice Programs, U.S. Department of Justice, Washington, DC.

Edelson, J. L., & Bible, A. L. (2001). Collaboration for women's safety: Partnerships between science and practice on women beating. In *Sourcebook of violence against women* (pp. 73–95). Thousand Oaks, CA: Sage.

Erez, E., & Ammar, N. (2003). *Violence against immigrant women and systemic responses: An exploratory study*. Report submitted to National Institute of Justice in fulfillment of requirements for Grant #98-WTVX-0030. US Department of Justice, Washington, DC.

Facer, K., & Enright, B. (2016). *Creating living knowledge: The connected communities programmed, community–university partnerships and the participatory turn in the production of knowledge*. Bristol: Arts and Humanities Research Council.

Fais, B. O., & Rahman, A. M. (1991). *Action and knowledge: Breaking the monopoly with participatory action-research*. New York, NY: Apex.

Freir, P. (1982). Creating alternative research methods: Learning to do it by doing it. In Hall et al. (Eds.), *Creating knowledge: A monopoly: Participatory research in development* (pp. 29–40). Toronto, Canada: International Council on Adult Education.

Fuller, D., & Kitchin, R. (Eds.). (2004). Radical theory/critical praxis: Academic geography beyond the academy. In *Radical theory, critical praxis: Making a difference beyond the academy* (pp. 1–20). Victoria, Canada: ACME e-book series/Praxis (e) Press. Retrieved from http://www.praxis-epress.org/availablebooks/radicaltheorycriticalpraxis.html. Accessed on July 2008.

Fonnow, M. M., & Cook, J. A. (1991). *Beyond methodology: Feminist scholarship as lived Research.* Bloomington, IN: Indiana University Press.

Gilfus, M., Fineran, S., Cohan, D., Jensen, S., Hartwick, L., & Spath, R. (1999). Research on violence against women: Creating survivor-informed collaborations. *Violence Against Women, 5*, 1194–1212.

Godin, B., & Gingras, Y. (2000). Impact of collaborative research on academic science. *Science and Public Policy, 27*, 65–73.

Gondolf, E., Yllo, K., & Campbell, J. (1997). Collaboration between researchers and advocates. In G. K. Cantor, & J. Jasiniki (Eds.), *Out of the darkness: Contemporary research* (pp. 255–267). Thousand Oaks, CA: Sage.

Greenwood, D. J., & Levin, M. (2006). *Introduction to action research: Social research for social change.* Thousand Oaks, CA: Sage.

Hall, B. L. (1992). From margins to center? The development and purpose of participatory research. *The American Sociologist, 23*, 15–28.

Harkness, J. (2003). Questionnaire translation. In J. Harkness, F. J. R. Van De Vijuver, & P. Moher (Eds.), *Cross-cultural survey methods* (pp. 19–34). New Jersey, NJ: John Wiley & Sons.

Haviland, M., Frye V., & Rajah, V. (2008). Harnessing the power of advocacy research collaborations: Lessons from the field. *Feminist Criminology, 3*, 247–275.

Hill-Bailey, P. (1997). Finding your way around qualitative methods in nursing research. *Journal of Advanced Nursing, 25*, 1, 18–22.

Horowitz, C. R., Robinson, M., & Seifer, S. (2009). Community-based participatory research from the margin to the mainstream are researchers prepared? *Circulation, 119*, 2633–2642.

Hyman, I., Forte, T., Mont, J. D., Romans, S., & Cohen, M. M. (2006). Help seeking rates for intimate partner violence (IPV) among Canadian immigrant women. *Health Care for Women International, 27*, 682–694.

Hyman, I., Mason, R., Guruge, S., Berman, H., Kanagaratnam, P., & Manuel, L. (2011). Perceptions of factors contributing to intimate partner violence among Sri Lankan Tamil immigrant women in Canada. *Health Care for Women International, 32*, 779–794.

John-Steiner, V. (2000). *Creative collaboration.* New York, NY: Oxford University Press.

Kilpatrick, D. G., Resick, P. A., & Williams, L. M. (2001). Fostering collaborations between violence against women researchers and practitioners. *Social Insight, 6*, 29–36.

Kindon, S., & Elwood, S. (2009). More than methods: Reflections on participatory action research in geographic teaching, learning and research. *Journal of Geography in Higher Education, 33*, 19–32.

Kone, A., Sullivan, M., Senturia K., Chrisman, N. J., Ciske, S. J., & Krieger, J. W. (2000). Improving collaboration between researchers and communities. *Public Health, 115*, 243–248.

Korten, D. (1980). Community organization and rural development: A learning process approach. *Public Administration Review, 40*, 480–511.

Koss, M. P., & White, J. W. (2008). National and global agendas on violence against women: historical perspective and consensus. *American Journal of Orthopsychiatry, 78*, 386–393.

Kwan, M. P. (2001). Quantitative methods and feminist geographic research. In P. Moss (Ed.), *Feminist geography in practice: Research and methods* (pp. 60–71). Oxford: Blackwell.

Lennett, J., & Colten, M. E. (1999). A winning alliance: Collaboration of advocates and researchers on the Massachusetts mothers survey. *Violence Against Women, 5*, 1118–1139.

Macpherson, H., Davies, C., Hart, A., Eryigit-Madzwamuse, S., Rathbone, A., Gagnon, E., … Dennis, S. (2017). Collaborative community research dissemination and networking: experiences and challenges. *Gateways, 10*, 298–312.

Minkler, M. (2000). Using participatory action research to build healthy communities. *Public Health Reports, 115*, 119–197.

Minkler, M. (2005). Community-based research partnerships: Challenges, and opportunities. *Journal of Urban Health, 82*(2S), 3–12.

Mog, J. M. (2006). Managing development programs for sustainability: Integrating development and research through adaptive management. *Society & Natural Resources*, *19*, 531–546.

Naples, N. A. (2003). *Feminism and method: Ethnography, discourse analysis, and activist research*. New York, NY: Routledge.

Perilla, J. L., Serrata, J. V., Weinberg, J., & Lippy, C. A. (2012). Integrating women's voices and theory: A comprehensive domestic violence intervention for Latinas. *Women & Therapy*, *35*, 93–105.

Perkins, D., & Wandersman, A. (1990). You'll have to work to overcome our suspicions: The benefits and pitfalls of research with community organizations. *Social Policy*, *21*, 32–41.

Ponic, P., & Jategaonkar, N. (2012). Balancing safety and action: Ethical protocols for photovoice research with women who have experienced violence. *Arts Health*, *4*, 189–202.

Reinharz, S. (1992). Feminist action research. In S. Reinharz (Ed.). *Feminist methods in social research* (pp. 175–196). New York, NY: Oxford University Press.

Riger, S. (1999). Working together: Challenges in collaborative research on violence against women. *Violence against Women*, *5*, 1099–1117.

Rynes, S. L., Bartunek, J. M., & Daft, R. L. (2001). Across the great divide: Knowledge creation and transfer between practitioners and academics. *Academy of Management Journal*, *44*, 340–355.

Schensul, J. J., & Stull, D. D. (1987). Introduction. In D. D. Stull & J. J. Schensul (Eds.), *Collaborative research and social change: Applied Anthropology in action* (pp. 1–8). Boulder, CO: Westview Press.

Schensul, S. L. (1987). Perspectives on collaborative research. In D. D. Stull & J. J. Schensul (Eds.), *Collaborative research and social Change: Applied anthropology in action* (pp. 211–219). Boulder, CO: Westview Press.

Schensul, J. J., Robinson, J., Reyes, C., Radda, K., Gaztambide, S., & Disch W. (2006). Building interdisciplinary/intersectional research partnerships for community-based mental health research with older minority adults. *American Journal of Psychology*, *38*, 79–93.

Small, S. A., & Uttal, L. (2005). Action-oriented research: Strategies for engaged scholarship. *Journal of Marriage and Family*, *67*, 936–948.

Snelgrove, S. R. (2014). Conducting qualitative longitudinal research using interpretative phenomenological analysis. *Nurse Researcher*, *22*, 20–25.

Stoecker, R., & Beckwith, D. (1992). Advancing Toledo's neighborhood movement through participatory action research: Integrating activist and academic approaches. *Clinical Sociology Review*, *10*, 198–213.

Stringer, E. T. (2013). *Action research*. Thousand Oaks, CA: Sage.

Sullivan, M., Bhuyan, R., Senturia, K., Shiu-Thornton, S., & Ciske, S. (2005). Participatory action research in practice: A case study in addressing domestic violence in nine cultural communities. *Journal of Interpersonal Violence*, *20*, 977–995.

Sullivan, M., Kone, A., Senturia, K., Chrisman, N. J., Ciske, S. J., & Krieger, J. W. (2001). Researcher and research-community perspectives: Towards bridging the gap. *Health Education Behavior*, *28*, 130–149.

Torres, M. E., & Fine, M. (2004). Remembering exclusions: Participatory action research in public institutions. *Qualitative Research Psychology, 1*, 15–37.

Vaughan, E., Murdolo, A., Murray, L., Davis, E., Chen, J., Block, K., … Warr, D. (2015). ASPIRE: A multi-site community-based participatory research project to increase understanding of the dynamics of violence against immigrant and refugee women in Australia. *BMC Public Health*, *15*, 1283. *Open Access* https://bmcpublichealth.biomedcentral.com/articles/10.1186/s12889-015-2634-0

Warren, M. R., Calderón, J., Kupscznk, L. A., Squires, G., & Su, C. (2018). Is collaborative, community-engaged scholarship more rigorous than traditional scholarship on advocacy, bias, and social science research. *Urban Education*, *4*, 445–472.

Weaver, R., & Ammar, N. (1991). A collaborative approach to applied survey research. *Sociological Practice Review*, *2*, 275–280.

White, J. W., Yuan, N. P., Cook, S. L., & Abbey, A. (2013). Ethnic minority women's experiences with intimate partner violence: Using community-based participatory research to ask the right questions. *Sex Roles*, *69*, 226–236.

Williams, L. (2004). Researcher–advocate collaborations to end violence against women: Toward liberating methodologies for action research. *Journal of Interpersonal Violence*, *19*, 1350–1357.

Wray, K. B. (2002). The epistemic significance of collaborative research. *Philosophy of Science*, *69*, 150–169.

Wright, K., Williams, P., Wright, S., & Gedjeyan, H. (2011). Ties that bind: Creating and sustaining community–academic partnerships. *Gateways: International Journal of Community Research and Engagement*, *4*, 83–99.

Wynne, B. (2006). Public engagement as a means of restoring public trust in science hitting the notes, but missing the music? *Community Genet*, *9*, 211–220.

CHAPTER 9

THE USES AND LIMITS OF PHOTOVOICE IN RESEARCH ON LIFE AFTER IMMIGRATION DETENTION AND DEPORTATION

Sarah Turnbull

ABSTRACT

Purpose – *This chapter critically reflects on the author's failed attempt to incorporate visual methods in follow-up research on immigration detention and deportation in Britain. In particular, it considers the uses and limits of participant-generated visuals, and the specific method of photovoice, which were originally conceived as a means to explore themes of home, identity, and belonging in and through practices of detention and release or expulsion.*

Methodology/approach – *This chapter discusses the visual method of photovoice to consider the uses and limits of participant-generated visuals.*

Findings – *Drawing on the notion of research "failure," this chapter highlights the challenges and limitations of photovoice in follow-up research with individuals who were detained and/or deported, pointing to various methodological, logistical, ethical, and political issues pertaining to the method itself and the use of the visual in criminological research.*

Originality/value – *Criminologists are increasingly considering the visual and the power of photographic images within criminological research, both as objects of study and through the use of visual methodologies. This shift toward the examination, as well as integration, of images raises a number of important methodological, ethical, and political questions worthy of consideration, including instances where visual methods like photovoice are unsuccessful in a research project.*

Methods of Criminology and Criminal Justice Research
Sociology of Crime, Law and Deviance, Volume 24, 151–164

ISSN: 1521-6136/doi:10.1108/S1521-613620190000024014

Keywords: Photovoice; immigration detention; deportation; visual criminology; research failure; ethics

INTRODUCTION

This is an article written from a sense of failure. Gillian Rose (1997, p. 305)

In 2013, I began a mostly qualitative research project on the lived experiences of immigration detention and deportation in the United Kingdom (UK), with specific focus on the themes of identity, home, and belonging. The project commenced with a multi-sited ethnography of four immigration removal centers (IRCs) over one year and included formal interviews, focus groups, and a survey. The second phase of the project involved following up with participants who had been released into the British community or deported to other countries to explore what life was like after detention and/or deportation. As part of this follow-up research, I attempted to integrate a visual component in which participants would be given digital cameras to document their lives after detention or deportation. Known as photovoice, the aim of incorporating this approach was to enable participants to record and showcase their own lives in ways that words alone could not, while also generating images that could be used in formal interviews as per the method of photo-elicitation.

I imagined at the beginning of the project that the photovoice component would generate a wealth of visual data on participants' lived experience of release to the British community or life after deportation and lead to enriched formal interviews. I expected that the method of photovoice would work in a particular way, along the lines of what I had read about in other studies utilizing the method, to reveal something novel about participants' lived experiences of border control. However, for a variety of reasons, utilizing the method of photovoice in this research project was, ultimately, unsuccessful.

The purpose of this chapter is to offer a critical reflection and discussion of where and how this methodological approach went "wrong," highlighting the tensions between research fantasy (as in expectations) and failure. It provides a situated account of methods in practice by speaking to the gap that emerged between the carefully planned research project and the use of methods in the field, which generated feelings of ambivalence and raised important questions about the ethics and politics of the visual in the context of the study and in criminological research more generally. In this chapter, I consider the uses and limits of participant-generated visuals and photovoice in particular, arguing that it is necessary to take account of our research failures as a means to contribute to and advance methodological discussions in criminology.

Criminologists have tended not to discuss the messiness of their research or what happens when projects do not go according to plan – or "succeed" – although this is changing. Indeed, "many accounts of research practice (not least guidelines to 'research ethics') reproduce an idealistic vision of research" (Horton, 2008, p. 378). Drawing on Rose (1997), Horton (2008, p. 365) observes that "the acknowledgement of 'failure' and uncertainty can often be revelatory and productive" (see also Ross & Call-Cummings, 2019; Vaswani, 2018). It is along this vein that this chapter was inspired and is intended to contribute to this special collection on methods of criminology and criminal justice.

This chapter is divided into two parts. First, I offer an overview of the research project and discuss its methodological approach, including the photovoice method. In the second section, I explore some of the methodological, ethical, and political challenges I encountered when attempting to draw on and incorporate the visual method of photovoice, reflecting on my failure with this approach. I then conclude with some reflections on the methodological contribution of thinking about research failure in the context of criminological research.

PICTURING LIFE AFTER DETENTION

As introduced above, photovoice was one of the methods used as part of a larger research project exploring migrants' experiences of immigration detention and deportation in Britain, with specific analytic attention paid to how ideas about home, identity, and belonging in (post)colonial, multicultural Britain shape experiences of detention and what happens when individuals are released into the community or deported. The research sought to explore the following questions: Who are the people detained at IRCs and where is (or are) their "home(s)"? Where do they "belong" and why? How do immigration detention and deportation make and remake the British homeland? How are Britain, Britishness, and ideas about "difference" constituted and reconstituted through practices of immigration detention and deportation? How do the experiences of immigration detention and deportation shape and reshape detainees' sense of identity, where they belong, and where or what "home" is? These questions and the broader project were informed by my background and training in criminology and commitment to an anti-racist feminist ethic.

The project had two main phases – although the timing of these overlapped – and involved a combination of research methods. The first phase was a multi-sited ethnography of four IRCs (Campsfield House, Yarl's Wood, Colnbrook, and Dover) between September 2013 and August 2014 with the aim to understand daily life in these detention centers. This ethnography included observation and interaction, along with formal interviews and focus groups with detainees as well as formal interviews with IRC staff (see Turnbull, 2016, 2017, 2018a; Turnbull & Hasselberg, 2017). I also administered the Measuring the Quality of Life in Immigration Detention survey across the four field sites (see Bosworth & Kellezi, 2015).

Undertaken primarily between January 2014 to December 2015, phase two of the study consisted of follow-up fieldwork with participants who had been released into the British community (e.g., on immigration bail, temporary admission, or leave to enter or remain) or subject to administrative removal or deportation. To carry out the follow-up fieldwork, I kept in contact with participants through a variety of means (e.g., email, text message, telephone, Facebook, and LinkedIn) once I concluded the fieldwork in the IRCs, as well as recruited additional participants through snowballing sampling. I conducted post-release interviews, both in-person (for participants in Britain) and via telephone or Skype (for participants who had been deported) (see Turnbull, 2018b, 2018c). It was during phase two of this study that I attempted to incorporate the method of photovoice.

What is Photovoice?

The method of photovoice was originally developed by Wang and Burgess in the 1990s "to enable Chinese village women to photograph their everyday health and work realities" (Wang, 1999, p. 185). Wang (1999, p. 185) defines photovoice as "an innovative participatory action research (PAR) method based on health promotion principles and the theoretical literature on education for critical consciousness, feminist theory, and nontraditional approaches to documentary photograph." The method involves providing participants with cameras so that they can "identify, represent, and enhance" their communities and perceived realities (Wang, 1999, p. 185). Photography thus provides a medium through which participants can "lend significance to their lived experiences" (Walsh, Rutherford, & Kuzmak, 2009, p. 303).

Although initially developed within the field of health promotion, photovoice has been used in research with diverse populations including homeless people (Miller, 2006; Walsh et al., 2009; Wang, Cash, & Powers, 2000), formerly incarcerated women (Fortune & Arai, 2014), women migrants (Pearce, McMurray, Walsh, & Malek, 2017), young migrants (Fassetta, 2016), young adults (Rania, Migliorini, Cardinali, & Rebora, 2015), students (Call-Cummings & Martinez, 2016; Stack & Wang, 2018), drug users (Copes, Tchoula, Brookman, & Ragland, 2018; Fitzgibbon & Healy, 2017), women under community supervision (Fitzgibbon & Healy, 2017; Fitzgibbon & Stengel, 2017), indigenous peoples (Brooks & Poudrier, 2014), and displaced persons (Weber, 2018). As Call-Cummings and Martinez (2016, p. 798) observe, photovoice "is a critical approach to empowering or 'unsilencing' groups often unheard by hegemonic research processes and powerful policy circles," which helps to explain why the method is particularly prevalent in research with marginalized or vulnerable groups.

In the context of criminological research and visual criminology specifically, photovoice has been used recently by Fitzgibbon and Healy (2017) in research with individuals on community supervision in England and Ireland based on the rationale that "images could provide a window onto the experience of supervision for those subject to it and also for the wider public for whom supervision is often invisible" (Fitzgibbon & Healy, 2017, p. 4). The authors note that images offer the greater potential to convey emotion, allowing audiences to feel what it would be like to be under community supervision. The study also involved photographic exhibitions to showcase the photographs taken and selected by participants

(Fitzgibbon & Healy, 2017). Relatedly, Fitzgibbon and Stengel (2017, p. 3) bring together two projects, the first involving women on community supervision in England and the second related to women injection drug users in Hungary, using photovoice to "provide an in-depth understanding of participants' realities." The authors conclude that:

> methodological strength of photovoice is that participants hold the power to take photographs of whatever they choose, and these images ultimately guide the generation of materials and analysis of the photovoice research. (Fitzgibbon & Stengel, 2017, p. 17)

In this sense, the goal is to have participants be co-researchers, thus shifting the traditional relationship and power imbalance between researcher and researched.

Indeed, as Carrabine (2012) has observed, criminologists are increasingly considering the visual and the power of photographic images within criminological and sociolegal research, both as objects of study and through the use of visual methodologies. This shift toward the examination, as well as integration, of images raises a number of important questions – and cautions – for criminological researchers and the field of visual criminology itself (Brown, 2014; Carrabine, 2014; Schept, 2014; Young, 2014). Importantly, Fitzgibbon and Stengel (2017) remind us that a method like photovoice does not magically remove power differentials in research nor inherently bring about social change.

Why Use Photovoice in This Study?

The integration of visual research methods into the research project was based on the idea that images can help convey experiences of life after detention – and for some, life after deportation – in ways that words alone could not. During the initial planning of the study, images were seen as being able to evoke or speak to the richer "textures" of people's lived experiences in relation to the main project themes – home, belonging, and identity – than those conveyed solely through ethnography, interviews, or focus groups. The goal with photovoice, and the related method of photo-elicitation, offered further insight into how detention impacts individuals upon their return "home" – whether this is in the UK or in another country. Visual images, I originally thought, would enrich and complement the textual data I had collected.

A second rationale was that as a method, photovoice is more a participatory-oriented approach to research in which participants can take, select, and contribute their own images (Call-Cummings & Martinez, 2016; Fitzgibbon & Stengel, 2017; Fortune & Arai, 2014) to express what is going on in their post-detention lives. Indeed, one of the broader goals of incorporating images in this project was to help make visible the daily lived experiences of border control that go beyond the sensational or extreme that often dominate media and public discourses (Gilligan & Marley, 2010; Lenette & Miskovic, 2016), to the more intimate and every day from the perspectives of those who live it. By giving participants cameras once they left detention or after they had been deported, the aim was that they may photograph or otherwise record their lives after detention and then select and comment on the images that had the most meaning to them.

The methodological approach I utilized first involved recruiting a sample of study participants who I had met in one of the four IRCs in which I conducted ethnographic fieldwork to remain involved with the project through the practice of photography. This was a small convenience sample of individuals with whom I had developed a rapport during the fieldwork (and most of whom I formally interviewed inside the IRCs) and who were interested in keeping in touch for follow-up interviews. To recruit potential participants, I explained the idea of the visual component of the project as an opportunity for them to document their "homes," notions of identity and belonging, and experiences of life after detention in the British community or after deportation. I told potential participants that they would be given a digital camera that was theirs to keep and that regardless of receiving the camera, they could stop participating in the research at any time. In total, I was able to recruit only six individuals – one woman and five men – who agreed (initially) to participate in the photovoice component.

I first piloted the method using a disposable camera with Hussain (a pseudonym), the first participant I recruited for the photovoice aspect of the study. I then purchased Hussain and each subsequent participant a digital camera for roughly £50 along with two memory cards (worth approximately £10). The models were simple to use and came with instructions in multiple languages. The camera models I purchased offered participants the option to make videos as well. I gave Hussain and one other participant their cameras during follow-up interviews after they had been released from detention into the British community. For two participants who were still in detention, I "deposited" the cameras into their personal belongings stored at the respective IRCs for when they were released (or deported). I also provided the above four participants with notepads to take "notes" (e.g., thoughts or ideas) as a type of "photo diary." The remaining two participants had already been deported, so I posted their cameras to them via Royal Mail and tracked the deliveries.

Along with the cameras, I endeavored to offer some guidance in terms of potential themes and feelings to explore, trying to make clear an idea that was arguably rather abstract. For Hussain, I handwrote him a list of "photograph ideas" that I gave to him along with his disposable camera and notepad:

(1) Photo journal (or video journal) – document a day: what you do, how you feel, where you go (or don't go) and take notes to explain.
(2) Keep the camera with you and take a photo of something that makes you (a) feel you belong or don't belong to the community, UK, etc.; or (b) feel like you are home or homesick; or (c) feel hopeful or frustrated and take notes to explain.
(3) Pick a theme or idea (e.g., "waiting", "boredom", etc.) and document this with images that capture how you feel.

I also provided technical instructions about how to submit the images, which typically involved the participant posting one of the memory cards to me so that they could continue to use the other memory card. In the one "successful" case with Hussain, I gave him a self-addressed stamped envelope so he could post the memory card and his photo diary (i.e., notes) back to me. When discussing the "instructions," I also revisited the issue of informed consent, including, for instance, the assurance to Hussain that he could stop participating at any time without having to return the camera. Further to the ethical imperative not to inadvertently cause pressure to participate, according to Mitchell, Hedayati, Rodriguez, Gordon, and Broyles (2016, p. 1307), assuring participants that the camera was theirs to keep is viewed to increase "ownership" of it so that it is better safeguarded and used.

As part of the methodology, a related aim was to then discuss the images participants submitted using photo-elicitation (see, e.g., Copes et al., 2018; Fitzgibbon & Stengel, 2017; Gariglio, 2016), an approach in which the images could be used as guides for participants' telling of their stories and experiences of life after detention. I developed a detailed consent form specifically for the visual images in which participants could select which materials (photographs or video) they agreed to contribute to the project as well as those that could be disseminated as part of communicating the findings. I conducted one follow-up interview with Hussain using photo-elicitation based on the first set of images he had taken during the pilot with the disposable camera. I developed two sets of the images, one to have in hard copy for the interview and the other for Hussain to keep, which he declined, stating that he did not want to remember that "dark time." We went through the images to discuss why he had taken them. During the interview, which was audio-recorded and transcribed, I also asked Hussain to indicate which images, if any, he gave permission to be used in the research. He stated that I could use all of them however I wanted, which was not an "ideal" response in terms of the method and the idea that participants ought to select those images with meaning to them (Fitzgibbon & Stengel, 2017). As with other follow-up research interviews in this study, Hussain was given an honorarium of £15 for his time and expertise.

In the end, I was unable to "successfully" utilize the method of photovoice in this research project. Only one participant, Hussain, was engaged for a time with taking and contributing images and discussing them with me. For example, he took photographs of his "no-choice" asylum-seeker accommodation, what it was like to live off of £35 per week in asylum-seeker support, how he traveled to report to the Home Office, waiting for his asylum interview, and trying to keep busy. I originally published some of these images and his story (based on his notes and the follow-up interview) as a blog post with the aim to make visible the lived experiences of border control (Turnbull, 2014).

In the following section, I outline a number of challenges that I encountered while attempting to incorporate this method, how I tried to overcome them, and where and how I think I failed.

THE CHALLENGES OF USING PHOTOVOICE

The participants in this project occupied highly precarious and/or emotionally difficult positions. I first met them in the context of immigration detention in which they were confined within prison-like institutions while facing deportation for indeterminate periods of time. I then tried to follow-up with them once they were released and/or deported, which were situations also marked by (at minimum) great uncertainty, precarity, and emotional upset (Klein & Williams, 2012; Turnbull, 2018c). In sum, then, participants were dealing with some challenging life circumstances during the time in which I was attempting to engage them with the research study.

The particular research methodology utilized in this study was contingent on the development and maintenance of strong researcher–participant relationships that could withstand the emotional, logistical, and practical effects of detention, release, and/or deportation. It often necessitated doing this across cultural, gender, and linguistic differences and over time, which presented a number of challenges (see Turnbull, 2018b). More generally, attempting to recruit participants in the context of immigration detention is especially difficult due to the highly uncertain, anxiety-provoking, distressing, and stressful nature of detention (see, e.g., Bosworth & Kellezi, 2017). A related issue was that the due to the cost of the cameras and the finite budget, I felt the need to be careful about recruiting a sample of participants who I thought would be the most likely to engage in the photovoice method. I intuitively attempted to select individuals with whom I felt I had developed strong relationships that could pass the test of time and distance. It was, however, difficult to recruit participants. This difficulty was, in part, due to the challenges I experienced in clearly conveying to participants the aims and purposes of photographic aspect of the research project. Despite trying to "sell" the project as being interesting and potentially fun (because who doesn't like to take photos?) and result in a free camera, I was unsuccessful in recruiting a sufficient number of participants to sustain the project if participants dropped off.

A second challenge, then, involved the attrition of participants. Five of the six participants who initially agreed to participate did not – as was their right – continue with the project. Three participants stopped responding to my attempts (via email, text message, and/or social media) to follow up with them and essentially dropped out of the study. For the remaining two participants, we kept in touch once they had been deported but one, as discussed below, did not receive his camera in the post and there was not scope in the project to send a new camera, while the other decided that he did not want to participate after all. The issue of participant attrition is not unique to photovoice as a method, but rather relates to the broader challenge of following up with participants over time and across geographical space. Attending to the reasons why participants do not "fully" participate or continue to stay involved in a research project, particularly involving a photographic element is, however, important (see Fassetta, 2016). According to Sharpe (2017, p. 240), "[r]efusal to participate in research can be interpreted as a self-protective strategy to avoid or minimize the potentially harmful emotional and material consequences of self-narration." Indeed, the request to photograph and otherwise document their lives may have been too great an intrusion on participants' lives and privacy, particularly given the context in which their lives had been subject to intense scrutiny and censure by the Home Office.

Another challenge related to the logistical and technical barriers is associated with getting the cameras to overseas participants and then retrieving the images. In relation to the first issue, the method of posting the cameras to overseas participants proved to be challenging. In addition to being highly costly, with the postage ending up costing more than the price of the camera, the reliability of the postal service varied. For instance, one camera I posted to South Asia was simply lost, whereas another one sat undelivered at the post office in its North African destination and was retrieved only due to the participant's personal connections to his country's postal service. In relation to the second issue of getting participants' images back, this initially posed a logistical problem, although in the end did not matter for this particular project. For participants in developing countries, access to the internet or to mobile data through which to submit digital photos was either expensive or unavailable. Posting the digital memory cards back to me was also not ideal as these could have been lost and also involved logistical challenges associated with pre-paying participants (e.g., through Western Union) for the postage costs so as not to burden them (e.g., through reimbursement).

A further challenge related to ethical issues associated with utilizing this particular methodology. I encountered several situations where I felt it was unethical to go past a certain point of "encouraging" participation. I often felt that it was too onerous a request to make of people who were leaving detention, some of whom faced deportation to places where their main concerns were for basic needs like shelter and food. Some participants suffered significant emotional and psychological distress due to their detention, and most encountered difficult situations once they were released from detention into the UK or returned to another country. I felt I could only make the opportunity available but could not press it further if there was no interest. As Sharpe (2017, pp. 237–238) observes, "[t]he methods of longitudinal qualitative research risk reproducing the everyday modes of surveillance experienced by" participants. Although this was not a longitudinal study, Sharpe's concern about the implications of "sociological stalking" is indeed a cogent reminder of how marginalized and vulnerable populations can be subjected to similar practices of surveillance and scrutiny by researchers as they are by the state (e.g., the Home Office) and other agents (e.g., solicitors, third sector professionals, etc.). Receiving a request by me for a follow-up interview or a friendly enquiry as to how their photographing was going could have likely contributed to what was already a difficult daily existence. In particular, and following Sharpe (2017), my requests for participation could be seen as yet another demand from an external actor in addition to demands experienced by former detainees in the UK such as reporting to the Home Office, communicating with solicitors, managing strained family relationships, dealing with asylum seeker support, and so forth. For those who had been deported, my requests could have been an unpleasant reminder of what had been experienced and potentially lost through detention and deportation, including their former lives in the UK.

Through this research project, I began to think that the model of photovoice I had been pursuing was "outdated," particularly given the ubiquity of smart phones with cameras and many younger people's familiarity with taking photos and sharing them through social media. In hindsight, my attempt to employ the photovoice method assumed particular levels of both technical competency and comfort with visual culture among participants. Researchers such as Yi-Frazier et al. (2015) have explored the feasibility of using the photo-sharing application Instagram to overcome the logistical challenges of implementing photovoice with adolescents, while others like DeBerry-Spence, Ekpo, and Hogan (2019) have considered the importance of using mobile phones to take photos as part of data collection. Although I was unable to "update" the technical aspect of the method, I raise it as a consideration for future photovoice research to potentially assist with participant recruitment and overcome possible barriers with participants who are widely dispersed. However, the technical aspect aside, the potential underlying disjuncture around participants' comfort level with taking photographs and the visual practice demanded by the method remain (see, e.g., Fassetta, 2016).

I also reached the conclusion that this method likely works best under certain conditions, in particular sites, and with specific populations. In the literature, researchers describe situations where the participants were located in a common geographic area and where the researchers could participate in the image-generating process, photo-elicitation focus groups, and public exhibitions (e.g., Fitzgibbon & Stengel, 2017). In my project, participants were diversely situated and located in disparate places. Had participant recruitment been successful, ideally, I would have had to have been creative in order to overcome the different time zones and technological resources to attempt a focus group via an online group video chat.

In attempting to utilize photovoice in this research project and receiving some photos from participants, important ethical and political questions started to emerge. I began thinking more deeply about the purpose of such images and what they could do to help us better understand the lived experiences of border control. At the outset, I admittedly did not think very carefully about how I would use the images contributed as part of the project; that is, how they would become "data" to analyze, tools to elicit discussions or conversations (photo-elicitation), and part of the "outputs" of the project in terms of images to share with wider audiences (e.g., my blog post, Turnbull, 2014). As the project progressed and the photovoice method turned out to be unsuccessful, I became to feel increasingly ambivalent about this aspect of the project and what I ought to do with the "archive" of images I had collected, including the contributions from Hussain.

The ethical and political implications of using images sent by participants were raised most profoundly when I received several photos via email from Dev (a pseudonym), one of the participants who had initially agreed to participate in the photographic component of the research but whose camera was lost in the post. Dev happened to be an avid photographer and after being deported to Bangladesh (see Turnbull, 2018c), he sent me a few photos of himself in his village, including swimming in a river and sitting on a riverboat. One image was of a beautiful sunset over the river and lush forest, framed by tree branches. I was first struck by the beauty of the images and of the sense of relief that Dev was at least "okay" enough after experiencing the traumatic rupture of being deported from an IRC to get in touch with me once he arrived in his village. Although these photos did not contribute to the project "officially" as part of the photovoice method, they gave me a sense of what I might have received if the method had worked.

The longer I reflected on these images from Dev, the more I was reminded of how "going home" was often framed by Home Office employees, IRC staff, and private security personnel as a "return" to various beautiful and "exotic" countries of origin. During my multi-sited ethnography, I observed IRC staff occasionally ask detainees why they would want to be in Britain given its miserable weather when they could be in the sun and surf of their home countries. Moreover, in a follow-up interview, Beata (a pseudonym), who was deported from an IRC to Namibia, expressed her astonishment that she "was thrown on a plane by English immigration officers who regard coming here to deport Namibians as a holiday, and casually discuss how they are going to enjoy it." Although such comments about the British weather are cliché and working people often combine business trips with leisure opportunities, the problematic imagining of detainees' post-deportation lives as sunny beach vacations minimizes detained people's own choices and aspirations as well as the reasons why they migrated in the first place and may not want to return. Moreover, such framings diminish the violence of detention and deportation and the numerous, long-lasting harms caused.

Although the potential for Dev's photo of the sunset to be "read" and consumed via a western touristic gaze seemed especially problematic to me, similar ethical and political questions exist around how Hussain's photos of "no-choice" asylum-seeker accommodation could also be "read" and understood by audiences. For instance, despite what looked to me as the apparent substandard accommodation provided to asylum-seekers like Hussain, the images could also be read into or by broader right-wing discourses of the British state providing housing and benefits to so-called undeserving non-citizens. However, despite the original framing of the photovoice method in this project as giving participants the opportunity to share their experiences and lives through photography, my own role in the process has become increasingly clear, particularly in the sense of strong feelings about which images were okay to show (i.e., Hussain's photos) and those that were not (i.e., photos like those shared by Dev). Despite the goal of "empowering participants" with a visual method like photovoice, Copes et al. (2018, p. 483) concede that "as researchers we acknowledge that it is also our job to synthesize the totality of the findings, analyze them, and interpret them." Although images are multivocal and audiences will differently interpret them, there are risks involved with sharing images, particularly when it may inadvertently reproduce dominant narratives that counter the ethical or political aims of the research. Consequently, the images collected as part of this project remain archived.

CONCLUSION

This chapter has provided an account of some of the challenges and opportunities of using the visual research method of photovoice in the course of undertaking criminological research on life after immigration detention and deportation. In doing so, this reflective discussion has, in Horton (2008, p. 363) words, "entail[ed] owning up to a range of experiences and emotions – uncertainty, fallibility, nervousness, self-doubt – which (still) seem to sit uncomfortably with contemporary ideals about what make a 'good researcher.'" Even as criminology as a discipline has tended not to delve into the "messiness" of research practice, this chapter aims to encourage the dialog forward, recognizing the importance of speaking to research "failure." Indeed, like Horton (2008, p. 364), I find methodological writing that "gestures towards imperfections, disappointments and angsts in/of others' research practices" to be the most useful to me as a researcher.

In the context of growing pressure by academic funders and institutions for researchers to be increasingly "creative" by incorporating or utilizing new or "innovative" methods in the course of carrying out research, it may be useful to think about challenges of "innovating." Successful grant applications often require methodological innovation and the turn to visual, arts-based, and participatory methodologies can look particularly appealing, especially in relation to research impact – even if the research topics or contexts do not lend themselves easily to such methods.

In writing this conclusion, I have grappled with how to frame this experience and articulate what it contributes to methodological discussions. For instance, framing it simply as "lessons learned" risks suggesting neat solutions to messy problems. On the other hand, too much focus on the failure risks returning to the idea that if I had only applied the method "correctly" and not, for example, as an additional qualitative tool, that the project would have been "successful." The primary contribution of this reflection is its attempt to come to terms with "failure" in research. Attending to the "messiness" of research necessitates recognition that we navigate a variety of choices as researchers and often things do not go according to plan.

ACKNOWLEDGMENTS

I would like to thank the women and men who participated in the study and the IRC managers and Home Office for allowing research access. This study was generously supported by the European Research Council under Mary Bosworth's Starting Grant (2012–2017) [no. 313362]. I am grateful to members of Birkbeck's Criminology Research Group, and Tanya Serisier and Rachael Dobson in particular, for their helpful comments on an earlier draft of this chapter. Many thanks to editors Mathieu Deflem and Derek Silva for inviting this contribution.

REFERENCES

Bosworth, M., & Kellezi, B. (2015). Quality of life in detention: Results from MQLD questionnaire data collected in IRC Campsfield House, IRC Yarl's Wood, IRC Colnbrook, and IRC Dover, September 2013–August 2014. Retrieved from https://www.law.ox.ac.uk/sites/files/oxlaw/mqld.pdf. Accessed on February 1, 2019.

Bosworth, M., & Kellezi, B. (2017). Doing research in immigration removal centres: Ethics, emotions and impact. *Criminology & Criminal Justice*, *17*(2), 121–137.

Brooks, C. M., & Poudrier, J. (2014). Anti-oppressive visual methodologies: Critical appraisal of cross-cultural research design. *Qualitative Sociology Review*, *10*(4), 32–51.

Brown, M. (2014). Visual criminology and carceral studies: Counter-images in the carceral age. *Theoretical Criminology*, *18*(2), 176–197.

Call-Cummings, M., & Martinez, S. (2016). Consciousness-raising or unintentionally oppressive? Potential negative consequences of photovoice. *The Qualitative Report*, *21*(5), 798–810.

Carrabine, E. (2012). Just images: Aesthetics, ethics and visual criminology. *British Journal of Criminology*, *52*(3), 463–489.

Carrabine, E. (2014). Seeing things: Violence, voyeurism and the camera. *Theoretical Criminology*, *18*(2), 134–158.

Copes, H., Tchoula, W., Brookman, F., & Ragland, J. (2018). Photo-elicitation interviews with vulnerable populations: Practical and ethical considerations. *Deviant Behavior*, *39*(4), 475–494.

DeBerry-Spence, B., Ekpo, A. E., & Hogan, D. (2019). Mobile phone visual ethnography (MpVE): Bridging transformative photography and mobile phone ethnography. *Journal of Public Policy & Marketing*, *38*(1), 81–95.

Fassetta, G. (2016). Using photography in research with young migrants: Addressing questions of visibility, movement and personal spaces. *Children's Geographies*, *14*(6), 701–715.

Fitzgibbon, W., & Healy, D. (2017). Lives and spaces: Photovoice and offender supervision in Ireland and England. *Criminology & Criminal Justice*, *19*(1), 3–25.

Fitzgibbon, W., & Stengel, C. M. (2017). Women's voices made visible: Photovoice in visual criminology. *Punishment & Society*, *20*(4), 411–431.

Fortune, D., & Arai, S. M. (2014). Rethinking community within the context of social inclusion as social justice: Implications for women after federal incarceration. *Studies in Social Justice*, *8*(1), 79–107.

Gariglio, L. (2016). Photo-elicitation in prison ethnography: Breaking the ice in the field and unpacking prison officers' use of force. *Crime, Media, Culture*, *12*(3), 367–379.

Gilligan, C., & Marley, C. (2010). Migration and divisions: Thoughts on (anti-) narrativity in visual representations of mobile people. *Forum: Qualitative Social Research*, *11*(2). Retrieved from http://www.qualitative-research.net/index.php/fqs/article/view/1476. Accessed on February 1, 2019.

Horton, J. (2008). A 'sense of failure'? Everydayness and research ethics. *Children's Geographies*, *6*(4), 363–383.

Klein, A., & Williams, L. (2012). Immigration detention in the community: Research on the experiences of migrants released from detention centres in the UK. *Population, Space and Place*, *18*(6), 741–753.

Lenette, C., & Miskovic, N. (2016). 'Some viewers may find the following images disturbing': Visual representations of refugee deaths at border crossings. *Crime, Media, Culture*, *14*(1), 111–120.

Miller, C. J. (2006). Images from the streets: Art for social change from the homelessness photography project. *Social Justice*, *33*(2), 122–134.

Mitchell, M. A., Hedayati, D. O., Rodriguez, K. L., Gordon, A. J., & Broyles, L. M. (2016). Logistical lessons learned in designing and executing a photo-elicitation study in the veterans health administration. *The Qualitative Report*, *21*(7), 1303–1315.

Pearce, E., Mcmurray, K., Walsh, C. A., & Malek, L. (2017). Searching for tomorrow: South Sudanese women reconstructing resilience through photovoice. *Journal of International Migration and Integration*, *18*(2), 369–389.

Rania, N., Migliorini, L., Cardinali, P., & Rebora, S. (2015). Giving a face to immigration and integration processes: The use of photovoice with Italian young adults. *The Qualitative Report*, *20*(6), 780–798.

Rose, G. (1997). Situating knowledges: Positionality, reflexivities and other tactics. *Progress in Human Geography*, *21*(3), 305–320.

Ross, K., & Call-Cummings, M. (2019). Acknowledging and transcending 'failure': Lifeworld possibilities and system constraints. *International Journal of Social Research Methodology*, *22*(1), 97–109.

Schept, J. (2014). (Un)seeing like a prison: Counter-visual ethnography of the carceral state. *Theoretical Criminology*, *18*(2), 198–223.

Sharpe, G. (2017). Sociological stalking? Methods, ethics and power in longitudinal criminological research. Criminology and *Criminal Justice*, *17*(3), 233–247.

Stack, M., & Wang, F. (2018). Students' perceptions of belonging: A photovoice participatory action research project. *Canadian Journal of Action Research*, *19*(1), 48–66.

Turnbull, S. (2014). Life after detention: A photo story. Retrieved from https://www.law.ox.ac.uk/research-subject-groups/centre-criminology/centreborder-criminologies/blog/2014/01/life-after. Accessed on February 1, 2019.

Turnbull, S. (2016). 'Stuck in the middle': Waiting and uncertainty in immigration detention. *Time & Society*, *25*(1), 61–79.

Turnbull, S. (2017). Immigration detention and the racialized governance of illegality in the United Kingdom. *Social Justice*, *44*(1), 142–164.

Turnbull, S. (2018a). Living the spectre of forced return: Negotiating deportability in British immigration detention. *Migration Studies*. Published online July 17, 2018. doi:10.1093/migration/mny024

Turnbull, S. (2018b). Making sense of the shifting 'field': Ethical and practical considerations in researching life after immigration detention. In A. Fili, S. Jahnsen, & R. Powell (Eds.), *Criminal justice research in an era of mass mobility* (pp. 130–143). Abingdon: Routledge.

Turnbull, S. (2018c). Starting again: Life after deportation from the United Kingdom. In S. Khosravi (Ed.), *After deportation: Ethnographic perspectives* (pp. 37–61). Basingstoke: Palgrave Macmillan.

Turnbull, S., & Hasselberg, I. (2017). From prison to detention: The carceral trajectories of foreign-national prisoners in the United Kingdom. *Punishment & Society*, *19*(2), 135–154.

Vaswani, N. (2018). Learning from failure: Are practitioner researchers the answer when conducting research on sensitive topics with vulnerable children and young people? *International Journal of Social Research Methodology*, *21*(4), 499–512.

Walsh, C. A., Rutherford, G. E., & Kuzmak, N. (2009). Characteristics of home: Perspectives of women who are homeless. *The Qualitative Report*, *14*(2), 299–317.

Wang, C. C. (1999). Photovoice: A participatory action research strategy applied to women's health. *Journal of Women's Health*, *8*(2), 185–192.

Wang, C. C., Cash, J. L., & Powers, L. S. (2000). Who knows the streets as well as the homeless? Promoting personal and community action through photovoice. *Health Promotion Practice*, *1*(1), 81–89.

Weber, S. (2018). Participatory visual research with displaced persons: 'Listening' to post-conflict experiences through the visual. *Journal of Refugee Studies*. Published online July 20, 2018. doi:10.1093/jrs/fey038

Yi-Frazier, J. P., Cochrane, K., Mitrovich, C., Pascual, M., Buscaino, E., Eaton, L., …, Malik, F. (2015). Using instagram as a modified application of photovoice for storytelling and sharing in adolescents with type 1 diabetes. *Qualitative Health Research*, *25*(10), 1372–1382.

Young, A. (2014). From object to encounter: Aesthetic politics and visual criminology. *Theoretical Criminology*, *18*(2), 159–175.

CHAPTER 10

AGENCY RECORDS AS A METHOD FOR EXAMINING HUMAN TRAFFICKING

Valerie R. Anderson, Teresa C. Kulig and Christopher J. Sullivan

ABSTRACT

Purpose – *The purpose of this chapter is to examine the ways in which human trafficking has been measured through the use of agency record data.*

Approach – *The authors review the state of previous research on human trafficking using agency record data and the challenges that are important to consider when using agency records in the study of human trafficking.*

Findings – *Researchers have used agency records in a wide variety of ways to measure human trafficking victimization, perpetration, and patterns or case characteristics. Agency data provide unique contributions to understand human trafficking including the scope of the problem, predictors of victimization, and public perceptions of this crime. The authors describe the efforts to use agency records to estimate the prevalence of human trafficking in a statewide study.*

Value – *This chapter provides an overview of how agency records have been used in human trafficking research in recent years. Furthermore, this chapter includes a case study and methodological reflection on the use of agency records in a statewide human trafficking prevalence study. The authors conclude with a methodological reflection and considerations moving forward for future use of agency data in human trafficking research.*

Keywords: Human trafficking; agency records; existing data; measurement; victimization; prevalence

Methods of Criminology and Criminal Justice Research
Sociology of Crime, Law and Deviance, Volume 24, 165–178

ISSN: 1521-6136/doi:10.1108/S1521-613620190000024015

INTRODUCTION

Human trafficking—broadly defined as the exploitation of individuals commonly through commercial sex or involuntary servitude—is recognized as a complex criminal justice and social problem. Although it has received significant attention from government agencies, service providers, and the general public, there are still challenges to measure the complexities of this crime across public health, criminal justice, and social service contexts. One way researchers have attempted to understand and measure human trafficking is by partnering with agencies that are likely to interact with potential victims. In this way, existing agency records could provide insights into various aspects of trafficking victim's experiences, needs, and vulnerability factors.

Given the increased recognition that victims come into contact with a variety of agencies (e.g., Foot, 2016; Macy & Graham, 2012; Varma, Gillespie, McCracken, & Greenbaum, 2015), obtaining and analyzing agency records for social scientific research has become an increasingly popular tool. This increase in popularity is, in part, due to requirements for archiving funded research in publicly accessible data repositories. These repositories ensure that datasets are available for researchers to replicate findings and/or extend the research possibilities. In addition to formal grant-reporting requirements, many agencies have developed greater capacities to conduct research internally. The information that agencies gather is frequently used to track client progress, make data-driven decisions, or conduct evaluations of services and/or policies. Thus, agency records are oftentimes collected for different purposes than research alone (e.g., Finkelhor & Wells, 2003). Still, agency records are a powerful tool to study complex justice system phenomena such as human trafficking in populations that can be difficult to identify.

Throughout this chapter we describe measuring human trafficking using agency record data. In particular, we discuss (1) the scope of previous research using agency records to measure human trafficking, (2) challenges to consider when using agency records in the study of human trafficking, and (3) a brief case study and methodological reflection on using agency records to estimate the prevalence of human trafficking. Finally, we conclude by providing a summary and considerations for future use of agency records in human trafficking research.

WHAT ARE AGENCY RECORDS?

Scholars in criminology and criminal justice often rely on data previously collected by others, such as governmental or non-governmental agencies. This is often referred to as the analysis of existing data (Stewart & Kamins, 1993). Agency records can include any type of quantitative (e.g., numerical) or qualitative (e.g., case narratives) data and often involves large files (either paper or electronic) of documentation of interest to researchers. These records can provide rich information that is otherwise difficult or impossible for researchers to collect on their own and are especially useful for examining rare events or hidden populations. The use of agency records in criminal justice research is key to descriptive research (e.g., prevalence studies), explanatory research (e.g., theory testing), and applied research (e.g., program evaluation).

Types of Agency Records

There are various types of agency records collected by governmental and non-governmental organizations. Agency records can generally be classified into three distinct types: (1) public agency data, (2) non-public agency data, and (3) new data collected by agencies. Each of these, along with their strengths and limitations, will be described in this section.

First, *public agency data* are commonly used by social scientists. Often reported in the form of aggregated statistics and databases, public agency data includes formal reports of data collected by government agencies. For example, these may include annual reports produced by agencies. Public agency data also include databases available for analysis. For example, the Inter-university Consortium for Political and Social Research (ICPSR) archives data from federally funded studies. These data are publicly accessible to researchers. The utility of these data is subject to three important considerations: (1) data restrictions, (2) purpose of data collection and measures used relative to the goals of the research study, and (3) the agency or original research team's ability to archive all record data for a given project. Based on how records are collected and how variables are measured, researchers face more restrictions in terms of capabilities for specific questions and analyses. That is, since these data are not designed for research purposes, they may not be as useful in answering specific research questions identified by scholars. A related consideration is that researchers do not have control over the research process including data collection and data processing of public agency records. Archived data often have restrictions to use, publishing, and/or certain pieces of the record data may not be made publicly available (e.g., qualitative data in a mixed methods project). Still, a quick search for "trafficking" in ICPSR yields a number of potential databases including those on sex and labor trafficking (e.g., Raymond & Hughes, 2006; Zhang & Barrick, 2018).

Second, *non-public agency data* are often used by researchers either as a separate project or in addition to public agency data (e.g., augmenting publicly available information with non-publicly available information). Agencies often collect and compile data internally; however, these data are not publicly accessible. With permission from an agency and approval of an institutional review board, researchers may be provided access to non-public agency data, but this can vary widely. Variation in data sharing abilities typically comes from the nature of the data that were collected by the agency (e.g., vulnerable populations), level of interest the agency has in the particular project, and/or willingness to partner with researchers. Often when researchers are given access to non-public agency data they will need to develop a data sharing agreement or memorandum of understanding between the research team and the agency (or agencies). These typically involve detailed parameters about the use of data, storage and handling of data, length of time researchers may keep data, and provide legal protections for data sharing. Similar to public agency data, the researcher does not have control over the research process when using non-public agency record data. It is critical to receive a detailed codebook—or to develop one in tandem with the agency to ensure no miscommunications about how and why data are classified. Researchers must get to know the agency's record-keeping system and data as if they collected them directly. Non-public agency data often offer greater depth and scope of information than publicly available agency records, but also pose more difficulties in terms of obtaining the data and sometimes complications in ownership around dissemination.

Finally, *new data collected by agencies* for research purposes are often undertaken by agencies and/or in collaboration with researchers. In most cases of using public and non-public agency data, the research team does not have control over the process of data collection. When new data are being collected, this is often in collaboration with a partnering agency. That is, researchers have some degree of control and input into the research process (e.g., design of measures, data collection, format of database, and processing of data). The data are still being collected by the agency, but researchers will have varying degrees of collaborative capacity in the data collection and extraction process.

One of the greatest challenges for using agency records—whether that be public agency data, non-public agency data, or new data collected by agencies (possibly with some degree of collaboration with research team)—is that despite the researcher's goals, the data will likely not be all encompassing for research purposes. Government and non-governmental agencies maintain records that might provide insight into a topic of interest to a researcher, but it is important to keep in mind that these records *serve the interest of the agency*—not the researcher—and can cause problems for researchers (Becker, 2017). For example, data may be collected to for agency regulations or required for grant reporting purposes. Usually these data are collected for descriptive purposes and/or to keep track of cases. It is important to keep in mind that data reflect decisions by stakeholders within agencies—and the records they produce may be reflective of those decisions, and could be less useful for the purposes of the researcher's question(s).

Another complicating issue in agency records research is that organizations may not collect all of the variables of interest, be unable or unwilling to share all of the fields in their records, and/or differ in definitions across agencies. Thus, it is important to ask key questions such as the format of the data (e.g., paper copies, electronic records and file types, and databases used), how they are organized (e.g., by case, by victim, and by family), and the types of fields they routinely collect (e.g., sociodemographic variables and details of case). In order to determine compatibility and usefulness of specific agency records for a research project, it is paramount to explicitly link the research question to the sample and measures used by the agency early on in the process.

PREVIOUS RESEARCH ON HUMAN TRAFFICKING USING AGENCY RECORDS

Researchers have used agency records to measure human trafficking victimization, perpetration, and patterns or case characteristics. It is beyond the scope of this chapter to discuss all the ways in which researchers have collaborated with agencies to study trafficking. However, the following section highlights five ways that agency data have been used: (1) access to existing records (e.g., publicly available data and agency records); (2) official task force data; (3) capture–recapture methods; (4) multiple systems estimation (MSE); and (5) collaborations between agencies and researchers to collect new data.

First, scholars have been able to access existing agency data through publicly available databases or by gaining permission to access non-public records. As an example of the former, Reid and Piquero (2014) used longitudinal data from the Pathways to Desistance study, which gathered information from delinquent adolescents in two counties (Philadelphia County, PA and Maricopa County, AZ) as they transitioned into adulthood. The authors examined a subset of the data involving 114 youths with self-reported commercial sexual exploitation (CSE)/prostitution or an official arrest for prostitution. Under federal law, any minors who engage in commercial sex are automatically classified as trafficking victims (Victims of Trafficking and Violence Protection Act of 2000). Thus, the "prostitution" indicator was used to identify victims in a database that was not originally created to study trafficking. The authors found that substance use and selling drugs generally occurred prior to CSE/prostitution and there were high rates of repeated CSE/prostitution. Also, a small proportion of youth had chronic CSE/prostitution, which accounted for the majority of CSE/prostitution occurrences in the sample. In this context, early intervention may be particularly important when trying to prevent initial and repeat exploitation.

In the latter case, Reid, Baglivio, Piquero, Greenwald, and Epps (2017) obtained data from the Florida Department of Juvenile Justice on 68,218 youths with an arrest. A subsample of 913 youths was identified between 2009 and 2015 as suspected or known trafficking victims by the Florida Department of Children and Families. Using the 913 juveniles with trafficking reports, the authors created a matched sample from the justice-involved youths without any trafficking indicators to understand what factors differentiated these groups. After examining males and females separately, the authors found that they had different risk factors for trafficking. Girls were who experienced sexual abuse, emotional neglect, physical neglect, and family violence were more likely to be trafficking victims. Physical abuse experienced by girls decreased the odds of trafficking exploitation. Conversely, boys were more likely to be trafficking victims if they experienced emotional or sexual abuse. Overall, it seems that certain maladaptive experiences matter for victimization risk, but some types of abuse (such as sexual abuse) may be pervasive across genders.

Second and relatedly, official task force data has been used to inform our understanding of identified trafficking offenses. The Human Trafficking Reporting System (HTRS) provides detailed information on the incidents, victims, and offenders from a small number of federally funded task forces (Farrell & Reichert, 2017). A recent report on HTRS data identified 2,515 suspected incidents of trafficking between January 2008 and June 2010 (Banks & Kyckelhahn, 2011). Of these, only 389 incidents were confirmed to be human trafficking. Details on confirmed cases indicated that a majority of victims were females subjected to sex trafficking. Although the data are not nationally representative (Farrell & Reichert, 2017), they do provide a detailed overview of identified cases.

Third, capture–recapture methods are used to estimate the likelihood of identifying individuals within public agency records by two independent observers, resulting in a variety of different estimates (Farrell & de Vries, 2019). Capture–recapture methods can be used to measure prevalence with different types of agency records, especially publicly available data such as law enforcement records and newspaper reports. Prevalence is estimated by synthesizing data from two or more sources and then adjusting for overlapping observations to arrive at an estimate of indicated or at-risk cases. Recently, the International Labour Organization (ILO, 2017) has developed updated sex trafficking and labor trafficking estimates using capture–recapture methods by examining both public record data (e.g., data from the Institute of Medicine) and survey data from around the world. The ILO estimated there were approximately 25 million human trafficking victims (including sex and labor) around the world in 2016 by identifying victim reports that also appeared in public, or open-source, information (ILO, 2017). Without adding those public sources of data, there is a strong possibility that the true number of victims is underestimated.

Fourth, similar to capture–recapture methods, MSE is used to predict the known and unknown population sizes based on lists from separate agency records (Bales, Hesketh, & Silverman, 2015; Cruyff, van Dijk, & van der Heijden, 2017). While similar in approaches, MSE extends capture–recapture approaches through the use of non-public agency data (presumed to be more reliable than public agency data). Agency records, usually non-public data and/or new data collection efforts by agencies, are used to identify how frequently people are identified across one or more of the lists or the possibility of not being captured on any list (Farrell & de Vries, 2019). Analogous to capture–recapture methods, MSE requires the use of agency record data. However, it is distinct in that it does not use public data, but rather non-public agency data (e.g., lists of individuals who have received victim services from a non-governmental organization) or new data collection efforts by agencies working with human trafficking victims (e.g., lists of individuals who have been identified by specialty human trafficking courts). For example, a recent study using MSE identified that law enforcement and service agencies are likely only identifying 14–45% (depending on location) of human trafficking victims (Farrell et al., 2019). Therefore, these numbers should be used as a conservative baseline for estimating human trafficking victimization of youth. These findings indicate an increased need for training for law enforcement and other service providers, especially those at the frontline who are likely to interact with potential trafficking victims.

Fifth, some scholars have collaborated with agencies to collect new quantitative or qualitative data (e.g., Baldwin, Eisenman, Sayles, Ryan, & Chuang, 2011; Farrell, McDevitt, & Fahy, 2008; Love, Hussemann, Yu, McCoy, & Owens, 2018). In a recent report, Love et al. (2018) conducted interviews about perceptions of justice with survivors and key stakeholders in eight metropolitan sites in the United States. Victims were identified through service providers, whereas stakeholders were recruited due to their direct human trafficking case experiences (e.g., service providers, law enforcement officers, and prosecutor's office). Overall, victims and stakeholders reported that criminalizing the actions of victims while they were being trafficked reduced trust in the justice system and hindered participation in investigations. Furthermore, criminal justice stakeholders viewed justice as successful prosecutions, whereas most trafficking victims perceived justice as preventing their traffickers from doing more harm. In this way, stakeholders and victims have similar end goals (i.e., stop the trafficker from harming others), but not necessarily through the same mechanisms.

Each of the agency data sources described provides unique contributions to our understanding of human trafficking. The richness of the databases illuminates various aspects of trafficking experiences including the prevalence, predictors, and perceptions of these events. However, some data sources are easier to obtain and analyze than others. In this way, it is important to build rapport with agencies and establish the benefits of collaboration for both parties.

Challenges in Using Agency Records for Human Trafficking Research

As outlined throughout this chapter, there are a number of challenges for using agency records to study criminal justice issues. With regard to the case of human trafficking, these challenges range from understanding prevalence and case characteristics to evaluating service provision.

First, there is often a wide degree of variation in information collected by agencies. This is often due to the purpose of the agency and/or funder requirements if receiving some type of grant support for agency work. Second, there are often variations in definitions used by agencies and, more broadly, language used to describe human trafficking events and victimization. For example, definitions may vary across agencies, by statute (e.g., using the federal definition or state-specific definitions), as well as operational definitions within agency measures to identify human trafficking cases. Generally, definitions require the use of force, fraud, or coercion for commercial sex or labor, but there can be wide variation in terms of measuring these constructs at an agency-level. Researchers must also take into consideration the variation in completeness of data and variation in data format, both relatively universal issues in using agency records for research purposes. Finally, many agencies may not be able to share their data on human trafficking due to limited research capacity (e.g., lack of data systems management and personnel to complete) or inability to share information with researchers or other agencies due to privacy concerns. These reflect general considerations when using agency records for criminal justice research, but can be more pressing when measuring human trafficking (e.g., lack of a standardized definition of human trafficking across agencies, victim privacy concerns).

These methods are useful in the sense that they rely on data that are already routinely collected (e.g., official data, open source information, and public media reports). However, existing data for research purposes can be problematic for several reasons. First, this type of data provides details only on individuals who have been identified as being trafficked—missing the hidden population of individuals who may never be identified by these systems. Additionally, data collectors do not always share the same definitions for similar behaviors or experiences (e.g., trafficking victim recorded as a prostitution offender). Discrepancies in definitions can make comparisons or the integration across sources difficult. Finally, even if agencies collect detailed and accurate trafficking reports, they may be unwilling or legally unable to share detailed information on these cases for confidentiality reasons (see also Farrell & de Vries, 2019). As researchers continue to engage with key stakeholders to determine the best way to collect data and integrate sources to better understand human trafficking victimization and risk, these obstacles could become less pronounced over time.

USING AGENCY RECORDS TO ESTIMATE PREVALENCE: A METHODOLOGICAL REFLECTION

In this section, we describe a case study of using agency records in a statewide project examining the prevalence of human trafficking in Ohio (see Anderson, Kulig, & Sullivan, 2019). Over the last few years, a number of agencies in Ohio, both state and local, have collected data on human trafficking events. This project relied on two of the three forms of state and local agency record data discussed earlier—public agency data and non-public agency data. The study had a specific focus on youth and young adult victims of human trafficking. Over the course of the study we identified a number of agencies that have some type of information recorded on human trafficking victimization. This included child welfare, legal system, non-profit, and law enforcement data. Data collection for this project was ongoing over the course of 15 months in which partnering agencies provided data to the research team. Through the data collection process, we found that the extent of the information collected—and ability to share data—varied widely by agency. We reflect on this process and provide considerations for researchers interested in pursuing the use of agency records to measure human trafficking. This includes a discussion of (1) data availability, (2) data types and challenges for using existing reports, and (3) synthesizing data within and across agency records.

Data Availability

Over the last five years, several state and local agencies have collected systematic information on victims of human trafficking in Ohio. We identified dozens of agencies and reached out to initiate a data sharing process, which took almost a year and a half. This lead to the development of a number of new partnerships with agencies and the initiation of data sharing—in addition to a number of challenges in terms of data availability and agency capacity to share data.

The first key challenge we encountered was obtaining any data at all. We put in multiple requests for data that were publicly available as well as non-public agency record data. The success of these requests was affected by the degree of availability and the timeline for record retrieval or extraction. For example, some agencies agreed to partner with the research team, but were unable to share data that met the needs of the study. Oftentimes, agencies offered aggregate reports of information, but were not able to share specific information about victims. This posed a challenge to the team given the purpose of the project was to measure the scope of the problem while also reducing error in measurement by accounting for duplicate cases. Duplicate cases refer to situations where individuals may be identified by different agencies, but it might not be possible to indicate which, or how many, individuals in total might be counted more than once. This research problem is exacerbated by the fact that agencies that encounter human trafficking victims do not share information with other agencies who also identify or provide services to victims. Moreover, given the sensitive nature of human trafficking data, agencies might not legally be able to share data with other agencies and/or researchers. A final consideration in initiating data sharing was the development of data sharing agreements for each agency, which varied due to specific policies in place across agencies. Detailed data sharing agreements are not uncommon in criminal justice research, however, it is especially important to consider data sharing parameters when planning to use agency records in human trafficking research.

Timeline is a second aspect of research with agency records to consider. Even when agencies agree to partner and share data in some format, developing and maintaining those relationships takes an extensive amount of time. This became a challenge since we were on a deadline as the grant period was initially for a 12-month study. Researchers should set a realistic timeline to develop relationships given the time-consuming nature of the data collection process. Throughout this process, agencies were oftentimes limited in how much information they were able to share, if any. For example, a number of non-profit agencies did not have the data management infrastructure to extract and compile information to be included in the study. This process illuminated common challenges researchers face when trying to obtain data from agencies with limited capacity and resources (e.g., funding, staff training, and time) for data extraction and sharing. In this way, our study transformed from a study about estimating prevalence into a study that took stock of human trafficking data by comprehensively examining what type of data is available, in what format, and to whom. One key takeaway from this experience, both in terms of data availability and initiating the data sharing process, is that building relationships and maintaining those relationships with partnering agencies takes time.

Data Types and Format

As discussed earlier, agency records can take a wide variety of formats. Agency records can include quantitative or qualitative data and can involve small or large files. These files can be paper copies or electronic. In the case of the prevalence study, we collected all electronic records (e.g., Excel files, SPSS databases, and Word documents with lists of victims) from agencies. One of the first challenges we ran into was how "data" were defined and stored. For example, an agency agreed to share data, but provided the research team with word document of summary statistics. Upon further clarification of the type of "data" we were in need of for the purposes of our study, the agency was able to provide an Excel file with individual-level information about the cases provided in the summary sheet. This aided our efforts to count individuals both within and across records. This highlights the importance of clarifying exactly the type and extent of information that is required for the project, as agencies and researchers may have differing definitions of data. Deliberate steps must also be taken to ensure clarity on the nature of the records and the various fields within those records in order to limit the potential for error.

Another task for the human trafficking prevalence study included a detailed process of taking stock of information available on victimization across the state. Once we secured data from agencies, we transformed data into a consistent format. In reviewing the information provided, we found that agencies rarely collected the same level of details. The most common variables that were consistent across datasets included sociodemographic characteristics of victims (e.g., gender and age) and information about the type of human trafficking (e.g., sex trafficking, labor trafficking, or both). Beyond these "core" items, information collected and provided by agencies varied widely. Variable coverage must be considered in using agency record data as that can preclude meaningful conclusions based on the information that is provided. That is, high degrees of missingness can increase uncertainty about the number of victims and the nature of their cases. After preliminary reviewing and cleaning of the data, we were able to develop a spreadsheet that identified which variables were available across datasets. For example, each column of the spreadsheet indicated a data source and rows indicated each possible variable. Cells were checked if the agency data included that variable. This detailed review of the data provided us with (1) a comprehensive overview of the extent of variable coverage within and across datasets, (2) a sense of the extent of missing data, and (3) an assessment of the possibilities and limitations for the prevalence study.

Synthesizing Data

The final key challenge we ran into was making sense of all of the data we collected in terms of synthesizing information. Agencies were sending data at varying points in time during our study. Prior to conducting any data analysis we undertook an extensive processing protocol to ensure that data were as clean as possible. This was aimed at removing clear duplicate cases within each data set and maximizing the range of fields available for the analysis. We first developed a checklist of available data fields identified in the study proposal and refined that as we obtained data from sources. We then integrated information for each data file so that we had a common set of measures that could be used to identify redundant cases and describe pools of known victims and at-risk individuals. For example, some sources provided individuals' date of birth and others simply an indicator of minor/adult status. In the former case, the date of birth was used to further populate the age status indicator. This process led to a single, "stacked" database comprising eight sets of individual case records from the sources. The "stacked" file balanced potentially useful identification fields available in only some files with a core set of measures that were present in multiple data files.

This resulted in the first comprehensive examination and analysis of the types of agency record data pertaining to human trafficking currently available in the state of Ohio (Anderson et al., 2019). In the end, based on our examination of agency records, we were able to develop an estimate of the prevalence of human trafficking in Ohio as well as a series of lessons learned and recommendations for future research on human trafficking using agency records. One recommendation was the use of more standardized measures and systematic assessments across agencies. Another recommendation included training key stakeholders within agencies to identify victims. Through training agencies to identify trafficking victims, we will likely see more individuals in need of services. For example, we found that a majority of victims were identified in higher population density, urban counties across the state. That is, 80% of the identified cases came from the most populated counties in the state. This has specific policy and practice implications for where the state might direct resources in terms of victim identification (e.g., counties that need more training or resources) and also service delivery (e.g., areas where there is a larger amount of trafficking victims requires a higher degree of resources for identification purposes such as law enforcement or funding for non-governmental organizations providing services to victims).

Agencies have made progress toward measuring the prevalence of human trafficking through the systematic assessment and collection of information on victims. Albeit imperfect, our research draws upon these efforts, to provide a "cataloging" of the types of human trafficking data available in agencies across one state. This included reports and data from social service agencies and legal system agencies to estimate the number of young people affected by human trafficking. There are challenges and limitations when gathering and integrating multiple sources, as outlined in this chapter both generally regarding the use of agency records, and more specifically regarding the use of those records to estimate the prevalence of human trafficking. There are also advantages in using existing record data in this research and it is unrealistic to think that researchers could arrive at a comprehensive understanding of its relevant questions without such data. Thus, our findings went beyond the core goal of the project to estimate the prevalence of human trafficking by also providing space to consider (1) what is available through cataloging the types of information in agency records, (2) what is not available (and how to improve upon that), and, finally, (3) how researchers can use these existing agency records in creative ways.

CONCLUSION

In this chapter, we describe the use of agency record data to measure human trafficking victimization, perpetration, and case characteristics. In particular, we reviewed (1) previous research using agency records to measure human trafficking, (2) challenges to consider when using agency records in the study of human trafficking, and (3) a description of a study using agency records to estimate the prevalence of human trafficking. We conclude our chapter with a series of considerations for future research when using agency records to measure the crime of human trafficking.

One consideration for future research is building off of the recent work using innovative methods to estimate the number of human trafficking victims. In order to best estimate the number of human trafficking victims, more centralized data sharing systems or repositories need to be created among agencies collecting information on human trafficking. A cornerstone to this work is the development of concatenation systems whereby agencies develop encoded identifiers. For example, details from a victim's identifiers (Name: Jane Doe; Date of Birth: 01/01/1990; Social Security Number: 123-45-6789) could be scrambled and recoded (e.g., 19J01D01678990) to protect anonymity. This process would also allow MSE to determine more systematically whether cases are present in multiple data systems using capture–recapture methods (Bales, Hesketh, & Silverman, 2015; Farrell et al., 2019). This would be beneficial for both researchers and agencies to develop a standardized system to share information and protecting victim identities. This would not require a completely centralized system. That is, being realistic with the scope of agency record data, we would not expect all sources to have information to match on, but with some relatively minor changes we can improve our current systems.

As previously discussed, a recent study using this approach across three sites in the United States found that only 14–45% (depending on location) of victims were identified by social service and legal systems when using these methods and applying MSE (Farrell et al., 2019). This highlights the importance of integration additional methods and procedures—in addition to the use of agency record data—in the study of this complex social problem.

The second consideration for human trafficking agency research that we described in our study, was how agencies should begin measuring "core items" such as a history of child sexual abuse, chronic runaway behavior, homelessness, foster care, and juvenile court involvement. Recent human trafficking research has helped us identify these potential core items based on shared risk factors of youth human trafficking victims (Gibbs, Walters, Lutnick, Miller, & Kluckman, 2015; Reid et al., 2017). However, these core items will likely vary based on a number of characteristics (e.g., age of victim, sex trafficking compared to labor trafficking, and combinations of vulnerability factors). Differential coverage is to be expected across data sources and should be identified depending on the population served, but agencies can also take steps to improve this.

The third consideration to make utilizing agency records to study human trafficking is the use of public health approaches such as capture–recapture methods.

Drawing upon the previous example, when developing systems (or separate systems that collect somewhat uniform information), future research could benefit from using epidemiological methods to estimate prevalence. This can be accomplished, in part, through developing information sharing systems discussed above to account for similar information and duplicate cases. Scholars have suggested specific approaches recently including the use of probability sampling approaches, capture–mark–recapture techniques, and respondent-driven sampling to estimate the prevalence of human trafficking (Rothman et al., 2017).

Counting potential victims and at-risk individuals in an epidemiological manner is a crucial step in this process and can help to build awareness of the problem—and perhaps garner resources for responding to it. It is nevertheless important to look at how research might inform future policy and practice. The information needs are even greater, and will likely require other information-gathering approaches such as mixed methods approaches and qualitative interviewing to fashion responses that are well founded in an understanding of the processes that lead to human trafficking. Runaway status, for example, is an indicator of vulnerability for trafficking victimization, but additional individual and contextual factors that lead a youth to runaway must be identified and integrated to understand mechanisms that contribute to that at-risk status and respond to those cases effectively. Without precise prevalence estimates, we cannot fully understand the economic impact of human trafficking on individuals and communities as well as the extent of resources needed in agencies conducting anti-trafficking work (Rothman et al., 2017).

In sum, the use of agency records can be used for a wide variety of purposes with respect to research on human trafficking. Researchers have used agency records in a number of ways to measure the number of human trafficking victims, patterns of traffickers, case characteristics, and the provision of services. The insights we have been able to discern from using agency records have provided valuable information on both the scope of, and response to, human trafficking.

REFERENCES

Anderson, V. R., Kulig, T. C., & Sullivan, C. J. (2019). *Estimating the prevalence of human trafficking in Ohio.* Columbus, OH: Ohio Department of Public Safety.

Baldwin, S. B., Eisenman, D. P., Sayles, J. N., Ryan, G., & Chuang, K. S. (2011). Identification of human trafficking victims in health care settings. *Health and Human Rights, 13,* 36–49.

Banks, D., & Kyckelhahn, T. (2011). *Characteristics of suspected human trafficking incidents, 2008–2010.* Washington, DC: Bureau of Justice Statistics.

Becker, H. S. (2017). *Evidence.* Chicago, IL: University of Chicago Press.

Cruyff, M., van Dijk, J., & van der Heijden, P. G. M. (2017). The challenge of counting victims of human trafficking: Not on the record: A multiple systems estimation of the numbers of human trafficking victims in the Netherlands in 2010-2015 by year, age, gender and by of exploitation. *Chance, 30,* 41–49.

Farrell, A., & de Vries, I. (2019). Measuring the nature and prevalence of human trafficking. In J. A. Winterdyk & J. Jones (Eds.), *The Palgrave international handbook of human trafficking.* Palgrave Macmillan, Cham.

Farrell, A., McDevitt, J., & Fahy, S. (2008). *Understanding and improving law enforcement responses to human trafficking: Final report.* Boston, MA: Institute on Race and Justice, Northeastern University.

Farrell, A., Pfeffer, R., Dank, M., Hughes, A., Kafafian, M., Vincent, K., & Lockwood, S. (2019). *Capturing human trafficking victimization through crime reporting*. Washington, DC: U.S. Department of Justice.

Farrell, A., & Reichert, J. (2017). Using U.S. law-enforcement data: Promise and limits in measuring human trafficking. *Journal of Human Trafficking*, *3*, 39–60.

Finkelhor, D., & Wells, M. (2003). Improving data systems about juvenile victimization in the United States. *Child Abuse & Neglect*, *27*, 77–102.

Foot, K. (2016). *Collaborating against human trafficking: Cross-sector challenges and practices*. Lanham, MD: Rowman & Littlefield.

Gibbs, D. A., Walters, J. L. H., Lutnick, A., Miller, S., & Kluckman, M. (2015). Services to domestic minor victims of sex trafficking: Opportunities for engagement and support. *Children and Youth Services Review*, *54*, 1–7.

International Labour Organization (ILO). (2017). *Global estimates of modern slavery: Forced labour and forced marriage: Methodology*. Geneva, Switzerland: International Labour Organization.

Love, H., Hussemann, J., Yu, L., McCoy, E., & Owens, C. (2018). *Comparing narratives of justice: How survivors, criminal justice stakeholders, and service providers perceive justice in human trafficking cases*. Washington, DC: Urban Institute.

Macy, R. J., & Graham, L. M. (2012). Identifying domestic and international sex-trafficking victims during human service provision. *Trauma, Violence, & Abuse*, *13*, 59–76.

Raymond, J. G., & Hughes, D. M. (2006). International and domestic trends in sex trafficking of women in the United States, 1999–2000. Ann Arbor, MI: Inter-university Consortium for Political and Social Research [distributor]. https://doi.org/10.3886/ICPSR03438.v1

Reid, J. A., Baglivio, M. T., Piquero, A. R., Greenwald, M. A., & Epps, N. (2017). Human trafficking of minors and childhood adversity in Florida. *American Journal of Public Health*, *107*, 306–311.

Reid, J. A., & Piquero, A. R. (2014). On the relationships between commercial sexual exploitation/prostitution, substance dependency, and delinquency in youthful offenders. *Child Maltreatment*, *19*, 247–260.

Rothman, E. F., Stoklosa, H., Baldwin, S. B., Chisolm-Straker, M., Kato Price, R., Atkinson, H. G., & HEAL Trafficking. (2017). Public health research priorities to address US human trafficking. *American Journal of Public Health*, *107*, 1045–1047.

Stewart, D. W., & Kamins, M. A. (1993). *Secondary research: Information sources and methods*. Newbury Park, CA: Sage.

Varma, S., Gillespie, S., McCracken, C., & Greenbaum, V. J. (2015). Characteristics of child commercial sexual exploitation and sex trafficking victims presenting for medical care in the United States. *Child Abuse & Neglect*, *44*, 98–105.

Victims of Trafficking and Violence Protection Act of 2000, Pub. L. 106-386, 114 Stat. 1464, codified as amended at 22 U.S.C. §§ 7101-7110.

Zhang, S., & Barrick, K. L. (2018). Labor trafficking in North Carolina: A statewide survey using multistage sampling, 2014–2016. Ann Arbor, MI: Inter-university Consortium for Political and Social Research [distributor]. https://doi.org/10.3886/ICPSR36990.v1

CHAPTER 11

SEARCHING FOR EXTREMIST CONTENT ONLINE USING THE DARK CRAWLER AND SENTIMENT ANALYSIS

Ryan Scrivens, Tiana Gaudette, Garth Davies and Richard Frank

ABSTRACT

Purpose – *This chapter examines how sentiment analysis and web-crawling technology can be used to conduct large-scale data analyses of extremist content online.*

Methods/approach – *The authors describe a customized web-crawler that was developed for the purpose of collecting, classifying, and interpreting extremist content online and on a large scale, followed by an overview of a relatively novel machine learning tool, sentiment analysis, which has sparked the interest of some researchers in the field of terrorism and extremism studies. The authors conclude with a discussion of what they believe is the future applicability of sentiment analysis within the online political violence research domain.*

Findings – *In order to gain a broader understanding of online extremism, or to improve the means by which researchers and practitioners "search for a needle in a haystack," the authors recommend that social scientists continue to collaborate with computer scientists, combining sentiment analysis software with other classification tools and research methods, as well as validate sentiment analysis programs and adapt sentiment analysis software to new and evolving radical online spaces.*

Methods of Criminology and Criminal Justice Research
Sociology of Crime, Law and Deviance, Volume 24, 179–194

ISSN: 1521-6136/doi:10.1108/S1521-613620190000024016

Originality/value – *This chapter provides researchers and practitioners who are faced with new challenges in detecting extremist content online with insights regarding the applicability of a specific set of machine learning techniques and research methods to conduct large-scale data analyses in the field of terrorism and extremism studies.*

Keywords: Sentiment analysis; web-crawler; machine learning; terrorism; extremism; internet

INTRODUCTION

Violent extremists and those who subscribe to radical beliefs have left their digital footprints online since the inception of the World Wide Web. Notable examples include Anders Breivik, the Norwegian far-right terrorist convicted of killing 77 people in 2011, who was a registered member of a white supremacy web forum (Southern Poverty Law Center, 2014) and had ties to a far-right wing social media site (Bartlett & Littler, 2011); Dylann Roof, the 21 year old who murdered nine Black parishioners in Charleston, South Carolina, in 2015, and who allegedly posted messages on a white power website (Hankes, 2015); and Aaron Driver, the Canadian suspected of planning a terrorist attack in 2016, who showed explicit support for the so-called "Islamic State" (IS) on several social media platforms (Amarasingam, 2016).

It should come as little surprise that, in an increasingly digital world, identifying signs of extremism online sits at the top of the priority list for counter-extremist agencies (Cohen, Johansson, Kaati, & Mork, 2014), with the current focus of government-funded research on the development of advanced information technologies and risk assessment tools to identify and counter the threat of violent extremism on the Internet (Sageman, 2014). Within this context, criminologists have argued that successfully identifying radical content online (i.e., behaviors, patterns, or processes), on a large scale, is the first step in reacting to it (e.g., Bouchard, Joffres, & Frank, 2014; Davies, Bouchard, Wu, Joffres, & Frank, 2015; Frank, Bouchard, Davies, & Mei, 2015; Mei & Frank, 2015; Williams & Burnap, 2015). Yet in the last 10 years alone, it is estimated that the number of individuals with access to the Internet has increased threefold (Internet World Stats, 2019), from over 1 billion users in 2005 to more than 3.8 billion as of 2019 (Internet Live Stats, 2019). With all of these new users, more information has been generated, leading to a flood of data.

It is becoming increasingly difficult, nearly impossible really, to manually search for violent extremists, potentially violent extremists, or even users who post radical content online because the Internet contains an overwhelming amount of information. These new conditions have necessitated guided data filtering methods, those that can side-step – and perhaps one day even replace – the laborious manual methods that traditionally have been used to identify relevant information online (Brynielsson et al., 2013; Cohen et al., 2014). As a result of this changing landscape, governments around the globe have engaged researchers to develop advanced information technologies, machine learning algorithms, and risk assessment tools to identify and counter extremism through the collection and analysis of large-scale data made available online (see Chen, Mao, Zhang, & Leung, 2014). Whether this work involves finding radical users of interest (e.g., Klausen, Marks, & Zaman, 2018), measuring digital pathways of radicalization (e.g., Hung, Jayasumana, & Bandara, 2016), or detecting virtual indicators that may prevent future terrorist attacks (e.g., Johansson, Kaati, & Sahlgren, 2016), the urgent need to pinpoint extremist content online is one of the most significant challenges faced by law enforcement agencies and security officials worldwide (Sageman, 2014).

We have been part of this growing field of research at the International CyberCrime Research Centre (ICCRC), situated in Simon Fraser University's School of Criminology.[1] Our work has ranged from identifying radical users in online discussion forums (e.g., Scrivens, Davies, & Frank, 2017) to understanding terrorist organizations' online recruitment efforts on various online platforms (e.g., Davies et al., 2015), to evaluating linguistic patterns presented in the online magazines of terrorist groups (e.g., Macnair & Frank, 2018a, 2018b). These experiences have provided us with insights regarding the applicability of a specific set of machine learning techniques and research methods to conduct large-scale data analyses of extremist content online.[2] In what follows, we will first describe a customized web-crawler that was developed at the ICCRC for the purpose of collecting, classifying, and interpreting extremist content online and on a large scale. Second, we will provide an overview of a relatively novel machine learning tool, sentiment analysis, which has sparked the interest of some researchers in the field of terrorism and extremism studies who are faced with new challenges in detecting extremist content online. Third, we conclude with a discussion of what we believe is the future applicability of sentiment analysis within the online political violence research domain.

Before proceeding, however, it is necessary to outline how we conceptualize extremist content online. We define it as text-, audio-, and/or video-based online material containing radical views – counter to mainstream opinion – that may or may not promote violence in the name of a radical belief. At the ICCRC, we focus primarily on text-based extremist content that has radical right-wing or jihadi leanings. For the former, radical right-wing material is characterized by racially, ethnically and sexually defined nationalism, which is typically framed in terms of white power and grounded in xenophobic and exclusionary understandings of the perceived threats posed by such groups as non-whites, Jews, immigrants, homosexuals, and feminists (see Perry & Scrivens, 2016). For the latter, we define jihadi material as supportive of the creation of an expansionist Islamic state or khalifa, the imposition of sharia law with violent jihad as a central component, and the use of local, national, and international grievances affecting Muslims (see Moghadam, 2008).

EXTRACTING EXTREMIST CONTENT ONLINE: THE DARK CRAWLER

In recent years, researchers have shown a vested interest in developing web-crawler tools to collect large volumes of content on the Internet. This interest has made its way into terrorism and extremism studies in the past 10 plus years (e.g., Abbasi & Chen, 2005; Bouchard et al., 2014; Chen, 2012; Fu, Abbasi, & Chen, 2010; Zhang et al., 2010; Zhou, Qin, Lai, Reid, & Chen, 2005). Some researchers have used standard, off-the-shelf web-crawler tools that are readily available online for a fee, while others have developed custom-written computer programs to collect high volumes of information online. The Dark Crawler (TDC) is one example of this latter approach.

Web-crawlers, also known as "crawlers," "data scrapers," and "data parsers," are the tools used by all search engines to automatically map and navigate the Internet as well as collect information about each website and webpage that a web-crawler visits. There are many off-the-shelf web-crawler solutions available on the Internet for purchase, such as *Win Web Crawler,*[3] *WebSPHINX,*[4] *Black Widow,*[5] or *BeautifulSoup*.[6] Once an end-user decides on a website from which parsing will begin, the crawler recursively follows the links from that webpage until some user-specified condition is met (discussed below), capturing all content along the way. During this process, the software tracks all the links between it and other websites and, if an end-user so chooses, the software will follow and retrieve those links as well. The content, as it is retrieved, is then saved to the hard-drive of the user for later analysis. In short, the purpose of most web-crawlers is to simply save the retrieved content onto a hard-drive, essentially "ripping" a webpage or website because it contains content desired by the end-user. More advanced analytic capabilities usually are not part of the package.

Similar in spirit, TDC browses the World Wide Web, but since it is a custom-written computer program, it is much more flexible than the abovementioned process. In particular, TDC is capable of seeking out extremist content online, among other types of content, based on user-defined keywords and other parameters (discussed below). As TDC visits each page, it captures all of the content on that page for later analysis, while simultaneously collecting information about the content and making decisions as to whether the page includes extremist content. The idea of this approach is based on a combination of the work associated with the Dark Web project at the University of Arizona (see Chen, 2012) and a previous project at the ICCRC that identified and explored online child exploitation websites (e.g., Allsup, Thomas, Monk, Frank, & Bouchard, 2015; Joffres, Bouchard, Frank, & Westlake, 2011; Frank, Westlake, & Bouchard, 2010; Monk, Allsup, & Frank, 2015; Westlake & Bouchard, 2015; Westlake, Bouchard, & Frank, 2011). TDC has since demonstrated its benefit in investigating online networks and communities in general (e.g., Frank, Macdonald, & Monk, 2016; Macdonald & Frank, 2016, 2017; Macdonald, Frank, Mei, & Monk, 2015; Mikhaylov & Frank, 2016, 2018; Zulkarnine, Frank, Monk, Mitchell, & Davies, 2016) and extremist content online in particular (e.g., Bouchard et al., 2014; Davies et al., 2015; Frank et al., 2015; Levey, Bouchard, Hashimi, Monk, & Frank, 2016; Mei & Frank, 2015; Scrivens et al., 2017; Scrivens, Davies, & Frank, 2018; Scrivens & Frank, 2016; Wong, Frank, & Allsup, 2015).

TDC is a system that can be distributed across multiple virtual machines, depending on the number of machines that are available. The first of four steps, as expressed in Fig. 1, is to define a task along with its parameters. TDC can handle multiple tasks simultaneously, each of which is given a priority, specified by the end-user. The priority of each task is determined by the number of machines allocated to it. For example, if tasks I, II, and III are given priority 50, 80, and 70, respectively, then task I will receive 25% of the available resources (50/(50+80+70) = 0.25 = 25%). If more machines are added to TDC, then the absolute number of resources available for each task will increase but the relative amount of resources available for each task will remain the same.

Each task consists of four parameters to prevent it from perpetually crawling the Internet and wandering into websites and webpages unrelated to extremism. The parameters are as follows:

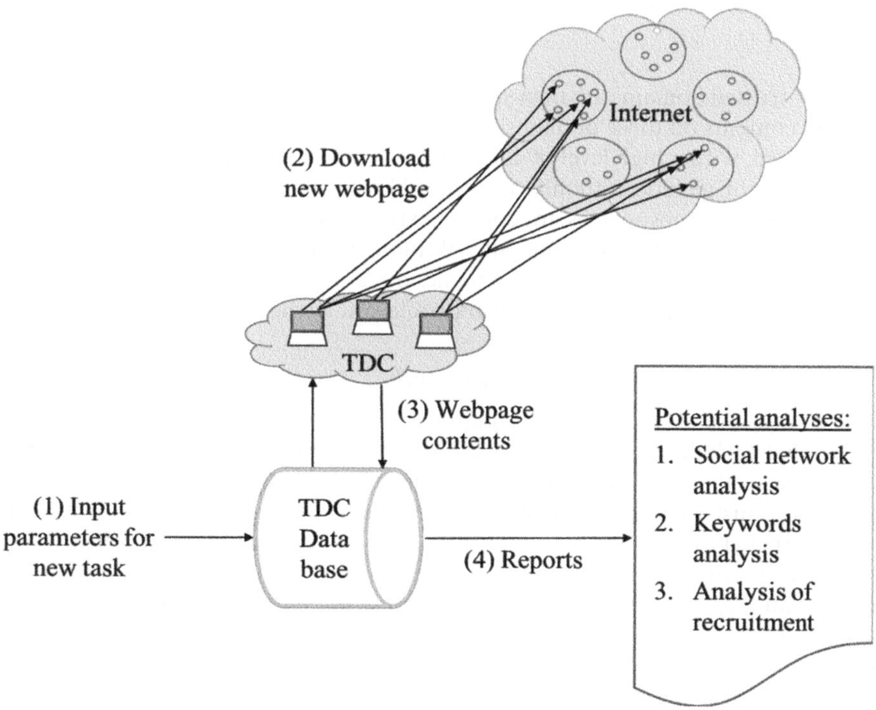

Fig. 1. Overview of The Dark Crawler.

Number of Webpages

For practical purposes, since the number of webpages on the Internet is infinite, restrictions must be placed on the number of webpages that are retrieved by the web-crawler. Theoretically, any web-crawler could crawl for a very long time and store the entire collection of webpages on the Internet. For our purposes at the ICCRC, however, this is infeasible for several reasons. First, the amount of storage that would be required to warehouse the extracted data is beyond the scope of any sensible research project. Second, webpages are created at a much higher rate than what can be extracted with TDC. Lastly, a copy of the "full Internet" is not required to draw meaningful conclusions about a particular topic under investigation; extracting large scale, representative samples, is more than adequate.

Number of Domains

The number of Internet domains that TDC will collect data on must be specified. When limiting a crawl to n pages, the crawler will attempt to distribute the sampling equally across all websites that it has encountered, meaning that TDC will sample similar numbers of pages from each of the sites it visits. As a result, at the end of the task, if w websites are sampled, all sites will have approximately the same number of pages retrieved ($=n/w$) and analyzed.

Trusted Domains

A set of trusted domains are then specified by the end-user, which tells the crawler that all contents on those domains should not be extracted. As an example, it can be assumed, with a high level of certainty, that a website such as www.microsoft.com does not include extremist material. Having said that, TDC is trained to assume that the website does not contain extremist content, and as such, it would not retrieve any pages from that site. Without having this mechanism in place, TDC could wander into a search engine, directing it completely off topic and making the resulting extracted network irrelevant to the specified topic and task.

Keywords

The purpose of TDC is to find, analyze, and map out the websites and webpages that include extremist content. To achieve this, TDC recursively retrieves all webpages that are linked from the webpage it is currently reviewing. However, since extremist webpages consist of a very small subset of all the webpages on the Internet (Frank et al., 2015), it would be expected that, unconstrained, TDC would very quickly start to retrieve webpages that are completely unrelated to extremism. As a result, some mechanism must be built into TDC that controls which webpages it uses in its exploration process. This is done through the use of keywords, which are user-specified words that have been found to be indicative of extremist content (e.g., Bouchard et al., 2014; Davies et al., 2015; Wong et al., 2015) and thus indicate to TDC that the pages being retrieved are on-topic. Within the extremist domain, such keywords could include *gun*, *weapon*, or *terror*. To make this mechanism more robust, though, a word counter can be included to TDC, which indicates a minimum threshold on the number of keywords that must exist on a page before the TDC considers it on topic.

Once a task has been decided, each webpage is downloaded by TDC (Fig. 1 – Step 2). If the downloaded page meets the parameters laid out above, then the page is considered "on topic," all page content is saved and all page links are followed out of it recursively (Step 3). The webpage contents are then stored in the database, and various reports and analyses can be performed (Step 4).

DATA MINING EXTREMIST CONTENT ONLINE: SENTIMENT ANALYSIS

The use of keywords presents a useful first step in identifying large-scale patterns in extremist content online (e.g., Chalothorn & Ellman, 2012; Bouchard et al., 2014; Davies et al., 2015; Wong et al., 2015). However, the use of single keywords may lead to misleading interpretations of content (Mei & Frank, 2015; Scrivens & Frank, 2016). If, for example, on a particular webpage, the words *gun* and *control* are found within close proximity of each other, it might be concluded that the page is discussing *gun control.* This would most likely not indicate an extremist page but more likely that the page was written by a proponent or opponent of gun ownership. This page, of course, is not relevant to TDC's data collection. On the other hand, a page containing the words *gun* and *control* could be discussing "controlling someone with a gun" within the context of kidnapping for example which, in this case, TDC should continue with its analysis. In other words, keywords can give an indication of the content within a webpage but cannot be used to determine exactly what that content is about. For a more complete understanding of the content of a specific piece of text, more powerful computational tools, such as sentiment analysis, are required.

Sentiment analysis, also known as "opinion mining," is a category of computing science that specializes in evaluating the opinions found in a piece of text by organizing data into distinct classes and sections, and then assigning a piece of text with a positive, negative, or neutral polarity value (Abbasi & Chen, 2005). Sentiment analysis also provides a more targeted view of textual data by allowing for the demarcation between cases that are sought after and those without any notable relevance. Sentiment analysis has been used in a wide variety of settings, including customer review analysis for products (e.g., Feldman, 2013), assessments of attitudes toward events or products on social media platforms (e.g., Ghiassi, Skinner, & Zimbra, 2013), and for various analyses of extremist content online (e.g., Bermingham, Conway, McInerney, O'Hare, & Smeaton, 2009, Chen, 2008; Williams & Burnap, 2015). Sentiment analysis has become increasingly popular in terrorism and extremism studies because, as the amount of "opinionated data" online grows exponentially, sentiment analysis software offers a wide range of applications that can help address previously untapped and challenging research problems (see Liu, 2012). Based on the notion that an author's opinion toward a particular topic is reflected in the choice and intensity of words he or she chooses to communicate, sentiment analysis software allows for identification and classification of opinions found in a piece of text (Abbasi, Chen, & Salem, 2008). Typically, this process occurs through a two-step process that produces a "polarity value":

(1) a body of text is split into sections (sentences) to determine subjective and objective content and
(2) subjective content is classified by the software as being either positive, neutral, or negative, where positive scores reflect positive attitudes and negative scores reflect negative attitudes (see Feldman, 2013).

Worth highlighting, though, is the fact that sentiment analysis is not without its limitations. It is estimated, for example, that 21% of the time humans cannot agree among themselves about the sentiment within a given piece of text (Ogneva, 2010), with some individuals unable to understand subtle context or irony. Understandably, sentiment analysis systems cannot be expected to have 100% accuracy when compared to the opinions of humans. Sentiment analysis does, however, provide insight into authors' expressions and reactions toward certain events or actions, for example, and one sentiment analysis program that has been widely used by criminologists in terrorism and extremism studies is *SentiStrength* (e.g., Frank et al., 2015; Levey et al., 2016; Macnair & Frank, 2018a, 2018b; Mei & Frank, 2015; Scrivens et al., 2017, 2018; Scrivens & Frank, 2016).

SentiStrength uses a "lexical approach" – which maintains that an essential part of understanding a language rests on the ability to understand the patterns of and meanings associated with language (see Lewis, 1993) – and is based on human coded data as well as various lexicons (i.e., dictionaries of phases and words). Although the program is designed for short informal online texts, there are features in place that allow longer texts to be analyzed (Thelwall & Buckley, 2013). *SentiStrength* analyzes a text by attributing positive, neural, or negative values to words within the text, and these values are augmented by "booster words" that can influence the values assigned to the text as well as negating words, punctuation, and other features that are uniquely suited for studying an online context (Thelwall & Buckley, 2013). One of the features of *SentiStrength* is its ability to analyze the sentiment around any given keyword. For example, the phrase "I love apples but hate oranges" can be analyzed for the sentiment around apples (resulting in a positive outcome) as well as oranges (resulting in a negative outcome). The words around a given set of keywords are compared to the sentiment dictionary and their resulting values make up the total sentiment score for any given text. Logically, a negative value implies negative sentiment for the ideas expressed in the text while a positive value implies overall support.

To analyze a given piece of text for multiple keywords, multiple iterations must be done, with each iteration consisting of an analysis of the same piece of text but with a different keyword (resulting in the sentiment toward that keyword). Due to the very specific nature of this procedure, it is necessary to input each form of a particular word being analyzed. For example, to analyze sentiment around the word *kill*, it is necessary to also analyze the words *kills*, *killing*, *killed*, and all other derivatives of the word. Multiple iterations of *SentiStrength* are then applied, each one returning the detected sentiment around the specific keyword and its derivatives. At the end of this process, each text is linked to multiple sentiment values, one for each keyword. Those multiple values are then averaged to produce a single sentiment score for any given piece of text.

THE FUTURE OF DETECTING EXTREMIST SENTIMENT ONLINE

There's been a shift in recent years in how researchers investigate online communities, ranging from the study of how extremists communicate through social media (e.g., Bermingham et al., 2009) to the analysis of users connecting through online health forums (e.g., Wang, Kraut, & Levine, 2012), for example. In short, researchers in this area are shifting from manual identification of specific online content to algorithmic techniques to do similar yet larger-scale tasks. The use of such analytical approaches is becoming increasingly apparent in criminology and criminal justice research (see Hannah-Moffat, 2018). This is a symptom of what some have described as the "big data" phenomenon – that is, a massive increase in the amount of data that is readily available, particularly online (see Chen et al., 2014).

Logically, a number of researchers who study how terrorists and extremists use the Internet have turned to sentiment analysis and other machine learning techniques to identify and, by extension, analyze content of interest on a large scale. In what follows, we will discuss what we believe is the future of the applicability of sentiment analysis to explore extremist content online, drawing from the recommendations of the below-listed studies in combination with our own experience with sentiment analysis. In short, we suggest that the future of sentiment analysis in exploring extremist content online should: (1) encourage social scientists and computer scientists to collaborate with one another; (2) consider a combination of analyses or more features to increase classifier's effectiveness; (3) continue to validate sentiment analysis programs; and (4) apply and adapt sentiment analysis to new and evolving radical online spaces.

Collaborations

In order to gain a broader understanding of online extremism, or to improve the means by which researchers and practitioners "search for a needle in a haystack," social scientists and computer scientists must collaborate with one another. Historically, large-scale data analyses have been conducted by computer scientists and technical experts, which can be problematic in complex fields such as terrorism and extremism research. Computer and technical experts tend to take a high-level methodological perspective, measuring levels of – or propensity toward – radicalization, or ways of identifying violent extremists, or predicting the next terrorist attack. But searching for radical material online without a fundamental understanding of the radicalization process or how terrorists and extremists use the Internet can be counterproductive. Social scientists, on the other hand, may be well-versed in terrorism and extremism research, but most tend to be ill-equipped to manage large-scale data – from collecting to formatting to archiving large volumes of information. Bridging the computer science and social science approaches to build on the strengths of each discipline offers perhaps the best chance to construct a useful framework for detecting extremist content online, as well as assisting authorities in addressing the threat of violent extremism as it evolves in the online milieu.

Combinations

A myriad of research shows that combining sentiment analysis with other methods and/or semantic-oriented approaches improves the detection of extremist content online, on three fronts. This, we argue, is the future in detecting extremist content online. First, research suggests that sentiment analysis software, in combination with classification software, is an effective method to detect extremist content online and on a large scale. In particular, combing sentiment analysis with classification software – which identifies similarities and differences in datasets and makes determinations about the data in a decision tree format – can pinpoint extremist websites (see Mei & Frank, 2015; see also Scrivens & Frank, 2016). In addition, combining sentiment analysis with affect analysis –a machine learning technique that measures the emotional content of communications – can detect and measure the intensity levels associated with a broad range of emotions in text found in online forums (see Chen, 2008; see also Figea, Kaati, & Scrivens, 2016). Research similarly suggests that the effectiveness of the sentiment analysis in detecting extremist content can be significantly boosted with additional classification feature sets, such as syntactic, stylistic, content-specific, and lexicon features (Abbasi & Chen, 2005; Abbasi et al., 2008; Yang et al., 2011).

Second, research suggests that combining sentiment analysis with commonly used research methods and frameworks in criminology and criminal justice research can aid in the detection of extremist content online. Social network analysis, for example, in combination with sentiment analysis can be used to identify users on *YouTube* who may have had a radicalizing agenda (see Bermingham et al., 2009), detect extremist content on Twitter (Wei, Sing, & Martin, 2016), and model online propaganda (see Burnap et al., 2014) and cyberhate (see Williams & Burnap, 2015) on Twitter following the Woolwich terrorism incident. In addition, combining sentiment analysis with geolocation software can be used to organize the opinions found on Twitter accounts using hashtags associated with IS (Mirani & Sasi, 2016). Lastly, sentiment analysis, in combination with an algorithm that incorporates criminal career measures (i.e., volume, severity, and duration) developed by Blumstein, Cohen, Roth, and Visher (1986), has been used to account for unique components of a users' online posting behavior and detect the most radical authors in a large scale sample of online postings (see Scrivens et al., 2017).

Third, in online political violence research, a growing emphasis has been placed on the integration of a temporal component with sentiment analysis – a combination that we believe is key to providing insight into the patterns and trends that characterize the development of extremist communities over time online.

For example, combining sentiment analysis with survival analysis has been a useful way to measure propaganda surges (see Burnap et al., 2014) and levels of cyberhate (Williams & Burnap, 2015) on Twitter over time after a terrorist attack. Other approaches that have proven to be effective in understanding temporal patterns in radical online communities include: (1) mapping users' sentiment and affect changes in extremist forums (see Figea et al., 2016); (2) identifying significant temporal spikes in extremist forums that coincide with real-world events (see Park, Beck, Fletche, Lam, & Tsang, 2016); and measuring the evolution of sentiment found in IS-produced online propaganda magazines (see Macnair & Frank, 2018b; see also Vergani & Bluic, 2015). Most recently, combining sentiment analysis with semi-parametric group-based modeling to measure the evolution of radical posting trajectories has shown to be an effective way to detect large-scale temporal patterns in radical online communities (see Scrivens et al., 2018).

Validation

Another common thread that binds together the aforementioned studies is the need to assess and potentially improve the classification accuracy and content identification offered by sentiment analysis software. Researchers, for example, have proposed that future work includes a "comparative human evaluation" component to validate a sentiment program's classifications (e.g., Chalothorn & Ellman, 2012; Figea et al., 2016). Macnair and Frank (2018a) further added that:

> computer-assisted techniques such as sentiment analysis, in conjunction with human oversight, can aid in the overall process of locating, identifying, and eventually, countering the narratives that exist within extremist media. (p. 452)

This technique would have humans rate opinions in sentences and compare the results to a sentiment analysis program. By comparing how a human might classify a piece of text to a sentiment analysis program, researchers can gain insight into the accuracy of sentiment analysis' classifications. Future studies should also integrate a qualitative understanding of how machine learning tools in general and sentiment analysis software in particular make decisions about the content that the tools analyze. Doing so may increase the reliability of the results and increase the likelihood of identifying radical content online (Scrivens & Frank, 2016).

Also, it is not yet clear which sentiment analysis program is the most accurate or effective overall in detecting extremist content online. Some research does, however, draw comparisons between the performance of several sentiment methods (i.e., *SentiWordNet*, *SASA*, *PANAS-t*, *Emoticons*, *SentiStrength*, *LIWC*, *SenticNet*, and *Happiness Index*) (see Gonçalves, Benevenuto, Araújo, & Cha, 2013), but comparisons of this sort have yet to be explored within the online political violence domain. One notable exception is the exploration of the linguistic patterns on Twitter following the Manchester attacks and the Las Vegas shooting terrorist attacks (see Kostakos, Nykänen, Martinviita, Pandya, & Oussalah, 2018). Comparing the results of *NLTK+SentiWordNet* and *SentiStrength* software, the authors concluded that *SentiStrength* performed at a higher level than the other applications. Building from that study, future work should continue to explore and test the wide variety of programs currently available to determine if there is indeed one 'superior' method, or if the appropriate methodology is context-specific. A combination of sentiment analysis tools could also be integrated into an analysis, in an attempt to cross-validate each other (Scrivens et al., 2017).

Adaptation

The ways in which violent extremists communicate online will continue to evolve, shifting from uses on traditional discussion forums and social media platforms to lesser known spaces on the Internet. For example, in addition to the use of dedicated extreme right forums and all major social media platforms, a diversity of more general online forums or forum-like online spaces are also hosting increasing amounts of extreme right content. These include the popular social news aggregation, web content rating, and discussion site Reddit and image-based bulletin board and comment site 4chan (Scrivens & Conway, in press). Sites such as these, which contrary to most mainstream social media platforms, do not have clear-cut anti-hate speech policies (see Gaudette, Davies, & Scrivens, 2018), may provide unique insight into the expressions and manifestations of virtual hate, especially on a large scale using sentiment analysis tool outlined in this chapter. In addition, a new generation of right-wing extremists are moving to more overtly hateful, yet to some extent more hidden platforms, including the likes of 8chan, Voat, Gab, and Discord (see Davey & Ebner, 2017). Similarly, between 2013 and 2016, IS's media production outlets developed content that was largely distributed via major (and some minor) social media and other online platforms. These included prominent IS presences not only on Facebook, Twitter, and YouTube, but also on Ask.fm, JustPaste.it, and the Internet Archive (Scrivens & Conway, in press). Having said that, as the ways in which extremists communicate online will undoubtedly evolve, so too must the ways in which researchers detect extremist content online. Sentiment analysis software, in combination with other means of analyzing data, should be applied to these increasingly popular platforms.

CONCLUSION

Since the advent of the Internet, violent extremists and those who subscribe to radical views from across the globe have exploited online resources to build transnational "virtual communities." The Internet is a fundamental medium that facilitates these radical communities, not only in "traditional" hate sites, web forums, and commonly used social media sites, but in lesser known, oftentimes more hidden spaces online as well (Scrivens & Conway, in press). Researchers and practitioners have attempted to identify and monitor extremist content online but increasingly have been overwhelmed by the sheer volume of data in these growing spaces. Simply put, the manual analysis of online content has become increasingly less feasible.

As a result, researchers and practitioners have sought to develop different methods of extracting data, especially through the use of web-crawlers, as well develop different methods for managing this large-scale phenomenon to sift through and detect extremist content. A relatively novel machine learning tool, sentiment analysis, has sparked the interest of some researchers in the field of terrorism and extremism studies who face new challenges in detecting the spread of extremist content online. Though this area of research is in its infancy, sentiment analysis is showing signs of success and may represent the future of how researchers and practitioners study extremism online – particularly on a large scale. This, however, will require that the social scientists continue to collaborate with the computer scientists, combining sentiment analysis software with other classification tools and research methods, validating sentiment analysis programs, and adapting sentiment analysis software to new and evolving radical online spaces.

NOTES

1. For more information, see https://www.sfu.ca/iccrc.html.
2. An array of machine learning techniques is used in the online political violence research terrain that are not discussed in detail in this chapter. For a list of some of these techniques, see Chen (2012).
3. For more information, see http://www.winwebcrawler.com.
4. For more information, see http://www.cs.cmu.edu/~rcm/websphinx.
5. For more information, see http://sbl.net.
6. For more information, see https://pypi.org/project/beautifulsoup4/.

REFERENCES

Abbasi, A., & Chen, H. (2005). Applying authorship analysis to extremist-group web forum messages. *Intelligent Systems, 20*(5), 67–75.

Abbasi, A., Chen, H., & Salem, A. (2008). Sentiment analysis in multiple languages: Feature selection for opinion classification in web forums. *ACM Transactions on Information Systems, 26*(3), 1–34.

Allsup, R., Thomas, E., Monk, B., Frank, R., & Bouchard, M. (2015). Networking in child exploitation – Assessing disruption strategies using registrant information. In *Proceedings of the 2015 IEEE/ACM international conference on advances in social networks analysis and mining (ASONAM)*, Paris, France (pp. 400–407).

Amarasingam, A. (2016). What Aaron told me: An expert on extremism shares his conversations with the terror suspect. *National Post*, August 11. Retrieved from https://nationalpost.com/news/canada/what-aaron-told-me-an-expert-on-extremism-shares-his-conversations-with-the-terror-suspect. Accessed on January 23, 2019.

Bartlett, J., & Littler, M. (2011). *Insight the EDL: Populist politics in the digital era*. London: Demos.

Bermingham, A., Conway, M., McInerney, L., O'Hare, N., & Smeaton, A. F. (2009). Combining social network analysis and sentiment analysis to explore the potential for online radicalisation. In *Proceedings of the 2009 international conference on advances in social network analysis mining (ASONAM)*, Athens, Greece (pp. 231–236).

Blumstein, A., Cohen, J., Roth, J. A., & Visher, C. A. (1986). *Criminal careers and 'career criminals.'* Washington, DC: National Academy Press.

Bouchard, M., Joffres, K., & Frank, R. (2014). Preliminary analytical considerations in designing a terrorism and extremism online network extractor. In V. Mago & V. Dabbaghian (Eds.), *Computational models of complex systems* (pp. 171–184). New York, NY: Springer.

Brynielsson, J., Horndahl, A., Johansson, F., Kaati, L., Martenson, C., & Svenson, P. (2013). Analysis of weak signals for detecting lone wolf terrorists. *Security Informatics*, *2*(11), 1–15.

Burnap, P., Williams, M. L., Sloan, L., Rana, O., Housley, W., Edwards, A., …, Voss, A. (2014). Tweeting the terror: Modelling the social media reaction to the Woolwich terrorist attack. *Social Network Analysis and Mining*, *4*, 1–14.

Chalothorn, T., & Ellman, J. (2012). Using SentiWordNet and sentiment analysis for detecting radical content on web forums. In *Proceedings of the 6th conference on software, knowledge, information management and application (SKIMA)*, Chengdu, China (pp. 9–11).

Chen, H. (2008). Sentiment and affect analysis of dark web forums: Measuring radicalization on the Internet. In *Proceedings of the 2008 IEEE international conference on intelligence and security informatics (ISI)*, Taipei, Taiwan (pp. 104–109).

Chen, H. (2012). *Dark web: Exploring and data mining the dark side of the web*. New York, NY: Springer.

Chen, M., Mao, S., Zhang, Y., & Leung, V. C. (2014). *Big data: Related technologies, challenges and future prospects*. New York, NY: Springer.

Cohen, K., Johansson, F., Kaati, L., & Mork, J. (2014). Detecting linguistic markers for radical violence in social media. *Terrorism and Political Violence*, *26*(1), 246–256.

Davey, J., & Ebner, J. (2017). *The fringe insurgency: Connectivity, convergence and mainstreaming of the extreme right*. London: Institute for Strategic Dialogue.

Davies, G., Bouchard, M., Wu, E., Joffres, K., & Frank, R. (2015). Terrorist and extremist organizations' use of the Internet for recruitment. In M. Bouchard (Ed.), *Social networks, terrorism and counter-terrorism: Radical and connected* (pp. 105–127). New York, NY: Routledge.

Feldman, R. (2013). Techniques and applications for sentiment analysis. *Communications of the ACM*, *56*(4), 82–89.

Figea, L., Kaati, L., & Scrivens, R. (2016). Measuring online affects in a white supremacy forum. In *Proceedings of the 2016 IEEE international conference on intelligence and security informatics (ISI)*, Tucson, Arizona, USA (pp. 85–90).

Frank, R., Bouchard, M., Davies, G., & Mei, J. (2015). Spreading the message digitally: A look into extremist content on the Internet. In R. G. Smith, R. C.-C. Cheung, & L. Y.-C. Lau (Eds.), *Cybercrime risks and responses: Eastern and western perspectives* (pp. 130–145). London: Palgrave Macmillan.

Frank, R., Macdonald, M., & Monk, B. (2016). Location, location, location: Mapping potential Canadian targets in online hacker discussion forums. In *Proceedings of the 2016 European intelligence and security informatics conference (EISIC)*, Uppsala, Sweden (pp. 16–23).

Frank, R., Westlake, B. G., & Bouchard, M. (2010). The structure and content of online child exploitation networks. In *Proceedings of the 10th ACM SIGKDD workshop on intelligence and security informatics (ISI-KDD)*, Washington, DC, USA, Article 3.

Fu, T., Abbasi, A., & Chen, H. (2010). A focused crawler for dark web forums. *Journal of American Society for Information Science and Technology*, *61*(6), 1213–1231.

Gaudette, T., Davies, G., & Scrivens, R. (2018). Upvoting extremism, part I: An assessment of extreme right discourse on Reddit. *VOX-Pol Network of Excellence Blog*. Retrieved from https://www.voxpol.eu/upvoting-extremism-part-i-an-assessment-of-extreme-right-discourse-on-reddit. Accessed on January 23, 2019.

Ghiassi, M., Skinner, J., & Zimbra, D. (2013). Twitter brand sentiment analysis: A hybrid system using n-gram analysis and dynamic artificial neutral network. *Expert Systems with Applications*, *40*(16), 6266–6282.

Gonçalves, P., Benevenuto, M., Araújo, F., & Cha, M. (2013). Comparing and combining sentiment analysis methods. In *Proceedings of the 1st ACM conference on online social networks*, Boston, MA, USA (pp. 27–38).

Hankes, K. (2015). *Dylann Roof may have been a regular commenter at neo-Nazi website The Daily Stormer*. Southern Poverty Law Center. Retrieved from http://www.splcenter.org/blog/2015/06/22/dylann-roof-may-have-been-a-regular-commenter-at-neo-nazi-website-the-daily-stormer. Accessed on January 23, 2019.

Hannah-Moffat, K. (2018). Algorithmic risk governance: big data analytics, race and information activism in criminal justice debates. *Theoretical Criminology*.

Hung, B. W. K., Jayasumana, A. P., & Bandara, V. W. (2016). Detecting radicalization trajectories using graph pattern matching algorithms. In *Proceedings of the 2016 IEEE international conference on intelligence and security informatics (ISI)*, Tucson, Arizona, USA (pp. 313–315).

Internet Live Stats. (2019). Total number of websites. Retrieved from http://www.internetlivestats.com/total-number-of-websites. Accessed on January 23, 2019.

Internet World Stats. (2019). Internet growth statistics. Retrieved from http://www.internetworldstats.com/emarketing.htm. Accessed on January 23, 2019.

Joffres, K., Bouchard, M., Frank, R., & Westlake, B. G. (2011). Strategies to disrupt online child pornography networks. In *Proceedings of the European intelligence and security informatics conference (EISIC)*, Athens, Greece (pp. 163–170).

Johansson, J., Kaati, L., & Sahlgren, M. (2016). Detecting linguistic markers of violent extremism in online environments. In M. Khader, L. S. Neo, G. Ong, E. T. Mingyi, & J. Chin (Eds.), *Combating violent extremism and radicalization in the digital era* (pp. 374–390). Hershey, PA: Information Science Reference.

Klausen, J., Marks, C. E., & Zaman, T. (2018). Finding extremists in online social networks. *Operations Research, 66*(4), 957–976.

Kostakos, P., Nykänen, M., Martinviita, M., Pandya, A., & Oussalah, M. (2018). Meta-terrorism: identifying linguistic patterns in public discourse after an attack. In *Proceedings of the 2018 IEEE/ACM international conference on advances in social networks analysis and mining (ASONAM)*, Barcelona, Spain (pp. 1079–1083).

Levey, P., Bouchard, M., Hashimi, S., Monk, B., & Frank, R. (2016). *The emergence of violent narratives in the life-course trajectories of online forum participants*. Canadian Network for Research on Terrorism, Security and Society Report, Waterloo, ON, Canada.

Lewis, M. (1993). *The lexical approach: The state of ELT and the way forward*. Hove: Language Teaching Publications.

Liu, B. (2012). *Sentiment analysis and opinion mining*. San Rafael, CA: Morgan and Claypool.

Macdonald, M., & Frank, R. (2016). The network structure of malware development, deployment and distribution. *Global Crime, 18*(1), 49–69.

Macdonald, M., & Frank, R. (2017). Shuffle up and deal: Use of a capture–recapture method to estimate the size of stolen data markets. *American Behavioral Scientist, 61*(11), 1313–1340.

Macdonald, M., Frank, R., Mei, J., & Monk, B. (2015). Identifying digital threats in a hacker web forum. In *Proceedings of the 2015 international symposium on foundations of open source intelligence and security informatics (FOSINT)*, Paris, France (pp. 926–933).

Macnair, L., & Frank, R. (2018a). The mediums and the messages: Exploring the language of Islamic State media through sentiment analysis. *Critical Studies on Terrorism, 11*(3), 438–457.

Macnair, L., & Frank, R. (2018b). Changes and stabilities in the language of Islamic State magazines: A sentiment analysis. *Dynamics of Asymmetric Conflict, 11*(2), 109–120.

Mei, J., & Frank, R. (2015). Sentiment crawling: Extremist content collection through a sentiment analysis guided web-crawler. In *Proceedings of the international symposium on foundations of open source intelligence and security informatics (FOSINT)*, Paris, France (pp. 1024–1027).

Mikhaylov, A., & Frank, R. (2016). Cards, money and two hacking forums: An analysis of online money laundering schemes. In *Proceedings of the 2016 European intelligence and security informatics conference (EISIC)*, Uppsala, Sweden (pp. 80–83).

Mikhaylov, A., & Frank, R. (2018). Illicit payments for illicit goods: Noncontact drug distribution on Russian online drug marketplaces. *Global Crime, 19*(2), 146–170.

Mirani, T. B., & Sasi, S. (2016). Sentiment analysis of ISIS related tweets using absolute location. In *Proceedings of the 2016 international conference on computational science and computational intelligence (CSCI)*, Las Vegas, NV, USA (pp. 1140–1145).

Monk, B., Allsup, R., & Frank, R. (2015). LECENing places to hide: Geo-mapping child exploitation material. In *Proceedings of the 2015 IEEE intelligence and security informatics (ISI)*, Baltimore, MD, USA (pp. 73–78).

Moghadam, A. (2008). The Salafi-jihad as a religious ideology. *CTC Sentinel, 1*(3), 14–16.

Ogneva, M. (2010). How companies can use sentiment analysis to improve their business. Retrieved from http://mashable.com/2010/04/19/sentiment-analysis. Accessed on January 23, 2019.

Park, A. J., Beck, B., Fletche, D., Lam, P., & Tsang, H. H. (2016). Temporal analysis of radical dark web forum users. In *Proceedings of the 2016 IEEE/ACM international conference on advances in social networks analysis and mining (ASONAM)*, San Francisco, CA, USA (pp. 880–883).

Perry, B., & Scrivens, R. (2016). Uneasy alliances: A look at the right-wing extremist movement in Canada. *Studies in Conflict and Terrorism, 39*(9), 819–841.

Sageman, M. (2014). The stagnation in terrorism research. *Terrorism and Political Violence, 26*(4), 565–580.

Scrivens, R., & Conway, M. (in press). The roles of 'old' and 'new' media tools and technologies in the facilitation of violent extremism and terrorism. In R. Leukfeldt & T. J. Holt (Eds.), *Cybercrime: The Human Factor*. New York, NY: Routledge.

Scrivens, R., Davies, G., & Frank, R. (2017). Searching for signs of extremism on the web: An introduction to sentiment-based identification of radical authors. *Behavioral Sciences of Terrorism and Political Aggression, 10*(1), 39–59.

Scrivens, R., Davies, G., & Frank, R. (2018). Measuring the evolution of radical right-wing posting behaviors online. *Deviant Behavior*.

Scrivens, R., & Frank, R. (2016). Sentiment-based classification of radical text on the web. In *Proceedings of the 2016 European intelligence and security informatics conference (EISIC)*, Uppsala, Sweden (pp. 104–107).

Southern Poverty Law Center. (2014). White homicide worldwide. Retrieved from https://www.splcenter.org/20140331/white-homicide-worldwide. Accessed on January 23, 2019.

Thelwall, M., & Buckley, K. (2013). Topic-based sentiment analysis for the social web: The role of mood and issue-related words. *Journal of the American Society for Information Science and Technology, 64*(8), 1608–1617.

Vergani, M., & Bluic, A. M. (2015). The evolution of the ISIS' language: A quantitative analysis of the language of the first year of Dabiq magazine. *Security, Terrorism, and Society, 2*, 7–20.

Wang, Y-C., Kraut, R., & Levine, J. M. (2012). To stay or leave? The relationship of emotional and informational support to commitment in online health support groups. In *Proceedings of the ACM 2012 conference on computer supported cooperative work*, Seattle, WA, USA (pp. 833–842).

Wei, Y., Singh, L., & Martin, S. (2016). Identification of extremism on Twitter. In *Proceedings of the 2016 IEEE/ACM international conference on advances in social networks analysis and mining (ASONAM)*, San Francisco, CA, USA (pp. 1251–1255).

Westlake, B. G., & Bouchard, M. (2015). Criminal careers in cyberspace: Examining website failure within child exploitation networks. *Justice Quarterly, 33*(7), 1154–1181.

Westlake, B. G., Bouchard, M., & Frank, R. (2011). Finding the key players in online child exploitation networks. *Policy and Internet, 3*(2), 1–25.

Williams, M. L., & Burnap, P. (2015). Cyberhate on social media in the aftermath of Woolwich: A case study in computational criminology and big data. *British Journal of Criminology, 56*(2), 211–238.

Wong, M., Frank, R., & Allsup, R. (2015). The supremacy of online white supremacists – An analysis of online discussions of white supremacists. *Information and Communications Technology Law, 24*(1), 41–73.

Yang, M., Kiang, M., Ku, Y., Chiu, C., & Li, Y. (2011). Social media analytics for radical opinion mining in hate group web forums. *Journal of Homeland Security and Emergency Management, 8*(1), 1547–7355.

Zhang, Y., Zeng, S., Huang, C.-N., Fan, L., Yu, X., Dang, Y., …, Chen, H. (2010). Developing a dark web collection and infrastructure for computational and social sciences. In *Proceedings of the 2010 IEEE international conference on intelligence and security informatics (ISI)*, Atlanta, GA, USA (pp. 59–64).

Zhou, Y., Qin, J., Lai, G., Reid, E., & Chen, H. (2005). Building knowledge management system for researching terrorist groups on the web. In *Proceedings of the 11th Americas conference on information systems (AMCIS)*, Omaha, NE, USA (pp. 2524–2536).

Zulkarnine, A., Frank, R., Monk, B., Mitchell, J., & Davies, G. (2016). Surfacing collaborated networks in dark web to find illicit and criminal content. In *Proceedings of the 2016 IEEE international conference on intelligence and security informatics (ISI)*, Tucson, AZ, USA (pp. 109–114).

INDEX

Printed and bound by CPI Group (UK) Ltd, Croydon, CR0 4YY

13/09/2026

14961061-0001